Marianne Burkhalter,
Christian Sumi (eds)

Konrad Wachsmann and the Grapevine Structure

Texts by

Marianne Burkhalter and
Christian Sumi

Fabio Gramazio, Matthias Kohler,
and Hannes Mayer

Andreas Burkhalter

Marko Pogacnik

PARK BOOKS

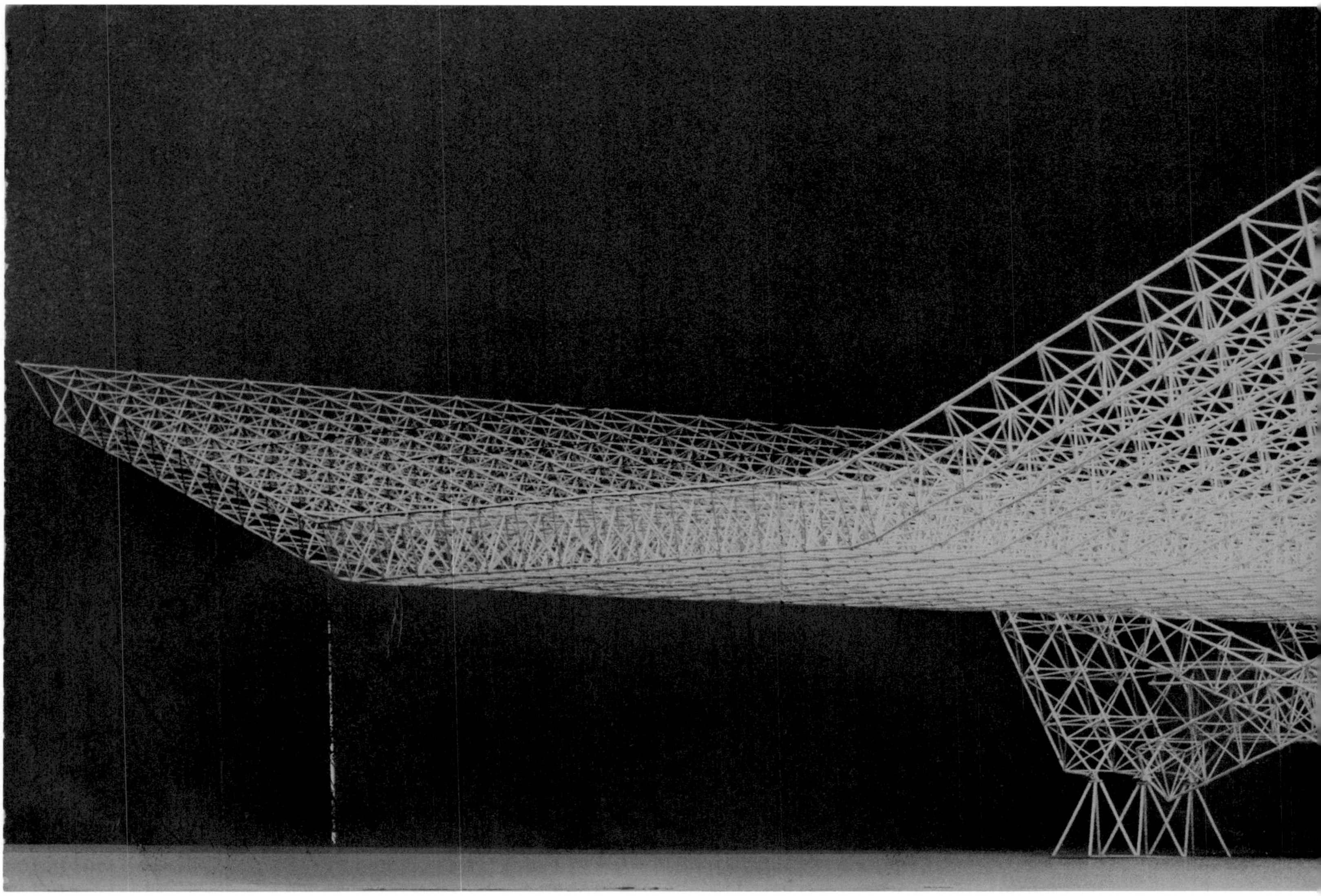

USAF Hangar for the US Air Force, model. Photograph by Harry Callahan, © The Estate of Harry Callahan; courtesy Pace/MacGill Gallery, New York

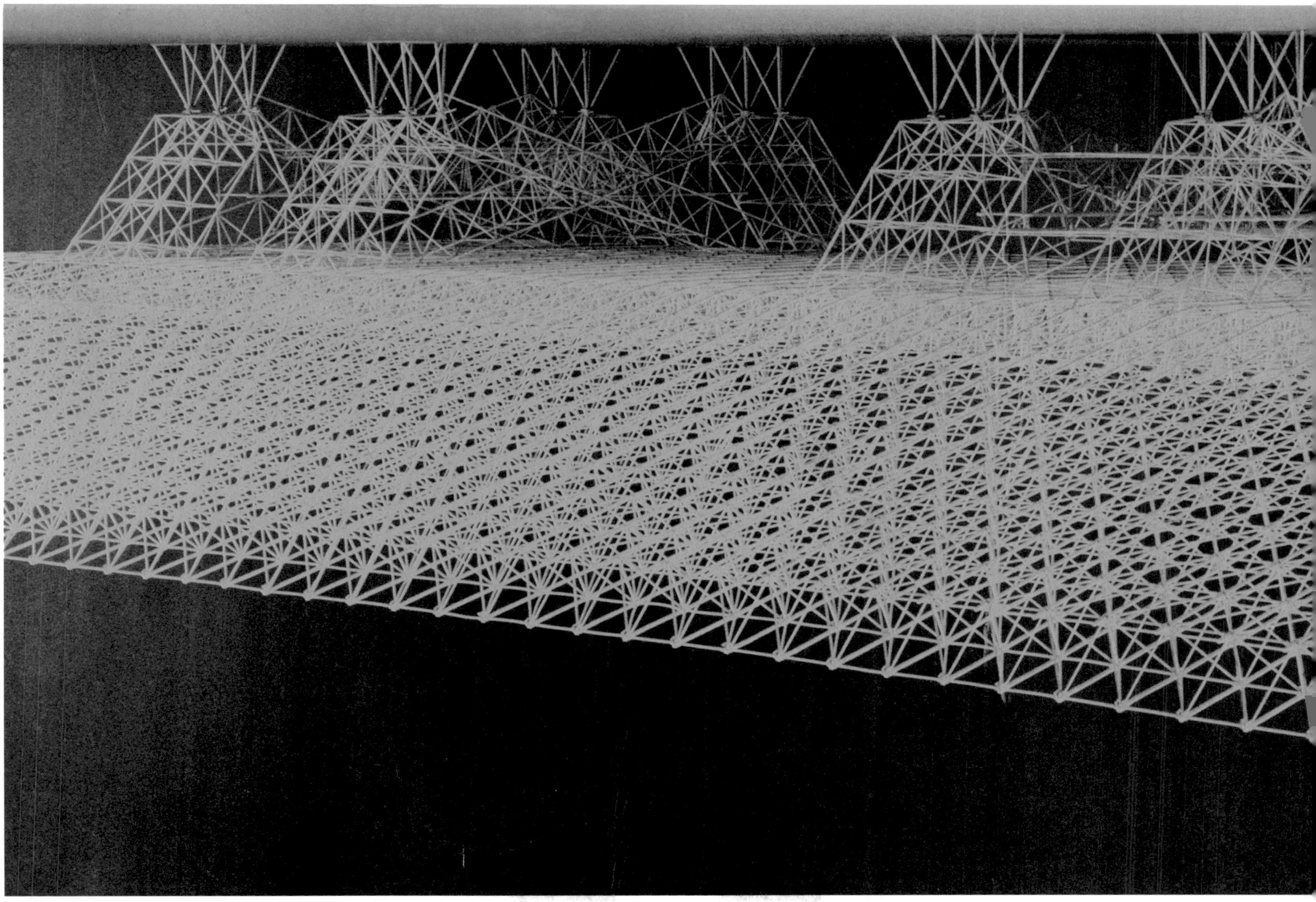

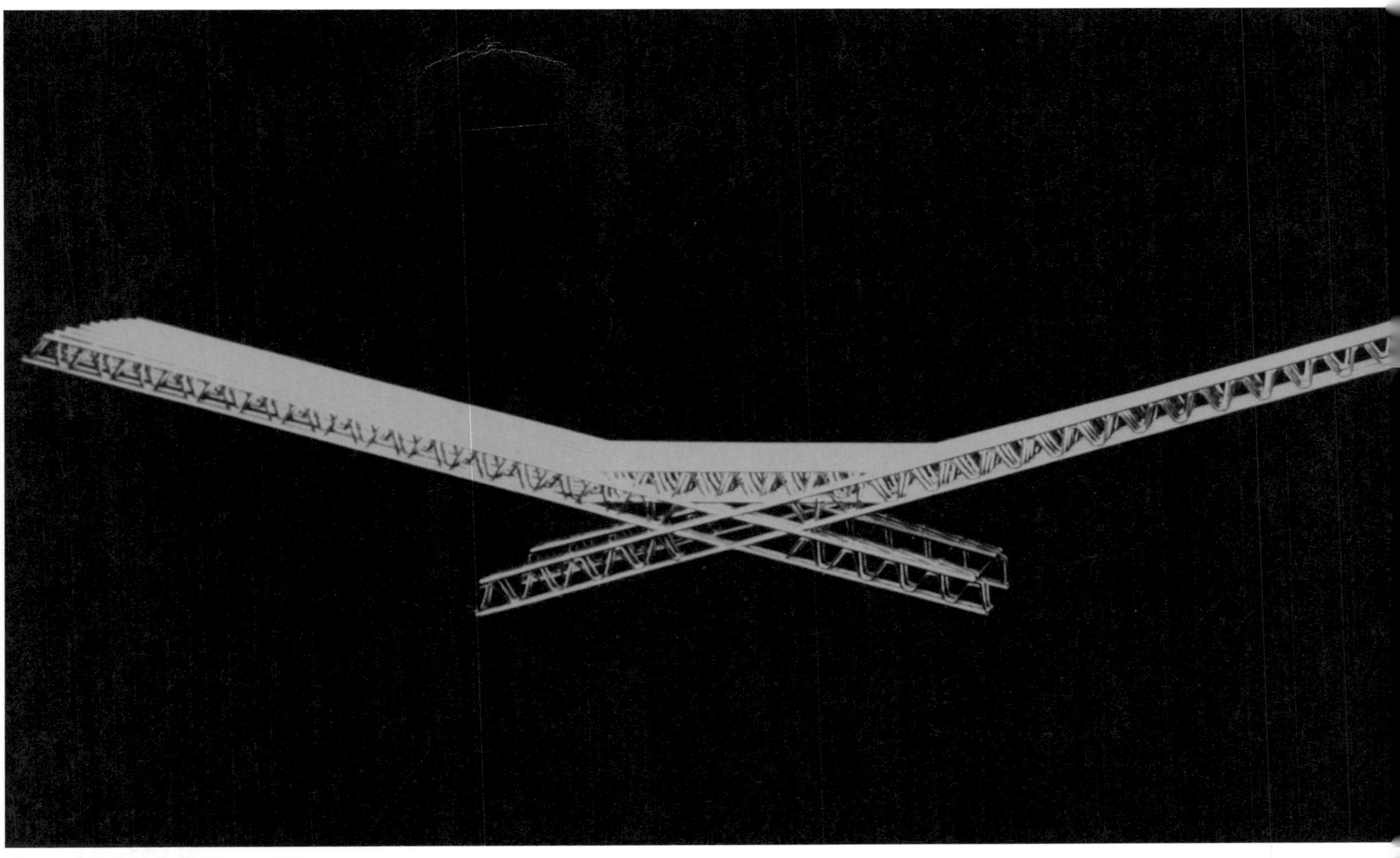

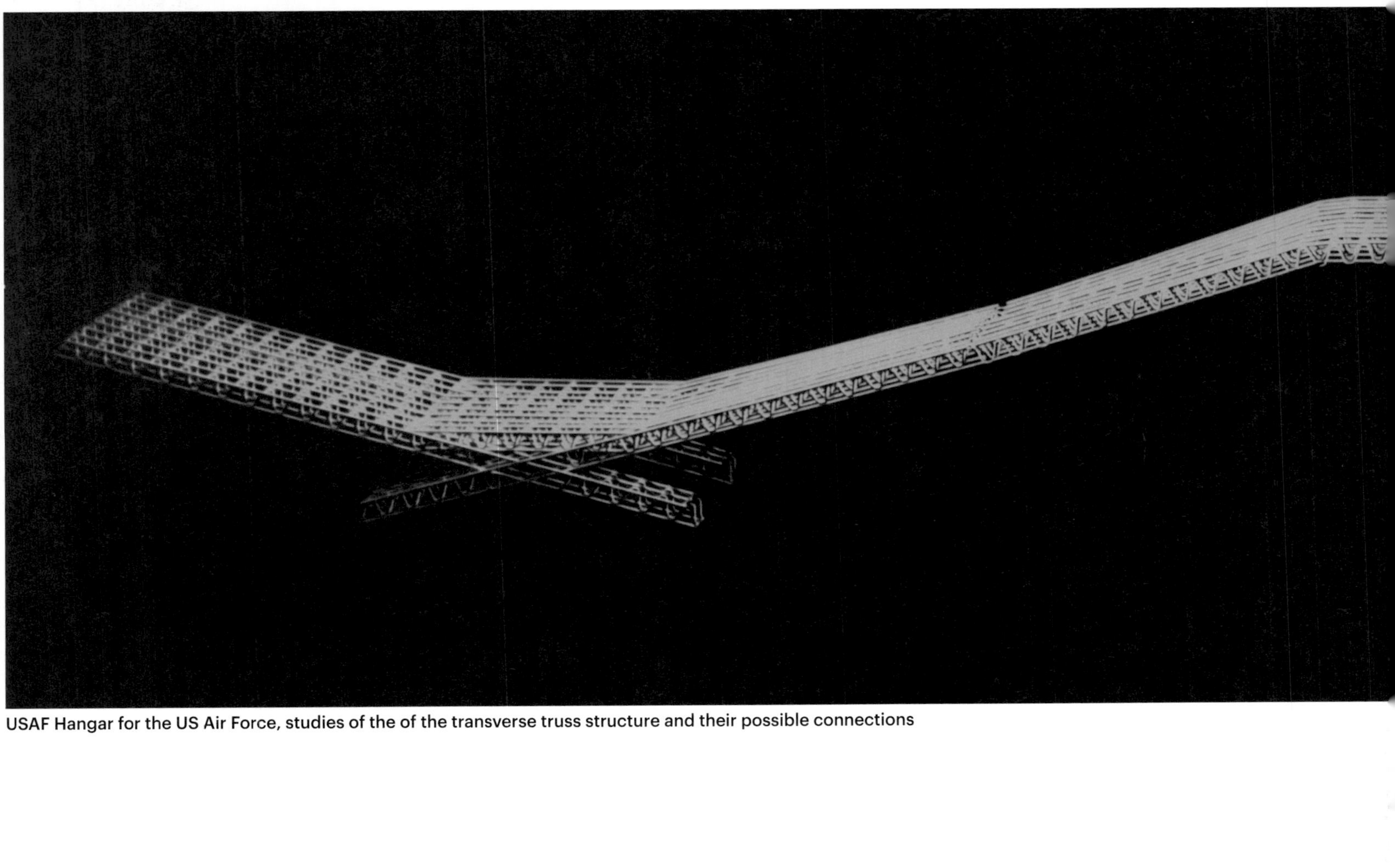

USAF Hangar for the US Air Force, studies of the of the transverse truss structure and their possible connections

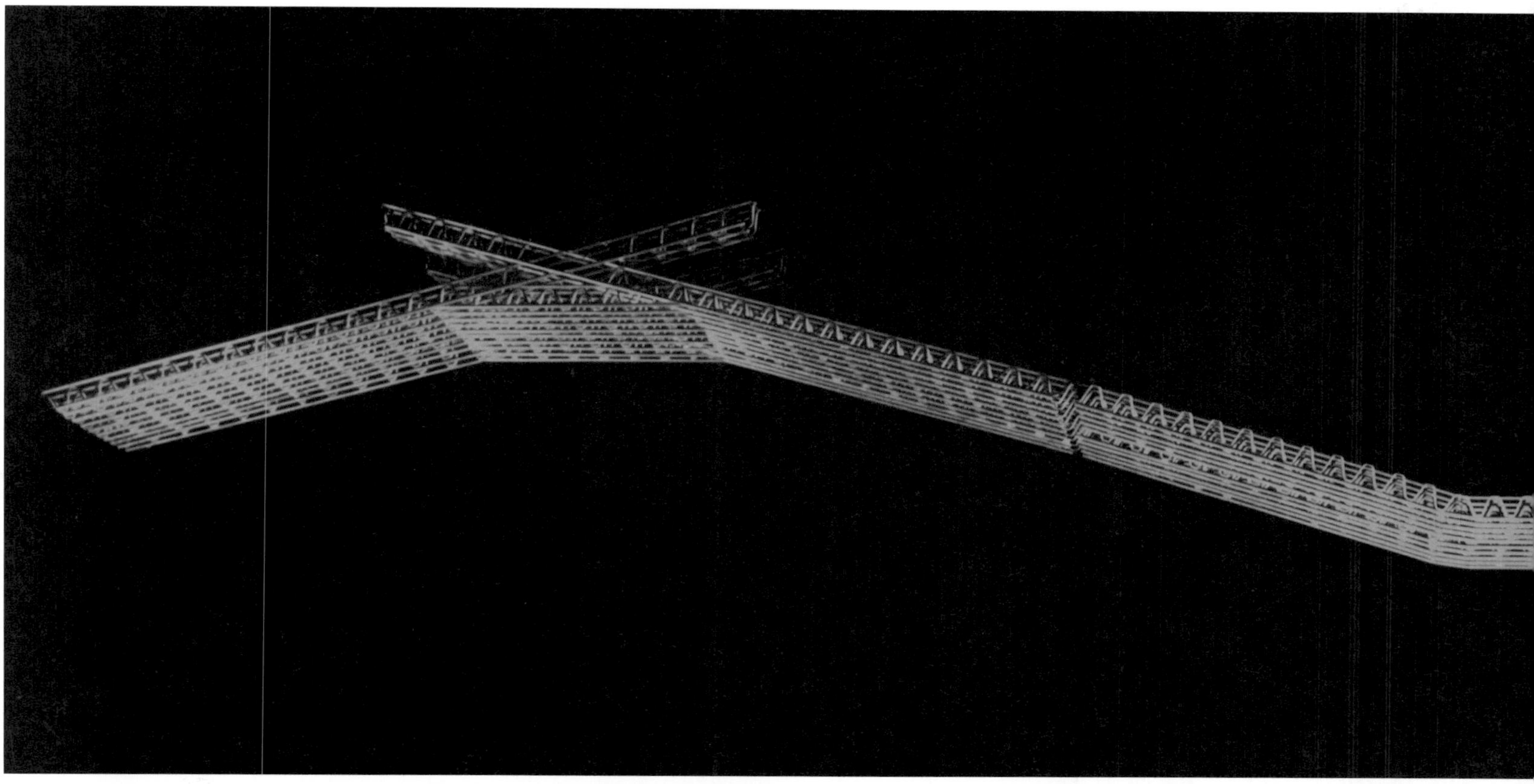

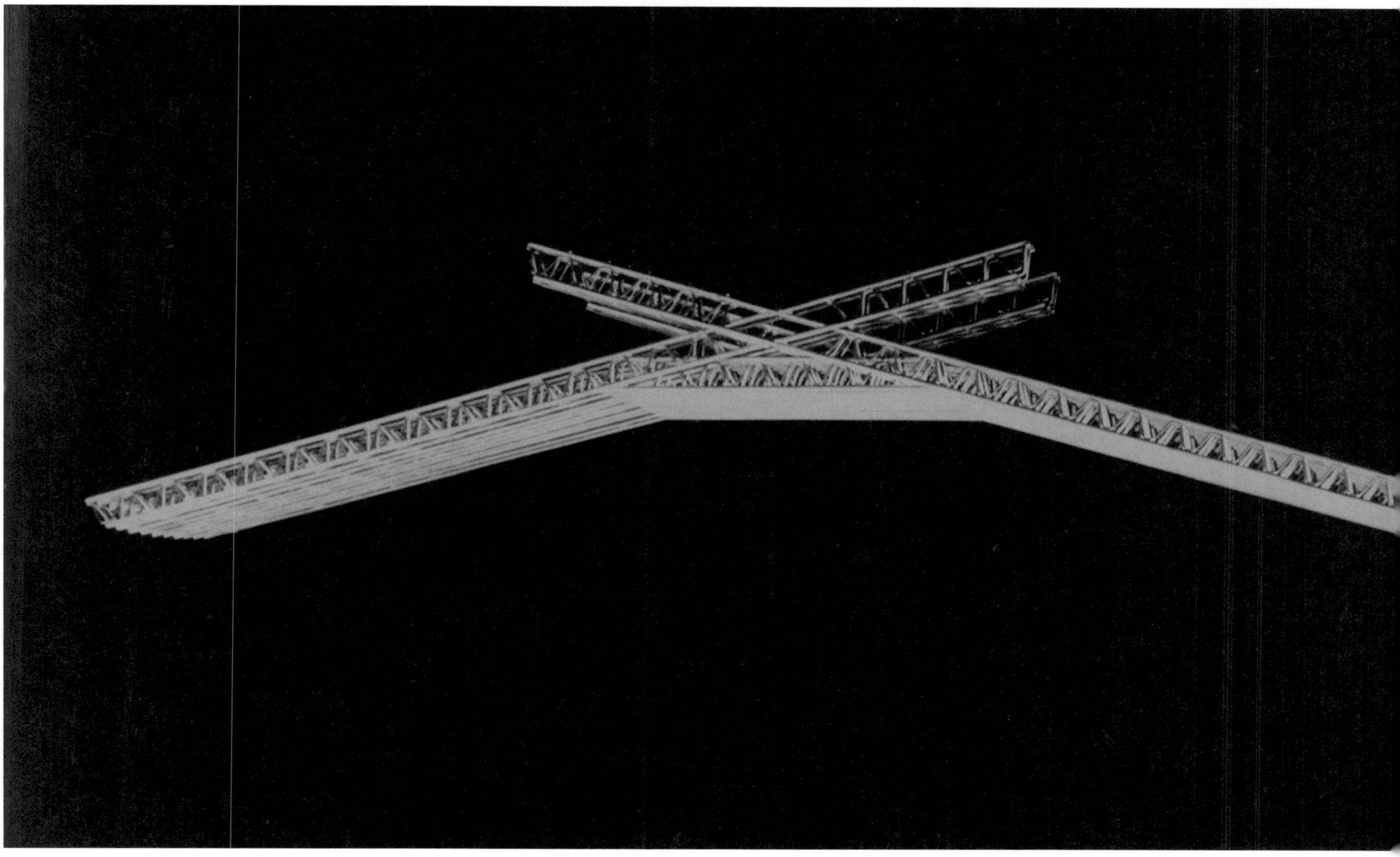

USAF, Production of the elements, Wachsmann (above and top right, left) in discussion with a collaborator, mold of the locking element, welded to the tube

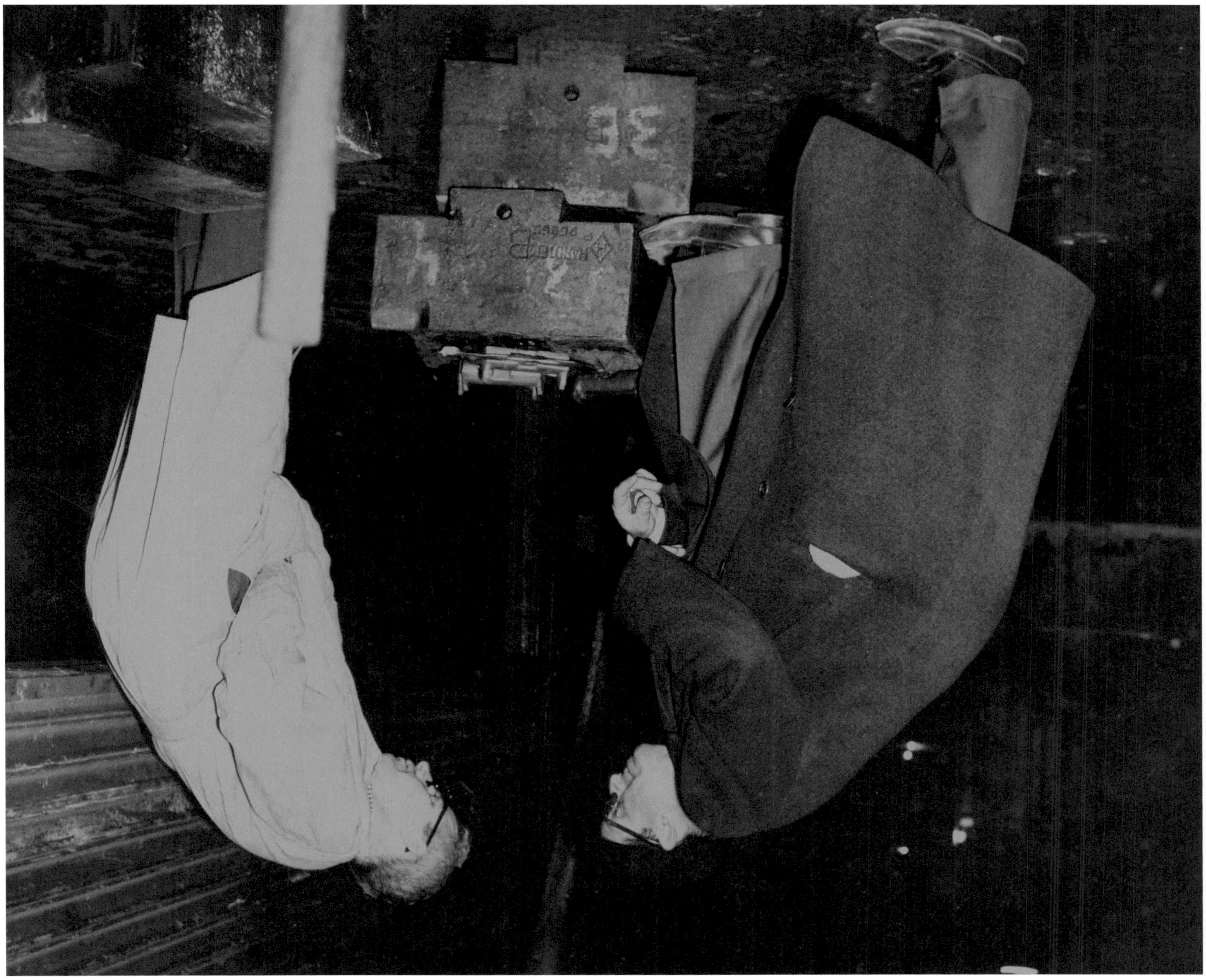

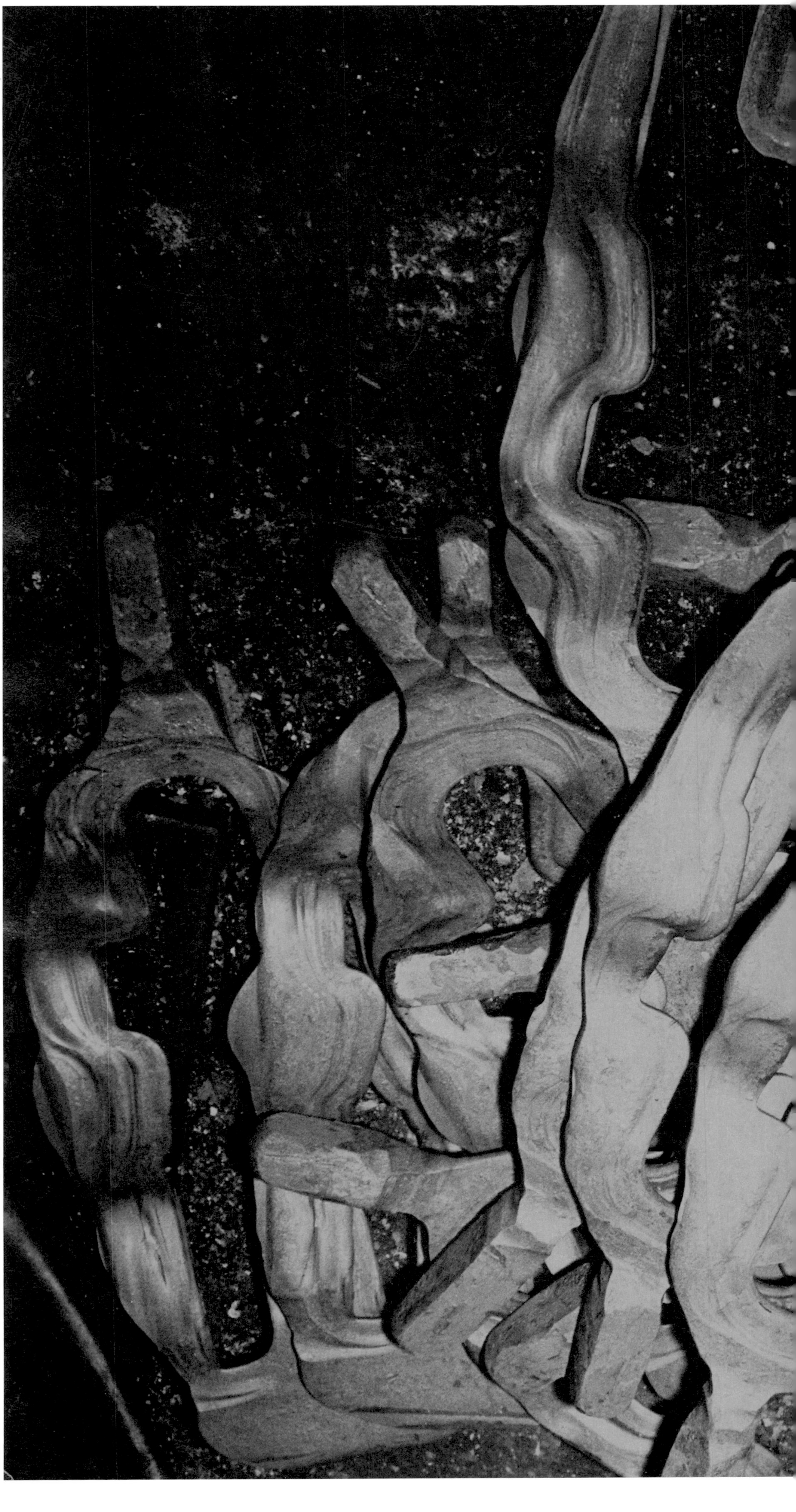

Remnants of the chain elements

Editorial note

In his book *The Turning Point of Building*, Konrad Wachsmann speaks of a "dynamic structure," while in a later manuscript for a planned exhibition the name "Vine Grape structure" appears. In the Konrad Wachsmann Archive at Akademie der Künste in Berlin, the project is filed under "Study of a Dynamic Structure 'Grapevine'." Today, two commonly used terms – "Structural Grapevine" and "Grapevine Structure" – have been established.

Content

Over the course of his entire life, Konrad Wachsmann was engaged in issues of construction and prefabrication. Together with Buckminster Fuller, he is the intellectual predecessor for contemporary "industrial construction," especially the High Tech movement. Architects from this movement, such as Piano and Rogers, refer to him explicitly.

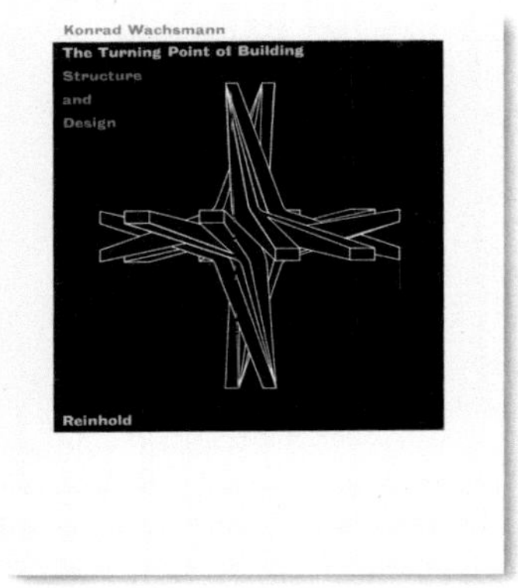

Born in 1901 in Frankfurt on the Oder, he completed an apprenticeship as a cabinetmaker and thereafter studied in Berlin with Tessenow and Poelzig. By the mid-1920s, he had become the chief architect for the timber construction firm Christoph & Unmack in Niesky, and built a weekend home for Albert Einstein in Caputh, near Berlin, published in his 1929 book *Holzhausbau (Building the Wooden House)*.[1]

Following his emigration to the USA, he focused intensively on a universal prefabricated panel, together with Walter Gropius, which subsequently led to the Packaged House System marketed by the General Panel Corporation beginning in 1941. Ironically, his first buildings realized in the US, the German and Japanese village of 1943, were largely destroyed immediately after completion. They had been commissioned by the US Army as a training ground for war preparations and to test new firearms.[2]

Shortly thereafter he developed space frame structures for US Army hangars (after 1951). In turn, both projects were published in 1959, in his pioneering book *Wendepunkt im Bauen (The Turning Point of Building)*.[3] With the Grapevine Structure (1953), he expanded upon his interest, working towards the development of infinite, self-generating structures, recalling on first sight the structure of the human brain. The LOM project (Localisation Orientation Manipulatur) finally marks a further step away from the construction of the joint to its localisation in space. During the famous Salzburg Seminars (1956–60), Konrad Wachsmann became a leading figure for an entire generation of young architects. In 1961, his publication *Aspekte* became available, featuring images from his time in Italy, organized by themes and accompanied by his commentary.[4]

Wachsmann is an architect, a man of the world, a philosopher[5] and a thinker of the not-yet-possible, characterized by a relentless, intuitive curiosity. He drives the industrialization of construction forward; his goal is a kind of architecture or, in Wachsmann's words, "the building of our time," ("das Bauen unserer Zeit") in which personal authorship is replaced by collective work.

One study of nine hinges that have been welded together is particularly illustrative. Its components are angled to generate a ring-like form. Six of these hinges would create a flat, two-dimensional ring, but by increasing the number to nine, the hinges buckle outwards, striving to find space and conquering the third dimension (see pp. 14, 15).

The following essays trace the stations described above. At its center is the Grapevine Project from 1953. The publication is fragmentary in character.

1
Konrad Wachsmann, *Holzhausbau*, Ernst Wasmuth Verlag AG Berlin, 1929. Neuauflage: Konrad Wachsmann, *Holzhausbau*, Birkhäuser Verlag, Basel 1995, with introductory texts by Michael Grüning und Christian Sumi. English edition: Konrad Wachsmann, *Building the Wooden House*, Birkhäuser Verlag Basel 1995. Regina Böhn, Daniela Däumler and Tobias Haag compiled the first comprehensive overview of Wachsmann's buildings for the firm of Christoph & Unmack in 1997 as an independent study at the Bauhaus University in Weimar. This work was expanded upon in 2017 by Livia Greuter, in an elective study project with Prof. Markus Peter at the ETH Zürich. (Archives of Christian Sumi).

2
See Mike Davis, *Dead Cities: A Natural History*, Chapter 3: "Berlin's Skeleton in Utah's Closet," New Directions, NY 2002.

3
Konrad Wachsmann, *Wendepunkt im Bauen*, Krauss-opf-Verlag, Wiesbaden 1959. English edition: Konrad Wachsmann, *The Turning Point of Building: Structure and Design*, Reinhold, NY 1961. Italian edition: Konrad Wachsmann, *Una svolta nelle costruzione*, Il Saggiatore, Milano 1960, foreword by G.C. Argan. New German edition: Deutsche Verlagsanstalt, Stuttgart 1989, foreword by Fritz Haller.

4
Konrad Wachsmann, *Aspekte*, Krausskopf-Verlag, Wiesbaden 1961.

5
Barbara Dafft describes the background of Wachsmann's philosophical thinking in her Master's thesis *Autopoisesis Die Genese des Grape Vine Project (1953) von Konrad Wachsmann*, ETH Zürich, 2009.

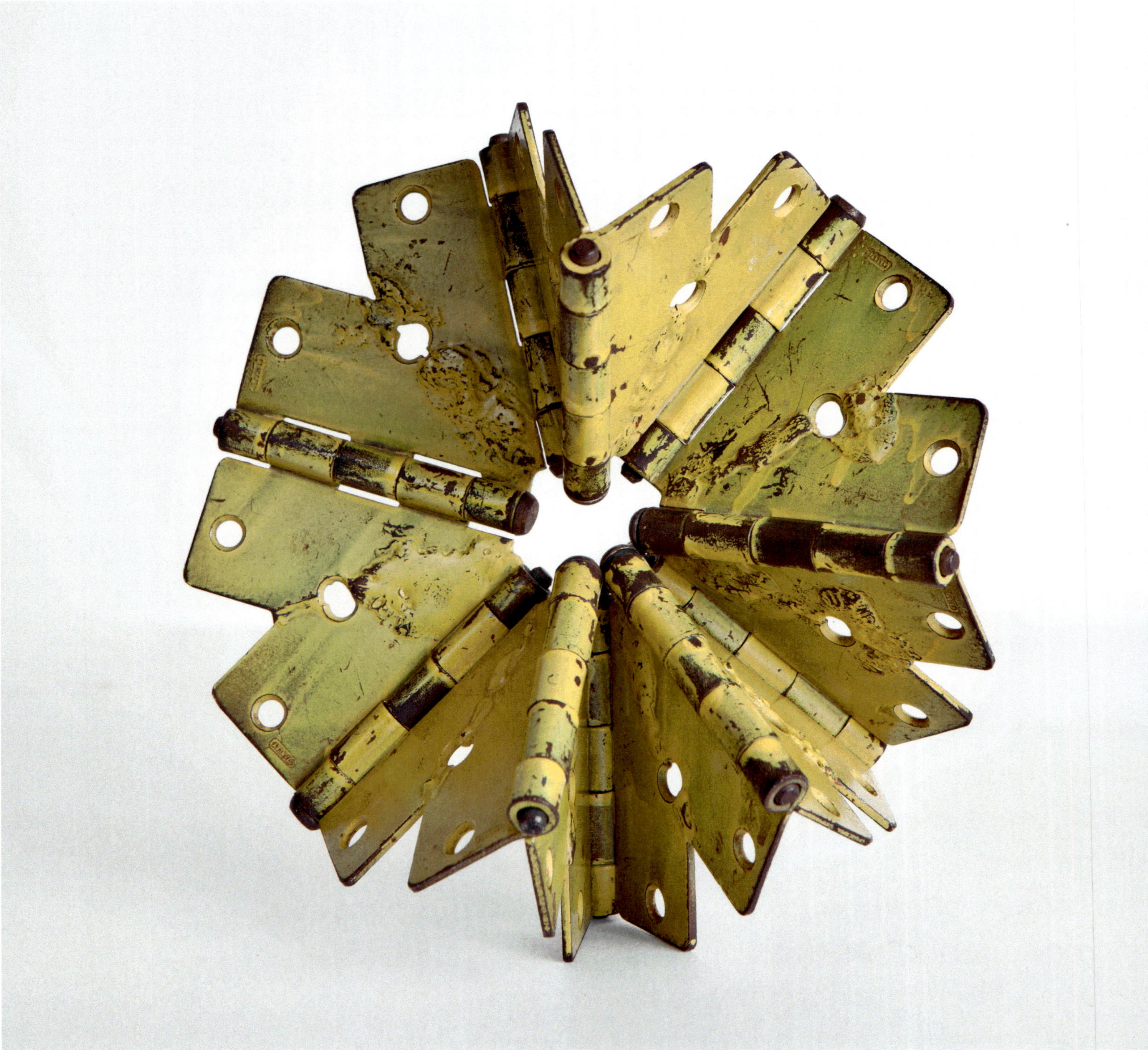

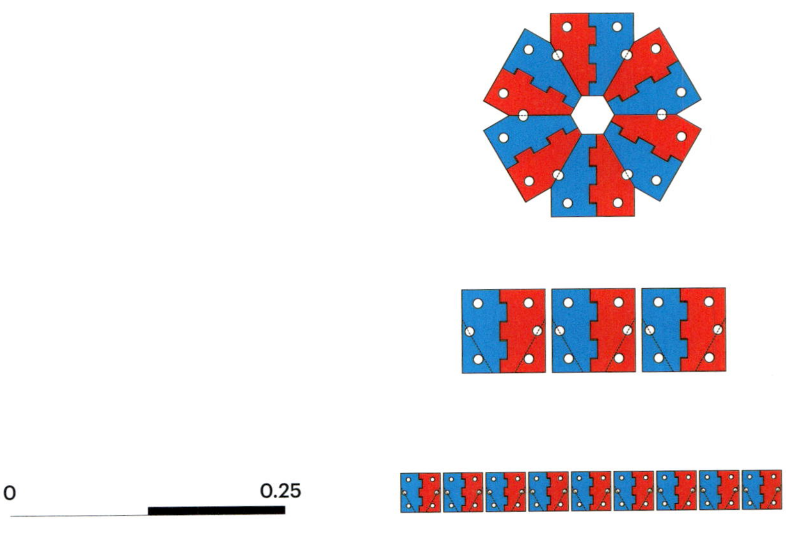

Nine hinges

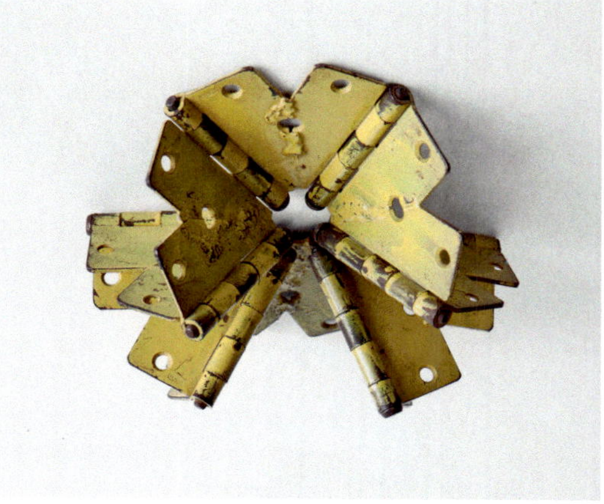

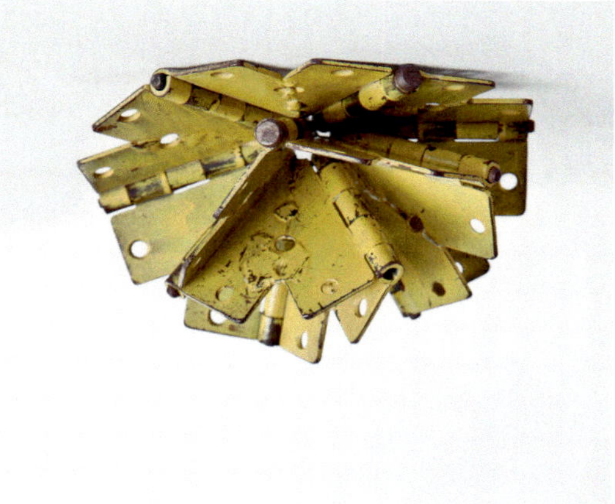

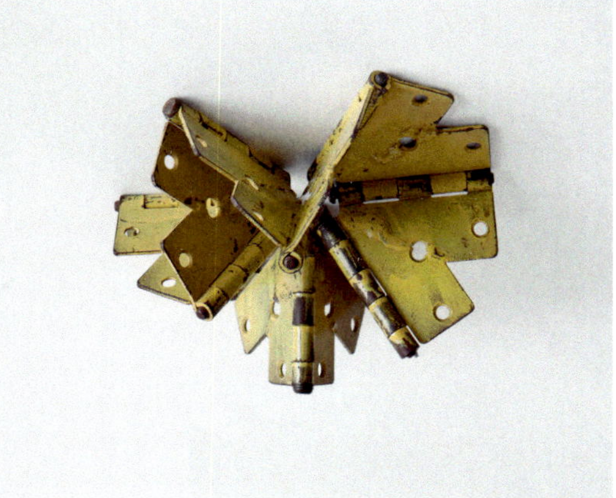

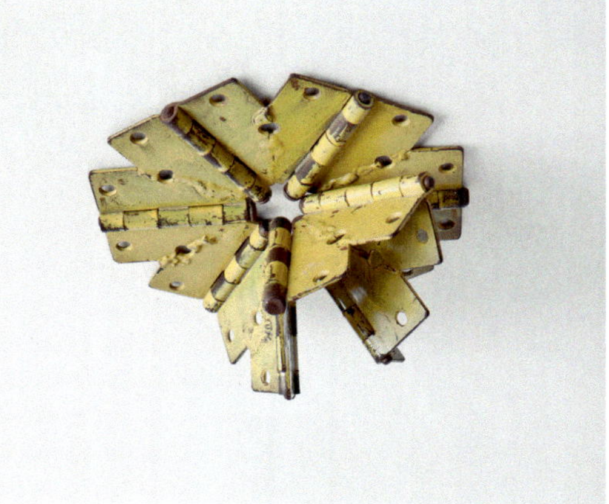
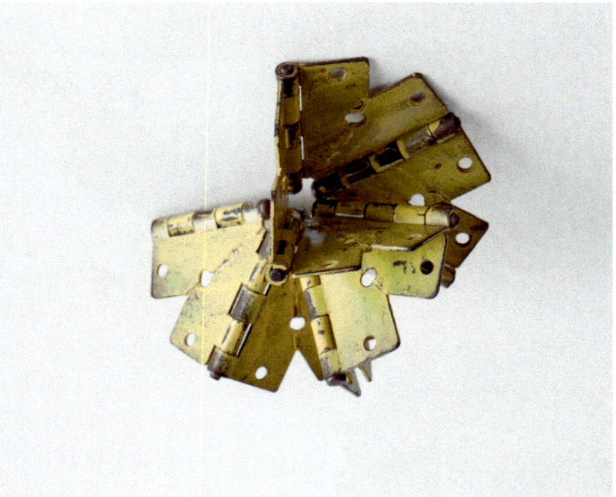

Image courtesy of the Aaron Siskind Foundation

Knots and Joints 1941–1951

Für den Antirationalismus ist die traditionelle Bildform nicht mehr alleiniger Ausdrucksträger, während im kritischen Realismus das Bild seine überlieferte Funktion beibehält. Weder der Irrationalismus noch der kritische Realismus fragen nach dem Stellenwert der kunstgeschichtlichen Struktur, dem Objektcharakter der Bildfläche, z. B. inwieweit der Bildausschnitt einer neuen Definition bedürfe, ebenso wird die Frage, ob die Fläche als grundsätzlich mobiles Element nicht Teil einer Gesamtstruktur geworden sei und die Bildfläche in einem neuen und grösseren Zusammenhang gesehen werden müsse, als irrelevant betrachtet. Auch wäre die These von der Ablösung des Bildes als Inhaltsträger durch die Aktion philosophisch zu begründen. Interessant hierbei ist, dass der Sozialbezug einen geringen Raum einnimmt.

Letztendlich bleibt die Frage nach der Einordnung der konstruktiven Kunstform in diese Zeit. Ist sie einem natürlichen Alterungsprozess unterworfen, oder ist sie dadurch, dass sie vom Besonderen auf das Allgemeine abzielt, in eine grössere kulturelle Entwicklung integriert? Im Zusammenhang damit müsste sich eine Standortbestimmung der konstruktiven Kunst ergeben.

Ich möchte auf zwei Ereignisse hinweisen, an denen erstmals das Zeitproblem der Entwicklung analoger additiver Strukturen erkennbar wird.

Um das Problem Zeit, Wirklichkeit und konstruktive Kunst, die auch mit methodischer, logischer, rationaler, struktureller Kunst bezeichnet werden könnte, zu erörtern, ist es richtig, nicht nur auf das Problem der Fläche, sondern ebenso auch auf das Problem des Raumes hinzuweisen. Keine andere Kunstform hat innerhalb der visuellen Gestaltung einen so grossen Anteil an der Entwicklung des für unsere Epoche charakteristischen Phänomens: des strukturellen Denkens. Die Frage, wieweit Kunst autonom sei, wäre dahingehend zu beantworten, dass jede Kunstform ihrer Zeit determiniert ist, jedoch als Erfindung und Ausdruck in einer dialektischen Beziehung zu der Epoche steht, selbst dann, wenn die Formulierung dieser Kunstform in einem äusseren Gegensatz zu den Forderungen des Tages und zu den allgemeingültigen Verhaltensweisen ist.

Zwei frühe Beispiele, eines der Flächenstrukturen und ein zweites räumlicher Strukturen, weisen auf Parallelprobleme hin.

Aus der Kontinuität geschichtlichen Denkens ist die Erwähnung der ersten Zäsur in der Kunstgeschichte aufschlussreich. Cézanne formuliert als erster Parallelführungen des Pinselstriches, durch Richtungsidentität beginnt die Verflüchtigung des Gegenstandes, ein Vorgang, der später im analytischen Kubismus und in vehementer Radikalität in den Meerbildern Mondrians 1913–1917 durchbricht. Abb. 3, 4.

8

9

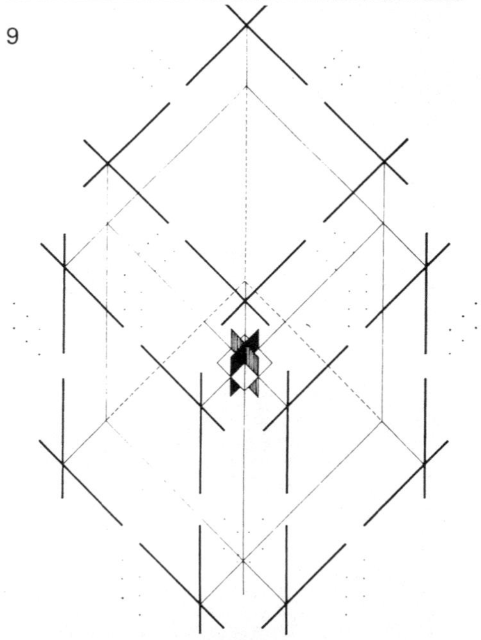

10

8
Theo van Doesburg, Kontra-Konstruktion 1923–1924. Achsial-dynamisches Konstruktionsprinzip. Die Systematisierung der Bauteile folgt der formal-räumlichen Vorstellung. Differenzierte Formung der individuellen Massverhältnisse von Länge, Breite und Abständigkeit der Elemente.

9
Konrad Wachsmann, Entstehung einer räumlichen Struktur durch Konzipierung von Flächenrastern, Modell. Die formale Vorstellung wird bestimmt durch die Möglichkeiten, die sich aus der Normung und der Kombination der Konstruktionsteile ergeben. Analog der Aufhebung der Individualität des Einzelelementes in der Kunst erfolgt die Standardisierung, die Einführung modularer und serieller Elemente in den Raum.

10
Konrad Wachsmann. Gedachte Elemente können in jeder beliebigen Beziehung zu einem angenommenen Rastersystem stehen, sie können sich zum Beispiel an ein solches anlehnen oder sich in einem immer gleichen Abstand davon befinden oder aber sich in einem exzentrischen, sich rhythmisch wiederholenden Raum befinden.

11

12

13
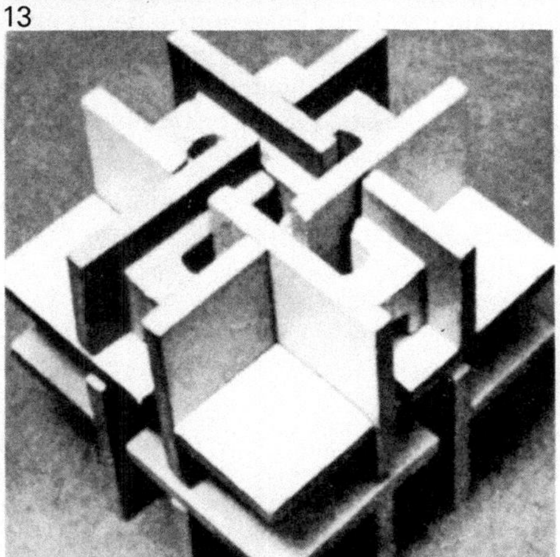

14
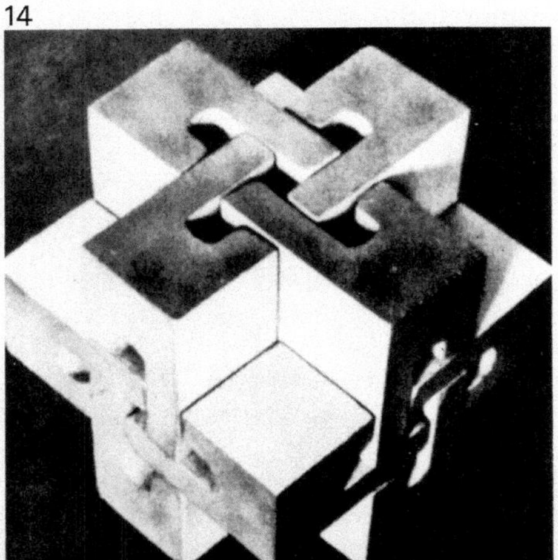

15

16
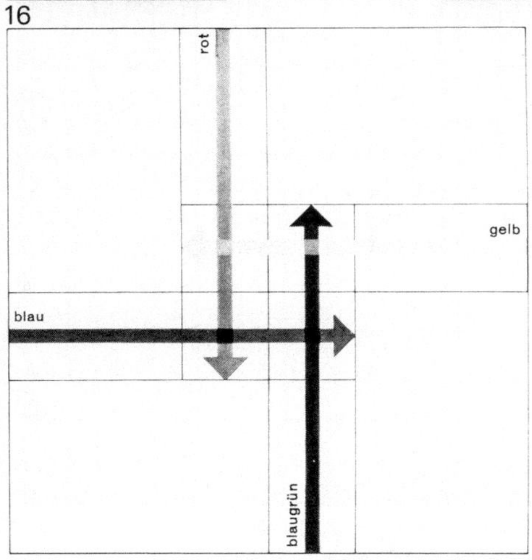

17

18
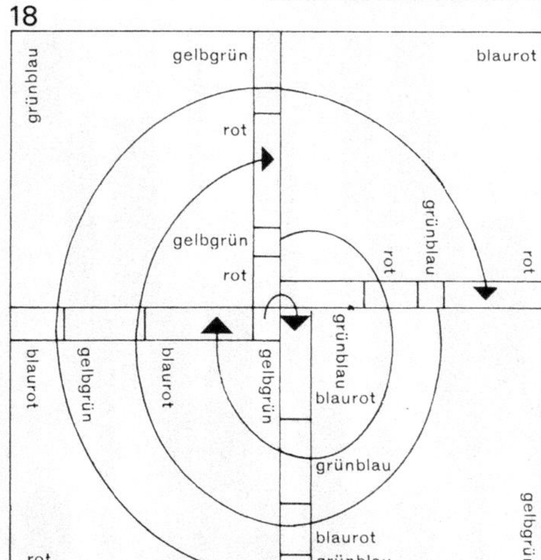

11, 12, 13
Konrad Wachsmann. Drei Beispiele für die Entstehung einer Verbindung von zwölf Elementen in einem Punkt mit gleichen Profilen als Basis eines universellen Bausystems für Trennwände.

14
Konrad Wachsmann, Modell einer Verbindung. Die Berührung von zwölf in drei Ebenen liegenden Platten im Mittelpunkt eines gedachten Würfels.

15
Richard Paul Lohse, Farbenergien in vier Richtungen 1952. Horizontal und vertikal gerichtetes Bewegungsmotiv mit quadratischem Zentrum. Der Bildaufbau erfolgt durch dreimal vier und zweimal zwei Farbrechtecke. Die diagonal angeordneten, sich durchdringenden Rechtecke um das Zentrum ergeben Verschränkungen und eine kommunizierende Bewegung von innen nach aussen und von aussen nach innen.

16
Richard Paul Lohse, Zentrum aus vier Quadraten als Ergebnis der vier Kreuzflächen 1962–1971, Schema. Aus der Verbindung der vertikalen roten mit der horizontalen gelben Rechteckfläche entsteht in der Kreisbewegung von links nach rechts das orangefarbene Quadrat, aus der gelben Fläche mit der vertikalen blaugrünen das hellgrüne Quadrat, aus der Verbindung der blaugrünen Fläche mit der blauen das dunkelgrüne und der horizontalen blauen Fläche mit der vertikalen roten das violette Quadrat. Durchdringung und Überlagerung ergeben die Konzentration nach innen und mit den Kreuzflächen nach aussen.

17
Richard Paul Lohse, Zentrum aus vier Quadraten als Ergebnis der vier Kreuzflächen 1962–1971.

18
Richard Paul Lohse, Vier Farbrhythmen an vier Feldern 1952–1968. Analog dem Typus der Farbenergien in vier Richtungen ist diese Gruppe aufgebaut, in denen vier verschränkte Kreuzflächen durch Vervielfachung des Flächenwertes eines Quadratmoduls rhythmisiert und in Kreisbewegungen vom Zentrum aus an die Bildbegrenzung geführt werden.

19

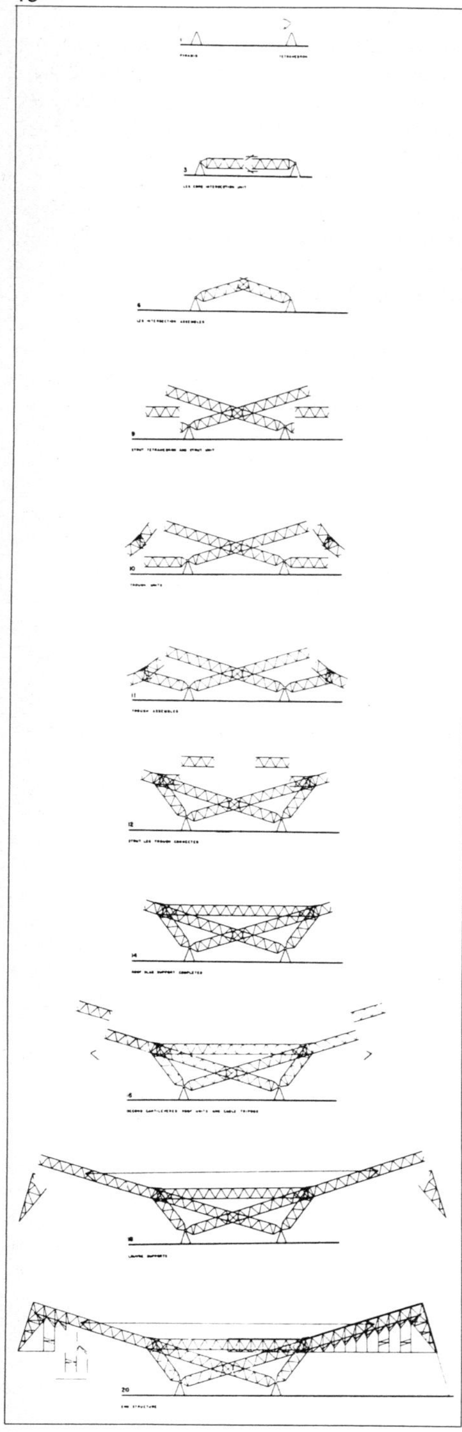

20

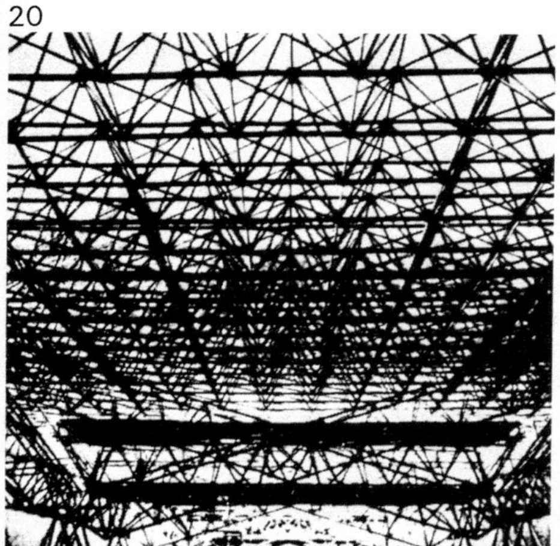

21

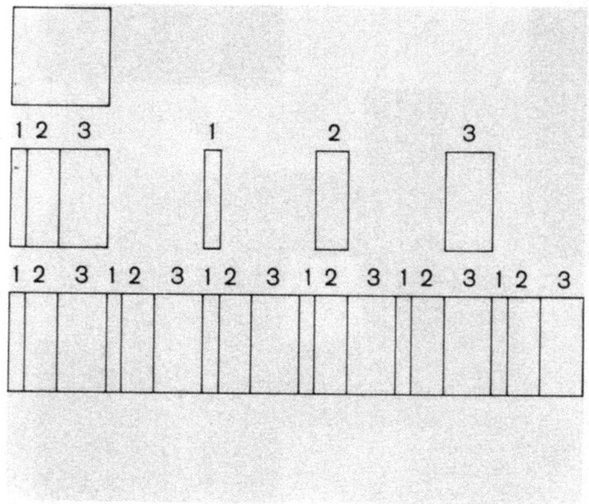

22

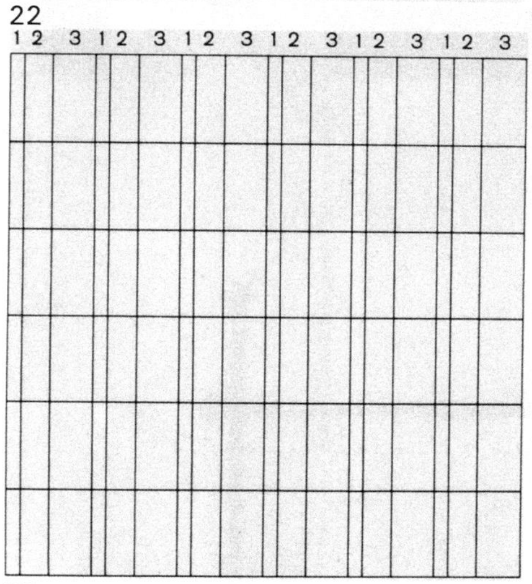

23

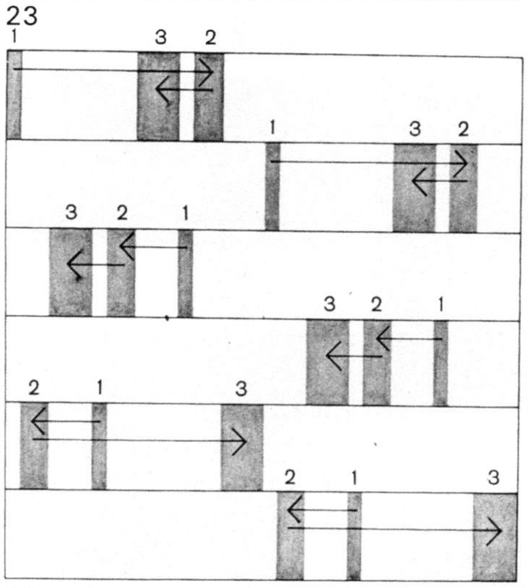

24

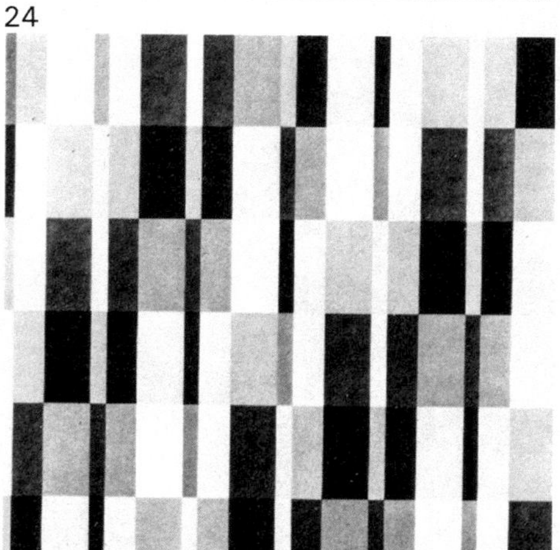

19
Konrad Wachsmann, Aufbau der Dachkonstruktion einer Halle. Die Verwendung eines Knotenpunktes, einer Stablänge, die Anwendung eines konstruktiven Systems, die rhythmische Wiederholung innerhalb der Dreidimensionalität einer modularen Ordnung bestimmen Struktur und Raum.

20
Konrad Wachsmann, Ausschnitt der Dachkonstruktion. Länge der Halle etwa 130 Meter, Auskragung von den Auflagepunkten der beiden Pyramiden etwa 150 Meter.

21
Richard Paul Lohse, Sechs horizontale Bänder mit je sechs formal gleichen Farbgruppen 1950–1955–1971. Die Grundwerte 1, 2, 3 eines Quadrates werden als Gruppe sechsmal horizontal gereiht.

22
Die Bildstruktur enthält die Werte: 36mal Wert 1, 36mal Wert 2, 36mal Wert 3.

23
Der additiven Reihung mit den Grundwerten 1, 2, 3 wird die diskontinuierliche Folge 1, 3, 2 zweimal, 3, 2, 1 zweimal, 2, 1, 3 zweimal entgegengesetzt.

24
Alle sechs Reihen enthalten sechsmal formal und farblich die gleichen Werte. Die drei Primärfarben sind mit je einem Sechstel und die drei Sekundärfarben ebenfalls mit je einem Sechstel an der Gesamtfläche vertreten. Die Primärfarben ergeben die dazwischenliegenden Sekundärfarben. Die Erweiterung erfolgt durch ein vertikales Folgeprinzip der Primär- und Sekundärfarben. Jede erweiterte Bilddimension enthält die gleichen Wert-, Proportions- und Farbanteile an der Reihe und an der Gesamtfläche.

Ein einzigartiges Ereignis leitet die Periode der Typisierung und additionellen Bildelemente ein. Insgesamt etwa 400 kurze senkrechte und waagrechte Linienelemente, die gegeneinander als Plus- und Minuszeichen gestellt sind und sich teilweise überkreuzen, sind zu einem Bild konzipiert. Der Titel des Bildes ‹Komposition mit Linien› stellt die Kulmination der Bilder mit dem Thema ‹Das Meer› dar. Es ist ein beunruhigendes Phänomen der Kunstgeschichte, dass das Vorbild in eine neue Kategorie verwandelt wird. In dieser Bildradikalität werden die Tendenzen zur Standardisierung, zur Anonymisierung der Bildelemente, zur Identifizierung von Bildmittel und Bildbegrenzung und zur Unlimitiertheit serieller Ordnungen erkennbar. Damit beginnt die Überwindung des durch das Bildmotiv bis anhin bestimmten individuellen Bildformates, die Bildfläche wird Teil eines Strukturfeldes. Analog der Normung und der Systematisierung erfolgt die Reduktion auf Grundformen, es formuliert sich die Farbfläche, deren Anonymität analog derjenigen der Chiffren ist und die den Ausdruck unlimitierter Dimensionen in sich trägt. Abb. 4

Von konstruktiver Kunst heute zu sprechen bedeutet auf ihren Realitätsbezug hinweisen. Um die Position dieser Kunst zu verstehen, wäre die Frage zu beantworten, in welcher Weise sie im Zusammenhang mit der Gestaltung der Umwelt steht. Wenn die Forderung an Kunst gerichtet wird, sie müsse einen totalen Ausdruck des Lebens vermitteln, so wird dieser Anspruch in einer Epoche der Ungleichzeitigkeiten und entgegengesetzter Entwicklungen, deren Vielschichtigkeit nicht mehr durchschaubar ist, irrelevant.

Keinesfalls ist es nun so, dass sich Parallelerscheinungen zu gleicher Zeit ereignen, dennoch lassen sich Tendenzen und Wirkungen einer ideologischen Grundwelle erkennen, auch bei grossen Zeitabständen. Analoge Ereignisse, die Anwendung ähnlicher Methoden, erstrecken sich vielmehr über eine längere Wegstrecke, oftmals überdeckt, einem unterirdischen Strom vergleichbar, um nach einem weit auseinanderliegenden Zeitraum in weiterentwickelten Formulierungen wieder aktiv zu werden. Vor allem in gleichartigen Beziehungen, in Masswerten, in der Methodengleichheit, in bestimmten Arbeitsvorgängen werden parallele Vorgänge auf der Fläche und im Räumlichen erkennbar. Je weiter Ereignisse grundsätzlicher Art auseinanderliegen, desto deutlicher wird der Grundplan einer Epoche. Eine Epoche rechnet mit Zeiten, nicht mit Zeit.

Mit einem zweiten, zeitlich zurückliegenden Beispiel möchte ich zeigen, wie Gleichungen, Anonymität der Mittel – Normung – Auswechselbarkeit – Kombinatorik, in räumlichen Vorgängen erkennbar werden.

Den Realisationen der heutigen Konstruktionssysteme sind die Entwicklungen vor 150 Jahren mit den Konstruktionen Ludons für Gewächshäuser in England, die später in grossen Dimensionen von Paxton realisiert wurden, vorausgegangen. Beispiel dafür ist der Bau des Kristallpalastes von 1859, dessen Systematik als eigentliche Zäsur in der Geschichte räumlicher Strukturen bezeichnet werden kann und damit in der Architektur die Periode des Denkens in Strukturen einleitet. Man muss das Konstruktionssystem eines Binderfeldes für den Kristallpalast von Paxton betrachten, um zu erkennen, dass hier eine Epoche neuer Raumkonzeption beginnt. Es ist folgerichtig, dass in diesem Augenblick die bisher unangetastete Hierarchie der Form, die am Anfang allen architektonischen Bemühens stand, aufgegeben werden muss und der neue Ausdruck sich aus dem Konstruktionssystem ergibt. Die Hilfsmittel erhalten die Bedeutung von Formmitteln, ein Phänomen, das für die nachfolgende Entwicklung räumlicher Strukturen entscheidend wird. Dass zu gleicher Zeit in London, ausgelöst durch die Elendssituation der Arbeiter, Sozialkämpfe geführt werden, zeigt einerseits die Diskrepanz zwischen Erfindung und Anwendung, andererseits wäre es undialektisch, Erfindung und sozialen Kampf gegeneinanderzustellen, vielmehr ergänzen sie sich und bestätigen einander in der Perspektive der Zeit. Niemand brauchte die Entdeckung von Kopernikus, am allerwenigsten die sich befehdenden Theologen.

Aufschlussreich für die grundlegende Verschiedenartigkeit des Raumbegriffs des Stijls und der neuen Auffassung von Struktur – Fläche – Raum ist der Ausspruch von Theo van Doesburg, 1922: Erst in unserer Zeit ist durch die führende Kunstart, die Malerei, der Weg gewiesen worden, den die Baukunst zu gehen hat... An dieser Definition zeigt sich der Unterschied zwischen den Thesen des Stijls und denen des strukturellen Denkens. Während im Stijl Malerei die Architektur bestimmen soll und der Raum als eine dynamisch-komplexe Einheit verstanden wird, bildet im strukturellen Prozess Flexibilität einer gesetzlichen Regel den Ausdruck. Struktur – Fläche – Raum sind als korrespondierende Einheiten zu verstehen.

Alle grossen Erfindungen in der Kunst und in räumlichen Kreationen tragen den Widerspruch in sich, was auch für die Raumkonstruktionen der Pionierzeit gilt. Vieles war gewonnen: Normung, Leichtigkeit der Konstruktion, Reihenprinzip, Auflösung der Fassade, Neuformulierung des Raumgedankens. Wohl ermöglichte die Standardisierung der Elemente additive Reihungen, wiederum aber nur für die Realisierung klassischer Grundrisse. Es erwies sich, dass das additive Prinzip in ein allseitig dynamisches übergeführt und die Widersprüchlichkeit zwischen Normung und Expansion neu überdacht werden müsse. Mehr und mehr verwandelte sich das additive Prinzip in ein Ordnungssystem von Bezügen, die Reihung in wechselseitige Mobilität.

Die Analogie zu Problemen der konstruktiven Kunst, insbesondere mit den Entwicklungen serieller Ordnungen, wird erkennbar. Das individuelle Element wird vereinheitlicht und zu einer kontrollier- und messbaren Grösse entwickelt mit der Absicht, eine strukturelle Identität zwischen Bildmittel und Bildbegrenzung herzustellen, und dem Ziel der Schaffung einer objektiven Rhythmik. Die Normung des Elements führt zur Bildung einer additiven Gruppenthematik, die Gruppe übernimmt die Aufgabe des Einzelelements. Die Komplexität des Problems gleicher Gruppen ergibt wiederum die Notwendigkeit einer Verbindung von Regelhaftigkeit und Flexibilität durch die Farbe. Von dieser Basis aus erfolgt auf der Grundlage kombinatorischer Systeme der Schritt zu differenzierten Farbstrukturen, Form und Farbe heben sich als Gegensatz auf. Es entstehen die Probleme grosser Zahlenordnungen und limitierter Farbfolgen, der Farbdurchdringung, der Farbmengengleichheit, der Farbkombinatorik.

In der Zeit, die mir zur Verfügung stand, versuchte ich Ihnen das Problem der Struktur von Fläche und Raum und Parallelen von Entwicklungen aufgrund ähnlicher Denkvorgänge aufzuzeigen. Analogien sind nicht zufällig, sondern deuten auf ähnliche Grundhaltungen hin.

Systematische Gestaltungsmethoden sind Parallelen zu den Strukturen unserer Zivilisation – obwohl identisch, stellen sie diese gleichzeitig in ihrer gesellschaftlichen Wirksamkeit in Frage –, durch die Verwendung objektivierter Mittel, die Durchschaubarkeit ihrer Methoden, die Möglichkeit zur Vorausberechenbarkeit sind sie in ihrer Denk- und Arbeitsweise modellhaft auf die Veränderung der Umwelt gerichtet.

Richard Paul Lohse

25
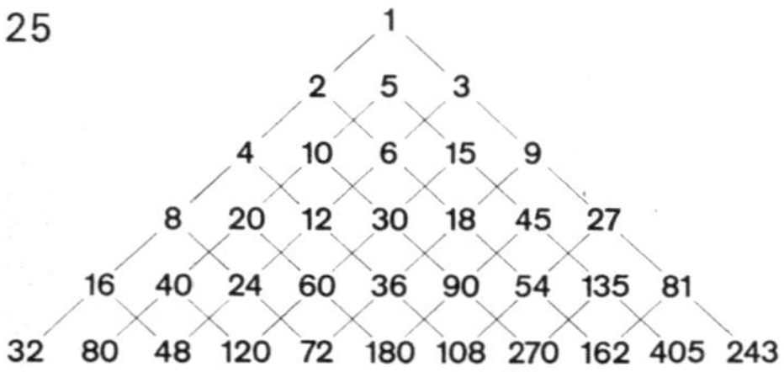

26
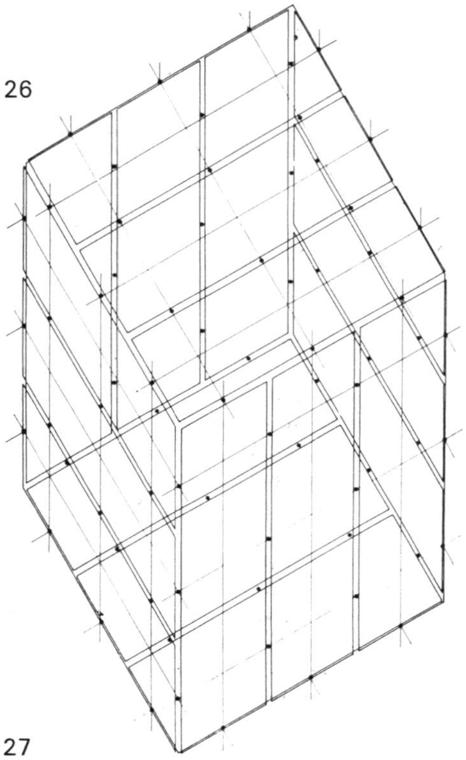

27
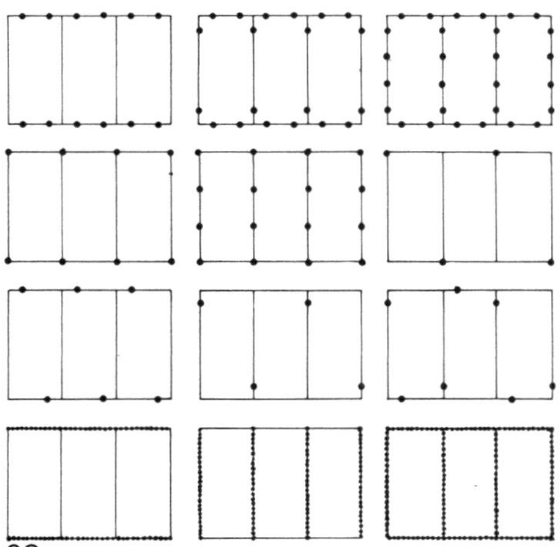

28
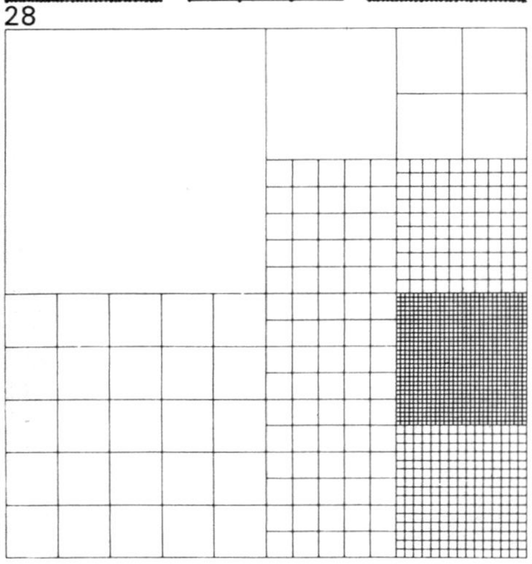

29
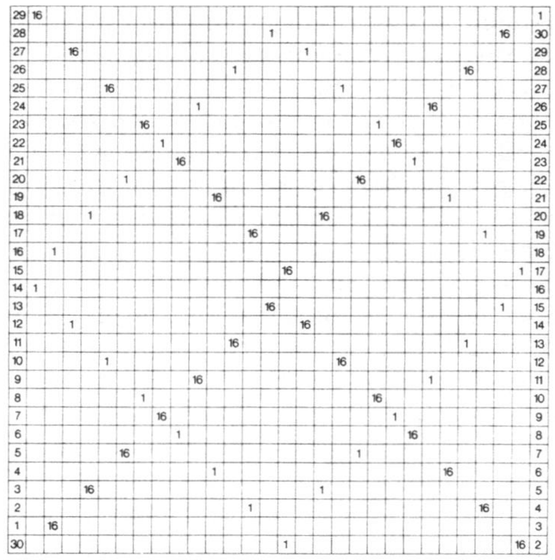

30
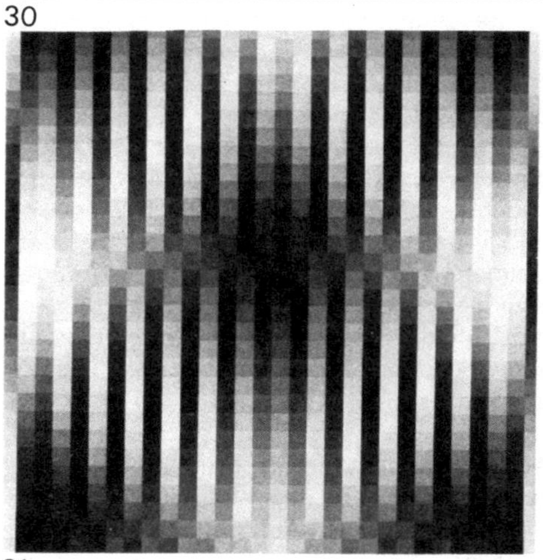

31
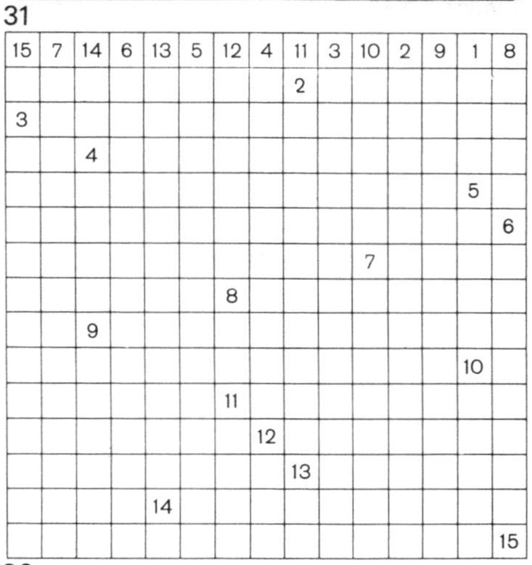

32
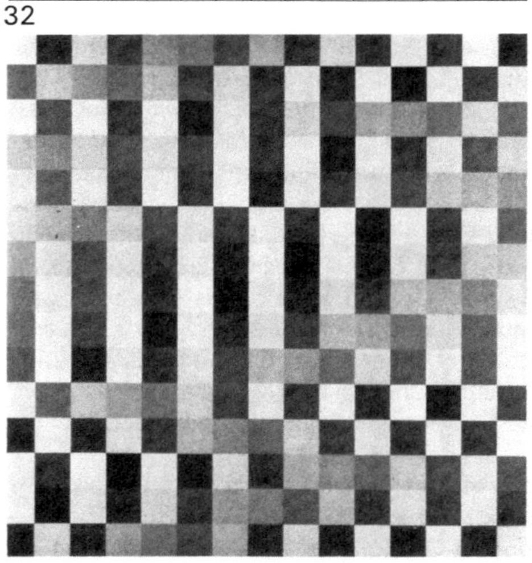

25
P. Bussat, Absolute Zahlenreihen des Moduls von 0,10 Meter.

26
Konrad Wachsmann, Diagramm eines Baukörpers, aus identischen Elementen zusammengesetzt. Modulare Ordnung der Verbindungen untereinander und ihre Beziehung zu den Bauelementen.

27
Konrad Wachsmann, Schema von Variationen der Verteilung von Verbindungspunkten beliebiger Bauelemente, die von Einzelpunkten in symmetrischer Anordnung über asymmetrische Beziehungen bis zu kontinuierlichen linearen Verbindungen führen.

28
Modularordnung der UdSSR, Grundmodul 0,10 Meter / 0,30 Meter, Planungsmodul 3,00, 6,00 oder 9,00 Meter.

29, 30
Richard Paul Lohse, Analyse zu Dreissig vertikale systematische Farbreihen in gelber Rautenform 1943–1970. Dreissigfache vertikale Wiederholung einer Spektralfarbreihe. Proportionale Identität der Anteile: Farbelement zu Farbreihe, Farbreihe zur Gesamtfläche, Mengengleichheit der Farben, Erweiterbarkeit, kombinatorisches Prinzip.

31, 32
Richard Paul Lohse, Schema zu Fünfzehn ineinandergehende systematische Farbreihen in drei horizontalen Gruppen 1943–1969. Diskontinuierliche Ordnung von kontinuierlichen Farbreihen des Spektrums. Farbmengengleichheit innerhalb der Reihe, innerhalb der Gesamtfläche.

Nachweis:
9–14, 19–20, 26, 27 Konrad Wachsmann, ‹Wendepunkt im Bauen›, Krausskopf-Verlag, Wiesbaden 1959;
25 P. Bussat, ‹Modularordnung im Hochbau›, Verlag Karl Krämer, Stuttgart;
28 Thomas Schmid/Carlo Testa, ‹Industrialisierung des Bauens›, Verlag für Architektur/ Artemis, Zürich 1969.

Bildauswahl, Typographie:
Richard Paul Lohse

On the occasion of the conferral of Zurich's 1972 Art Prize, Paul Lohse held a lecture entitled "Norming and Structural Principle" ("Normierung und Strukturprinzip") about "constructive art and parallel examples of structure, plane and space within one and the same developmental trajectory." The way this lecture uses the concepts *type, norming, systematization, serial order, exchangeability of means, controllability of means, anonymity of means, combinatory principles, kinetics*, etc. is interesting, in that it, of course, strongly recalls Konrad Wachsmann's vocabulary. Shortly thereafter, the journal *Werk* published the lecture, accompanied by six pages of images edited and laid out by Lohse, including typography.[1] On three of those pages, he juxtaposed his painting to three projects by Konrad Wachsmann. The successive images have a wonderful stringency in their argumentation, with concise captions, which we have placed ahead of the following technical analysis.[2]

1
Richard Paul Lohnse, "Norming as Structural Principle," in: *Werk* 3/74, pp. 347–354. Hubertus Adam later refers to this article and expands the discussion to the work of Fritz Haller, in: *Fritz Haller Architekt und Forscher*, op. cit., pp. 108ff.

2
The topic of "constructive art and industrial building" will not be pursued further here.

Christian Sumi

Knots and Joints[1]

1861

In Gottfried Semper's first volume of *Style*, p. 219 ff[2], he deals directly with knots made in hemp string. He writes, *"The knot is perhaps the oldest technical symbol..."*

1965

USM U. Schärer Söhne AG submits a patent for the USM ball joint for furniture. The "little sphere," the centerpiece of the eponymous furniture system, became the absolute *"technical symbol"* that Semper had described 100 years ago. It was developed by the Swiss architect Fritz Haller together with Paul Schärer Jr. Haller had completed research with Konrad Wachsmann between 1967 and 1971 at the Institute at UCLA.[3] Fritz Haller is considered as one of Konrad Wachsmann's most important collaborators at the institute.

In the same passage, Semper continues, *"Knots serve first of all to join the ends of two threads; their strength depends principally on friction."*

1951

Commissioned by the US Army, Konrad Wachsmann begins to study the nodal joints of his space frame system for his hangar constructions (USAF). In its definitive solution, the structural connection is achieved using a light, conical pin in soft steel, which is forced into the ring-shaped nodal joint construction using a hammer. The joint is compressed, its various elements wedged together and its "strength depends principally on friction," as Semper describes it.

In the case of both the knotted hemp string and the nodal joint of Wachsmann's USA hangar, the same mechanical principle is operational: friction created by pressure. This demonstrates the temporal persistence of technical processes, how they continue to develop through permanent transformation and are realized in diverse materials (hemp string and soft steel).[4]

The series of images shows the genesis of the components, beginning with the hook-like closure in the Packaged House in 1939, through the USAF hangar in 1951. The relationship between form and function of each component, and their interrelation, is the focus of the examination. It is based upon the various connective techniques and their mechanical principles.[5]

1
My thanks to Sonja Hildebrand, Marko Pogacnik and Akos Moravanszky for the references to Semper; to Dani Meier, Dr. Lüchinger and Meier Engineers for the references to various mechanical principles.
I also want to thank Georg Vrachliotis, who originated the comprehensive documentation of Frei Otto, an important Wachsmann student (*Denken in Modellen*, Georg Vrachliotis, Joachim Kleinmanns, Martin Kunz, Philip Kurz (eds), Spector Books, Leipzig 2017) and Steeve Sabatto, who has written his dissertation on Wachsmann in the USA (Steeve Sabatto, "Innovation technique et programmation technologique dans le contexte nord américain de l'après seconde guerre mondiale et de la Guerre Froide. L'oeuvre architecturale de Konrad Wachsmann (1942–1972) comme étude de cas," Ph.D. research manuscript, EHESS Centre Alexandre Koyré, February 2017) for the interesting conversations.

2
Gottfried Semper, *Style in the Technical and Tectonic Arts; or, Practical Aesthetics*. Harry Francis Mallgrave and Michael Robinson, trans. Getty Research Institute, 2004.

3
See Georg Vrachliothis, "Modell, Werkzeug und Metapher. Fritz Hallers Architekturforschung," in: *Fritz Haller*, op. cit. An important precedent for the USM nodal joint is, among others, the universal Mero nodal joint, also mentioned in *Turning Point*, op. cit.

4
In the most expansive sense, the topics discussed here on "technology, material, form" relate to Semper's theory.
See: Akos Moravanszky, *Stoffwechsel. Materialverwandlung in der Architektur*. Birkhäuser, Basel 2018, pp. 221ff.

5
For example: the bolt (hinged), the screw with slotted hole (shear, a small amount of bending because of the give between screw and hole), the fitted screw (compression, some shear), the pre-tensioned screw (compression/friction, comparable to the older technique of riveting), welding (seam, melting), wedging (compression), etc.

Gottfried Semper, *Der Stil in den technischen und tektonischen Künsten oder Praktische Ästhetik*, Munich 1860–63, p. 180.

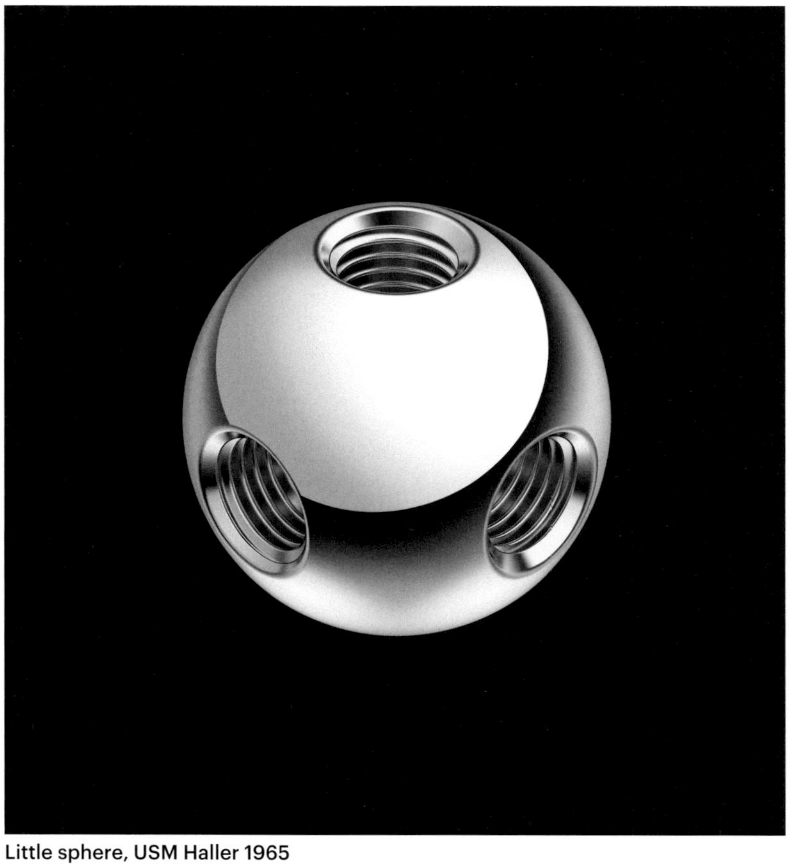

Little sphere, USM Haller 1965

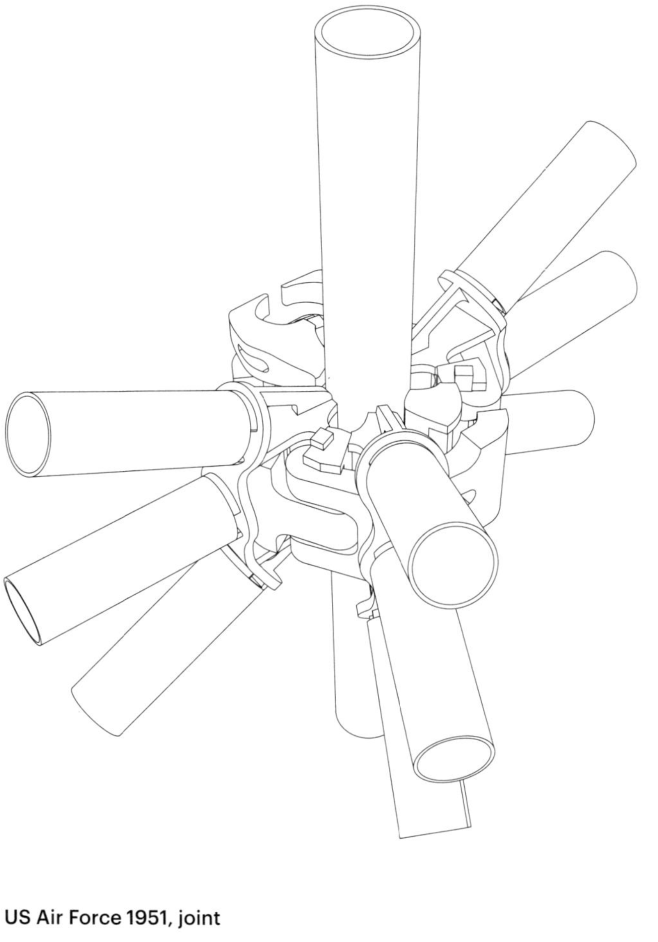

US Air Force 1951, joint

Drehungen bewerkstelligen, die miteinander oder gegeneinander laufen u. s. w. So bietet diese einfache Technik für stilistische Betrachtungen, die das Nützliche im Schönen sehen, den reichsten Stoff, deren Bearbeitung einem kunstphilosophischen Posamentier vorbehalten bleibt. Auch von diesem Prozesse besitzen wir Illustrationen, die älter sind, als unsere papierne Geschichte.[1]

§. 50.

Der Knoten.

Der Knoten ist vielleicht das älteste technische Symbol und, wie ich zeigte, der Ausdruck für die frühesten kosmogonischen Ideen die bei den Völkern aufkeimten.

Der Knoten dient zuerst als Verknüpfungsmittel zweier Fadenenden und seine Festigkeit begründet sich hauptsächlich auf den Widerstand der Reibung. Das System, welches durch Seitendruck die Reibung am meisten befördert, wenn die beiden Fäden in entgegengesetzten Richtungen nach ihrer Länge gezogen werden, ist das festeste. Andere Verhältnisse treten ein, wenn auf die Fäden nicht in dem Sinne ihrer Länge, sondern vertikal auf deren Ausdehnung eingewirkt wird, obgleich auch hier die nach der Längenrichtung der Fäden gehende Resultante der Spannung am meisten in Betracht kommt. Der Weberknoten ist unter allen der festeste und nützlichste, vielleicht auch der älteste oder doch derjenige, der in den technischen Künsten am frühsten figurirte. Die Seiler und Schiffer kennen eine Menge von Knotensystemen, über welche ich leider nur als Laie sprechen könnte. Manches auch für unsere

[1] S. Wilkinson's oft citirtes Werk über Aegypten. Vol. III. S. 144.

Auffassung Interessante liesse sich an ihre Spezifikation knüpfen, doch bleibt auch diess befugtern Händen überlassen.

Eine sehr sinnreiche und uralte Anwendung des Knotens führte zu dem Netzwerk, das auch die wildesten Stämme zu bereiten wissen und für Fischerei und Jagd benützen. Die Maschen des Netzes, dessen Knotengefüge hier beigegeben wird,[1] haben den Vorzug, dass die Zerstörung einer Masche das ganze System nicht afficirt, und leicht auszubessern ist. Hierin liegt zugleich das Kriterium des Netzgeflechts das in anderer Hinsicht die mannichfachsten Variationen gestattet in diesem einen Punkte aber sich unter allen Umständen gleich bleibt. Bei den Alten war der spanische Hanf zu Netzen der besste. Auch der kumanische hatte in dieser Beziehung Berühmtheit. Man machte Netze, worin Eber gefangen wurden, von so grosser Feinheit, dass ein einziger Mann so viel davon auf seinem Rücken tragen konnte, als hinreichte, um einen ganzen Wald damit zu umstellen. Doch diente dasselbe Geflecht in dichteren Maschen auch als Brustharnisch, wozu der Faden, obschon an sich fein, dennoch aus 3 bis 400 Einzelnfäden zusammengezwirnt war. Diese Industrie scheint bei den Aegyptern besonders geblüht zu haben.[2] Dieselben Aegypter machten auch Ziernetze aus Glasperlenschnüren, wovon sich mehrere sehr hübsche Exemplare erhielten. Dieser Schmuck war auch bei den Griechinnen, so wie bei den hetruskischen und römischen Damen gewöhnlich. In Indien dient das Netz als reiches Motiv für Kopfbedeckungen und Halsbänder, wobei der Geschmack in der Al-

[1] Es zeigt sich bei genauerer Anschauung dasselbe identisch mit dem Weberknoten.

[2] cfr. Plinius XIX. 1. und Herodot.

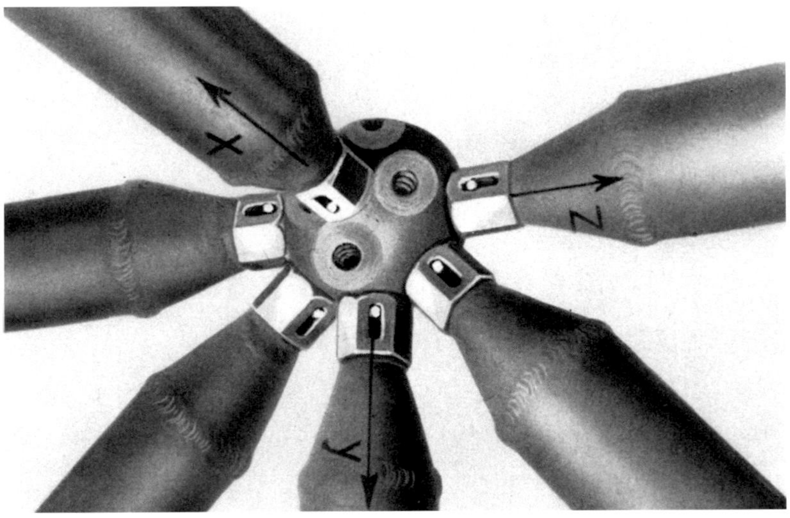

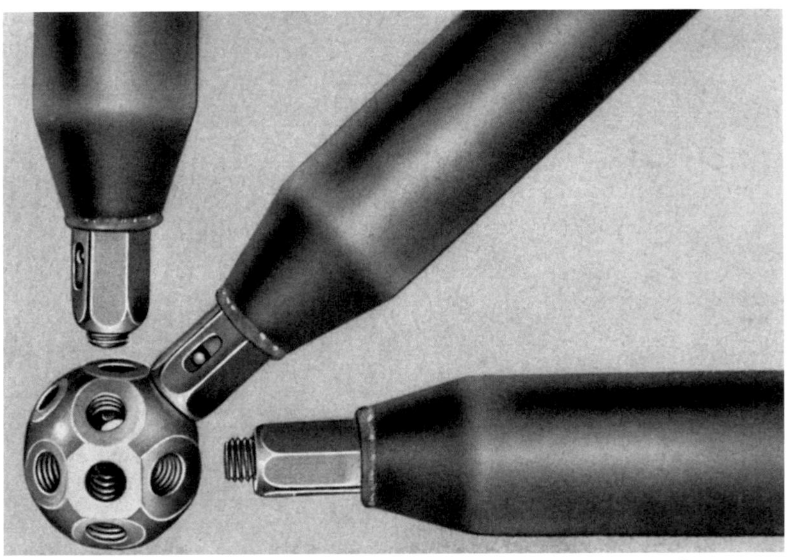

Max Meringhausen (1903–1988), Mero junction (Knotenpunkt) patented 1943, pulished in *Wendepunkt des Bauens* p. 133

USM – "Ulrich Schärer Münsingen" – stands for timeless design and the highest levels of quality. The successful Swiss company which specializes in furniture systems, USM U. Schärer Söhne AG, employs around 400 employees at its headquarters in Switzerland and at its sister companies in Germany, France, the USA, UK and Japan. The manufacturer with the Swiss production location is represented in over 40 countries worldwide via sales partners. USM Modular Furniture Haller was developed between 1962 and 1965. Its acceptance into the Design Collection of the Museum of Modern Art (MoMA) in New York (USA) at the end of 2001 is a high distinction and confirms the artistic character of the product. The famous classic is used in offices and public buildings as well as in the private sphere.

Packaged House, General Panel System, with Walter Gropius
Compression connection through panels' dead weight.

“In the winter of 1941 in Lincoln, Mass., Walter Gropius and I decided to design, in the most comprehensive way, a system of construction which would truly correspond to industrial requirements; our design later came to be known as the ‘General Panel System’.

“Wood construction was chosen, because at that time wood was the only available material combining the advantages of quality, quantity and economy. The intention was not to build a definite type of house but simply to design the most versatile possible prefabricated building element, suitable for easy assembly on the site by totally unskilled labor in any kind of one or two-story structure. It was also part of the general conception that windows, doors, glazing, fittings and mechanical installations should all be incorporated in the building elements in advance.

“After a series of preliminary investigations it was concluded that, assuming a standard connection and a standard section, it would be necessary to design a universal building system in which the individual element did not need to occupy a predetermined position, in other words, one in which every panel connection was the same vertically and horizontally.”

Konrad Wachsmann, *The Turning Point of Building*, op. cit., p. 140

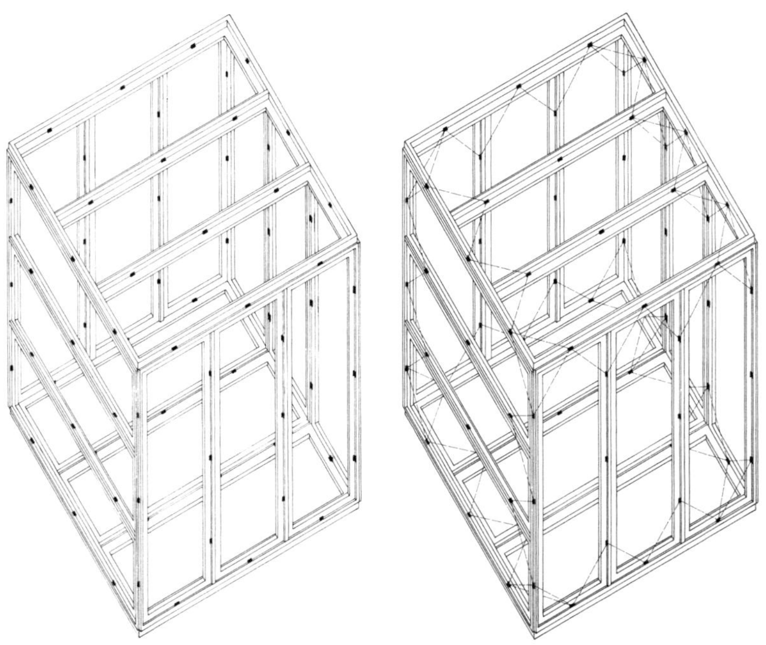

The frame structure with the metal hooks

211 Der ausgestanzte universelle Metallhakenverschluß, etwa eineinhalb Mal vergrößert, General-Panel-System

The Nodal Joint, Chronology[1]

The chronology demonstrates the development of the hook connection, comprising two cross pieces (red), a pin (blue) and screws or wedges (yellow). In advance of the chronology is an earlier project by Walter Gropius and a first scheme by Wachsmann from 1939.

Growing House 1932, Walter Gropius: (Förster und Kraft Prinzip)
The three champfered interior components of the wall are held in place with the U-shaped fasteners (red). Three single compression connections (yellow) result.

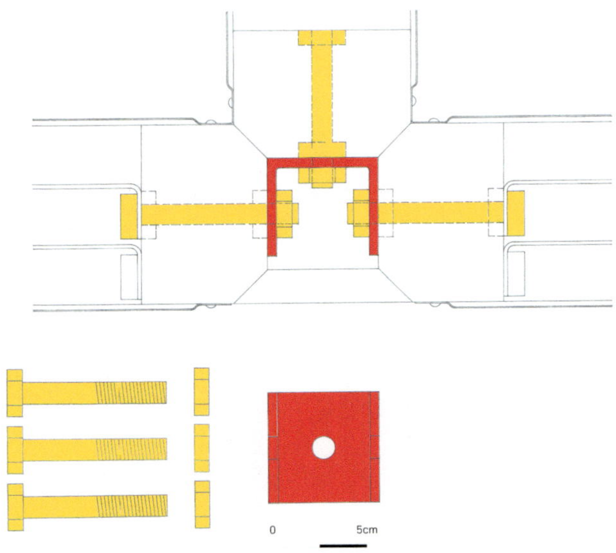

Growing House 1932, Walter Gropius

1. French scheme 1939:
The wall elements arrive on site with pre-mounted fasteners. The joint consists of three Connectors (Wachsmann): Two Y-shaped cross pieces (red) interlock in the center and are fixed in place by a spine (blue). The final locking element (yellow) pulls the two wedge-shaped elements at the wall's edges together with radial force and stabilizes the joint.

2. Reworking of the French scheme 1941:
Instead of screwing the cross pieces together on the diagonal the connection is made with a screw and counter-screw perpendicular to the panel (yellow), preventing the connecting element from tearing itself out. The locking element (yellow), can be released with a screwing action, allowing for the "internal pressure" to be regulated.

3. Packaged House System variation 1942:
The walls' cladding are slightly shifted against each other and organized by a nodal joint in a rotational orientation (see Wachsmann's cube). Because of this configuration, all wall connections are identical. The Y shape and spine connectors are replaced by 3 "flat" elements: two "crosspieces" (red), fixed with and pushed through and intersected by the "mainstay piece" (blue). The screws are replaced by wedges (yellow). The final wedge is driven on site, tangential to the joint. In the end, a cover strip is used to cover the aperture used for assembly. By now, four wall elements can also converge in a single joint.

4. TDU-1 variation:
Similar to variation 3 but with less expensive hardware: instead of cast elements, the system uses die cut and breaked sheet metal.

5. Patent variation 1945:
The "mainstay piece" has been subdivided into two diagonal hooks (blue) and the shape of the "crosspieces" is modified into "loops" (red). The joint is constrained and locked into place by the dead weight of the last vertical wall element to be lifted into place.

6. Turning Point variation:
Same as variation 5, except that instead of a tapered horizontal element, the element is bent.

1 The chronology was contributed by Daniel Gut. His work, with a comprehensive explanation, was written under the supervision of Bruno Krucker as an elective project for Prof. Arthur Rüegg at the ETHZ upon my encouragement, and was published in abridged form in: *Konstruktive Konzepte der Moderne*, Lehrstuhl Prof. Arthur Rüegg Zurich 2001, p. 138 ff. Steeve Sabatto provides a thorough chronology in: *Architecture industrialisée* op.cit. p. 170 ff

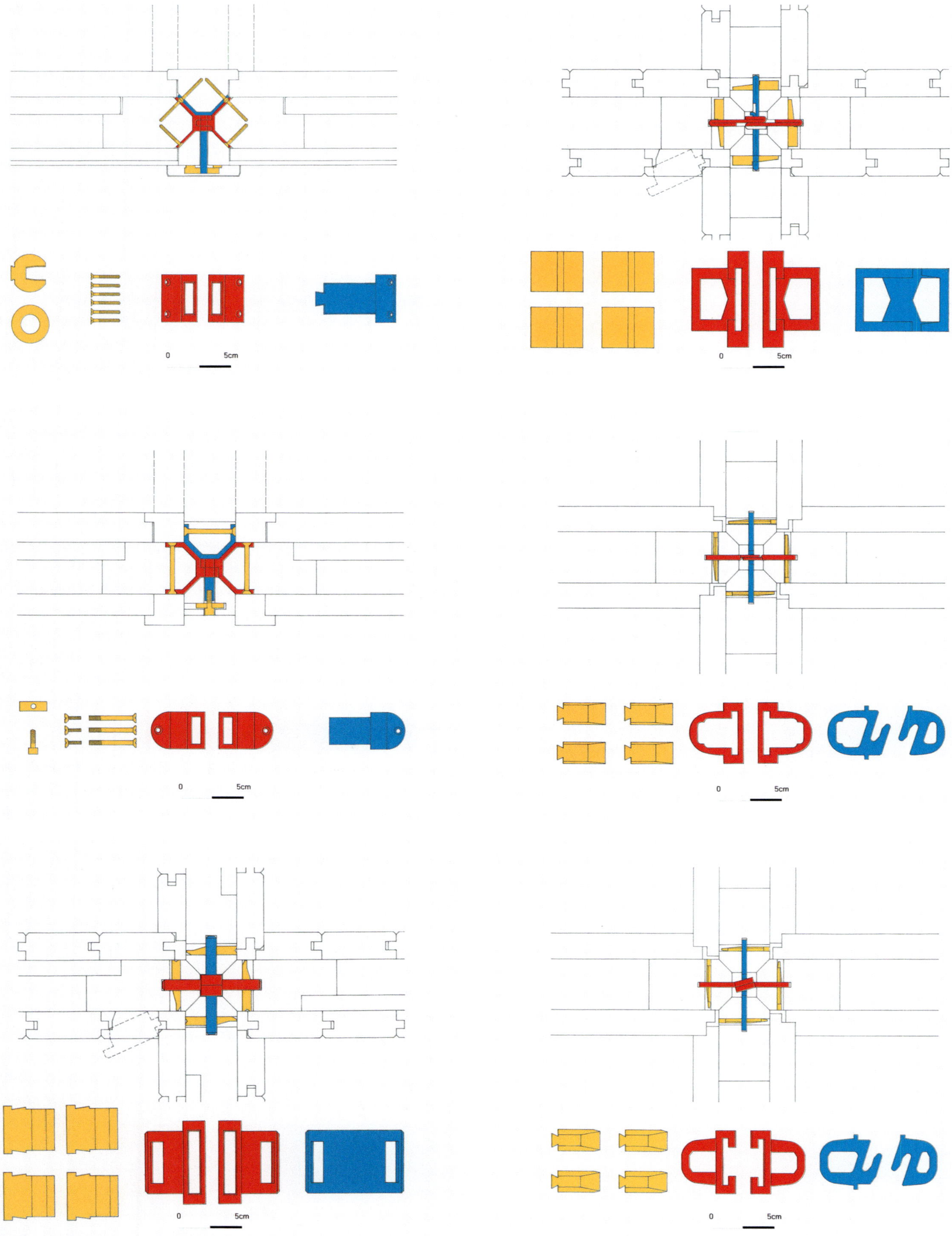

1 French scheme 1939
2 Reworking of the French scheme 1941
3 Packaged House System variation 1942
4 TDU-1 variation
5 Patent variation 1945
6 Turning Point variation

Wedging by means of shifting

"In New York during the period 1942–1943 I designed a partition wall system for the General Panel Corporation.

"Whereas, apart from a simple asymmetrical modification, the General Building System, described in the next section, has an essentially symmetrical panel connection, in this partition wall system the principle of the connection is based on a purely asymmetrical form which gives every element a definite direction. Like the building panel system, the partition wall method enables up to 12 panels to be joined to one point within an imaginary three-dimensional raster. In this case the filler strips of the General Panel Building System are replaced with a filler strip located inside the joint.

"However, the special feature of this design is that no mechanical connector of any kind is required to hold the individual elements together. As a result of the diagonally displaced relationship between the outer surfaces of the stressed-skin panels, the individual parts only need to be pushed together, after which they are no longer free to move in any direction."

Konrad Wachsmann, *The Turning Point of Building*, op. cit., p. 136

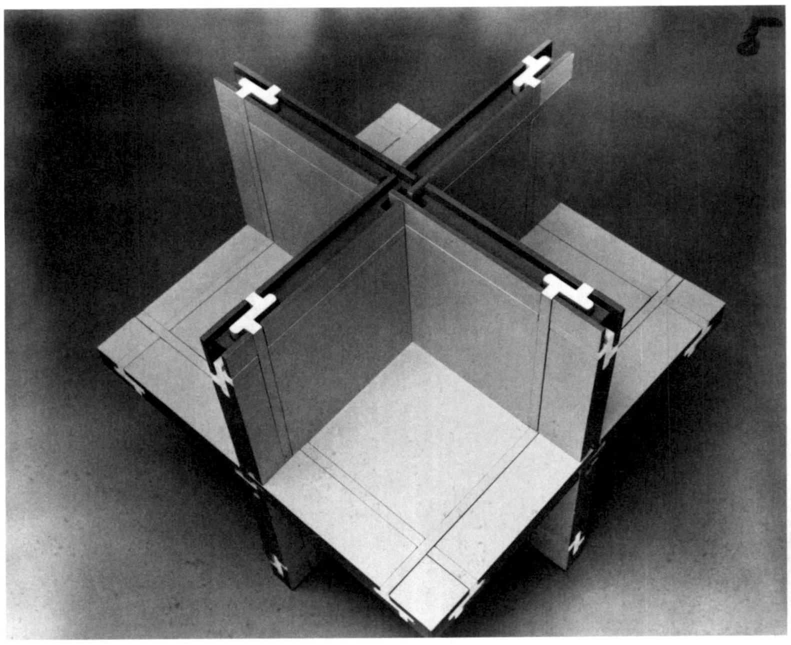

Three-dimensional joint as part of the wall and floor system

195 Die Entstehung einer Verbindung von 12 Elementen in einem Punkt mit immer gleichem Profil als Grundlage eines universellen Bausystems für Trennwände ◀

196 Die Berührung von 12 in drei Ebenen liegenden Platten im Mittelpunkt eines gedachten Würfels

197 Die Auflösung der Platten in rahmenbildende Stäbe

Joints, Reconstruction[1]

The photographic series of working models show the step-by-step genesis of the rotational, three-dimensional orientation of each component. The nodal joint, better known under the name "Wachsmann cube" comprises twelve elements: six square, six rectangular, of which three each are oriented counterclockwise and three clockwise.

This principle is the basis for the walls' vectorial, reciprocally offset orientation. The walls' cladding is shifted sufficiently relative to one another that they are wedged against one another at their juncture, so that mechanical joinery such as the hook connection used for the Packaged House are no longer needed. In other words, by applying the principle of three-dimensional rotation, the joint is stabilized by itself.

The nodal joint, in turn, generates the profile of the structural members, which frame the walls and ceilings of the partition wall system.[2]

1
Mark Gilbert reconstructed the "cube" in drawing. The basis is a photographic series in *Turning Point* on p. 136. The model-building workshop Zabrowski in Zurich rebuilt the cube in wood at a scale of 1:1. Based upon comparison with other wall constructions, the wall thickness is presumed to have been 7.5 cm. The cube has, in the meantime, been exhibited in various locations, among them 1996 in the Architektur Zentrum Vienna and 2010 at the Architecture Museum of the TU Munich.

2
With the cube, Fritz Haller perpetuated the cube as a central theme (rotation, vectorially oriented systems, etc). See Vrachliotis, op. cit. p. 78 ff.

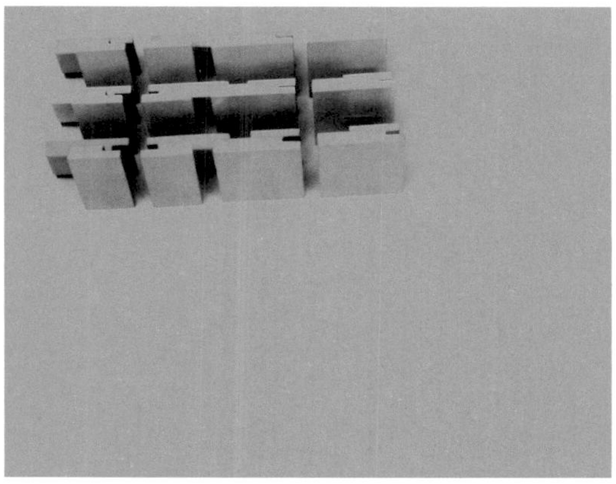

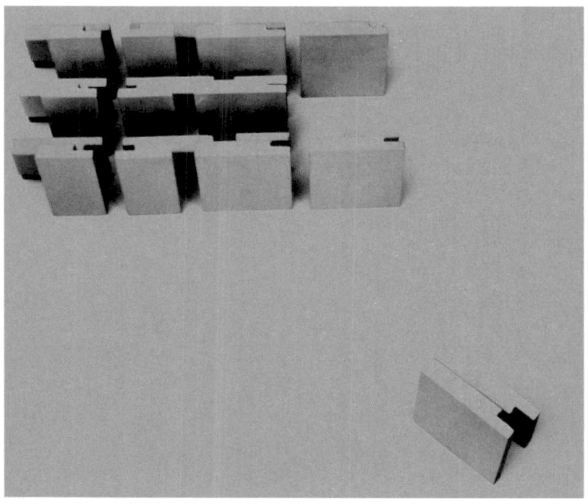
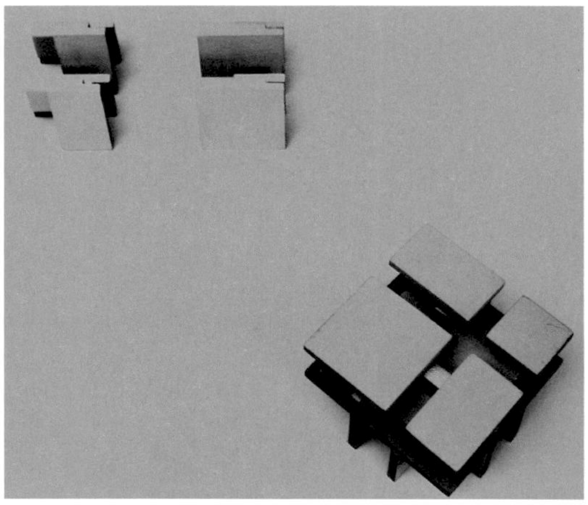
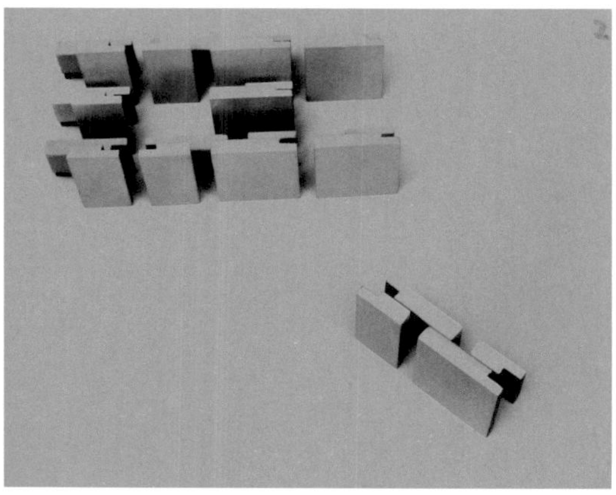
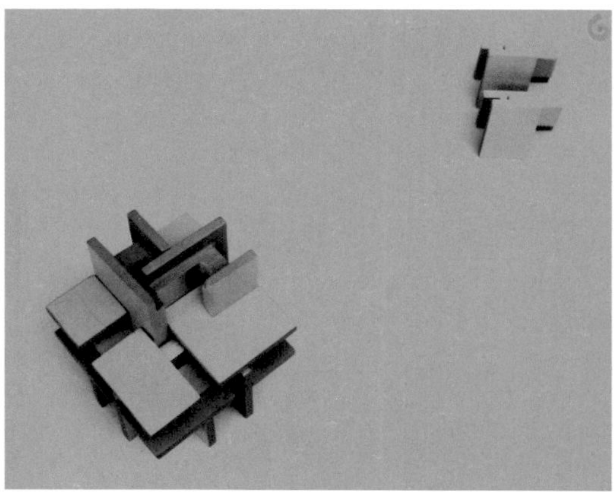
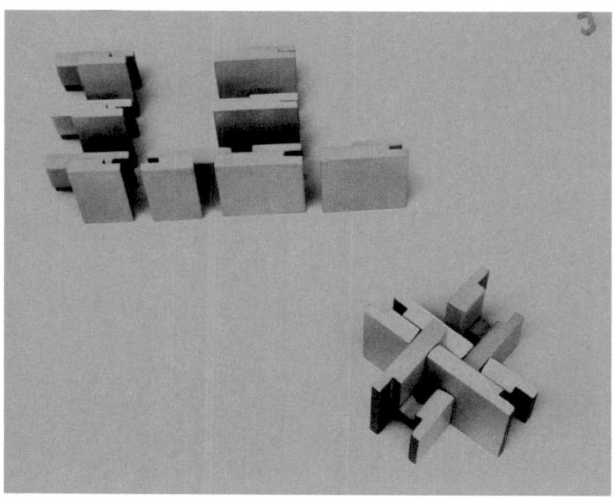

Development of the elements and their joinery

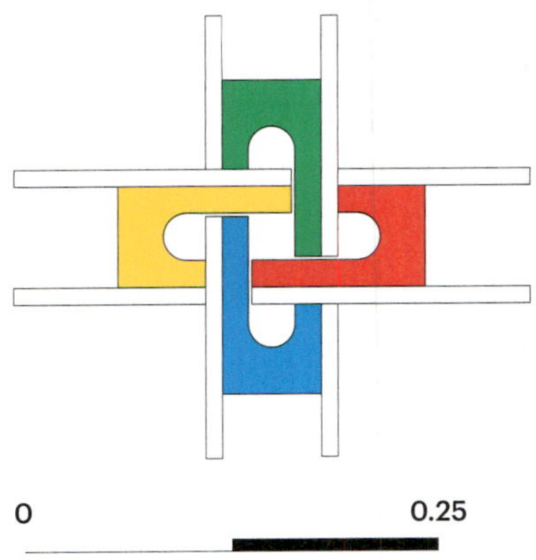

burkhalter sumi architekten: reconstruction 1:1 of the "cube"

Plan of the 4 rotated elements

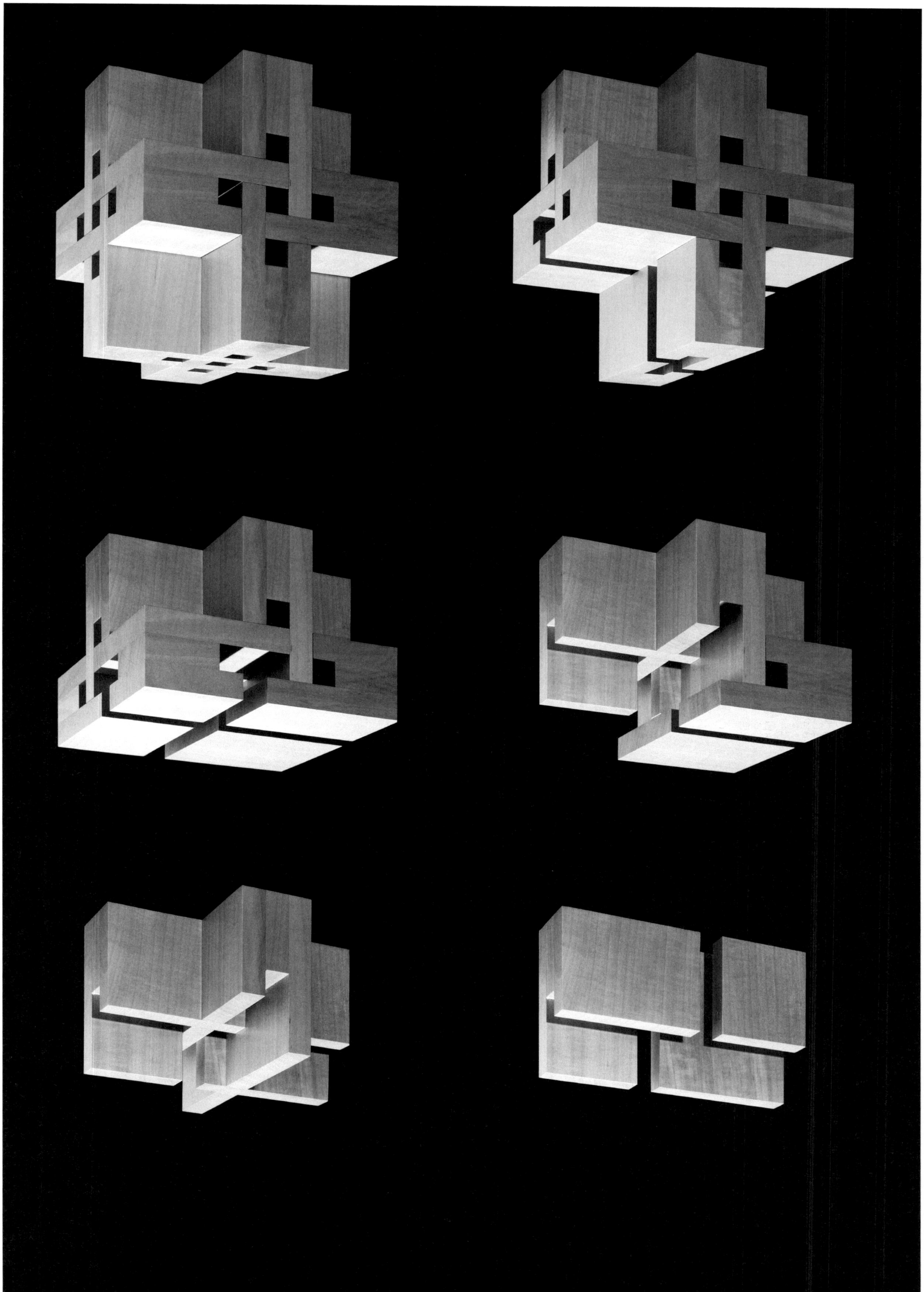

"During 1944–1945 I developed a wide-span structural system, on which I had already done some preliminary work in France towards the end of the Thirties. This system was subsequently named 'Mobilar Structure' and its further development was sponsored by the Atlas Aircraft Corporation.

"The problem was to try and utilize the advantageous statical properties of tubular cross sections in steel construction. The chief result of these investigations, which extended over 1½ years and for which I was again able to assemble a team of engineers, designers and technicians, was the development of a new truss joint and a movable wall panel assembly.

"The principal link in the joint is formed by a pair of stamped eye plates of different thicknesses, automatically spot-welded at each end of the tube, one on each side of the center-line. The center of the connection is formed by a pin which is passed through the openings in the eye plates at right angles to the axis of the tube. While the inside face of the thicker of the two eye plates coincides with the center-line of the tube, the second, thinner eye plate is mounted in such a way that it counteracts the eccentricity resulting from the reverse orientation of the pair of eye plates with which it mates."

Konrad Wachsmann, *The Turning Point of Building*, op. cit., p. 160

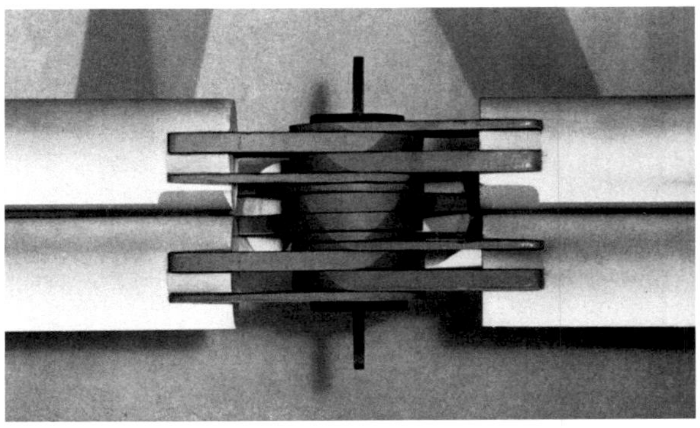

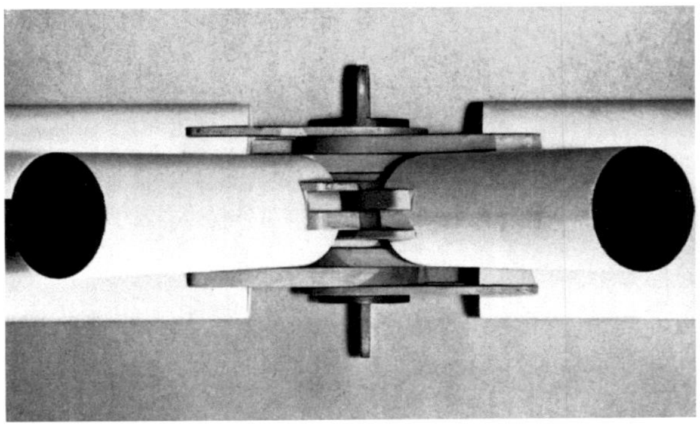

Eccentric connectors of the junction

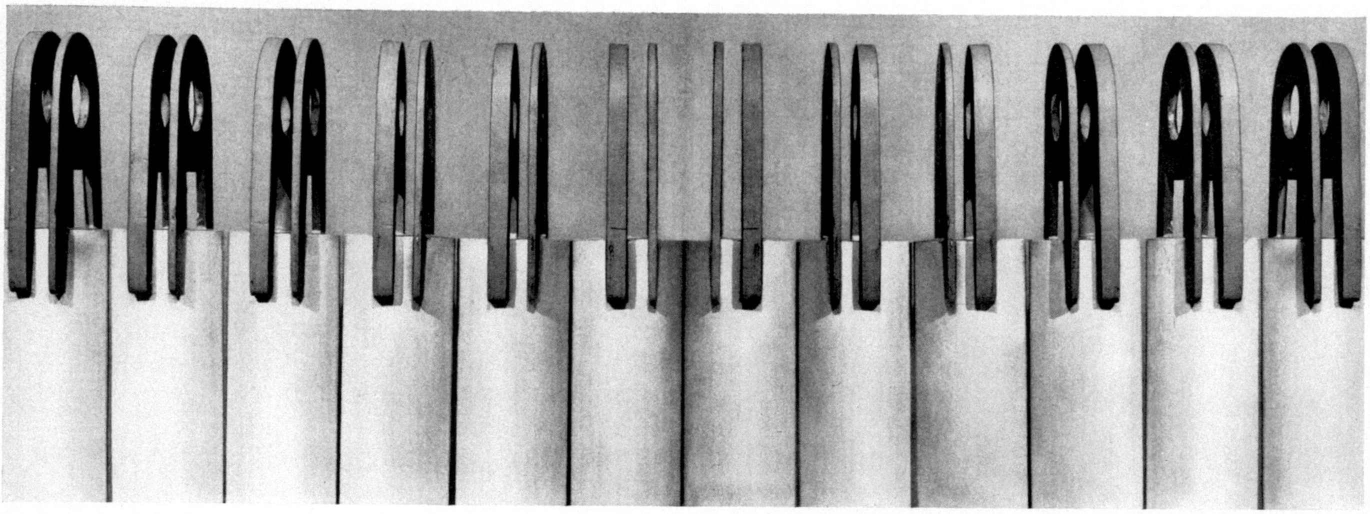

249 Das uniforme, standardisierte Massenprodukt. Die Augenplatten sind an beiden Rohrenden identisch

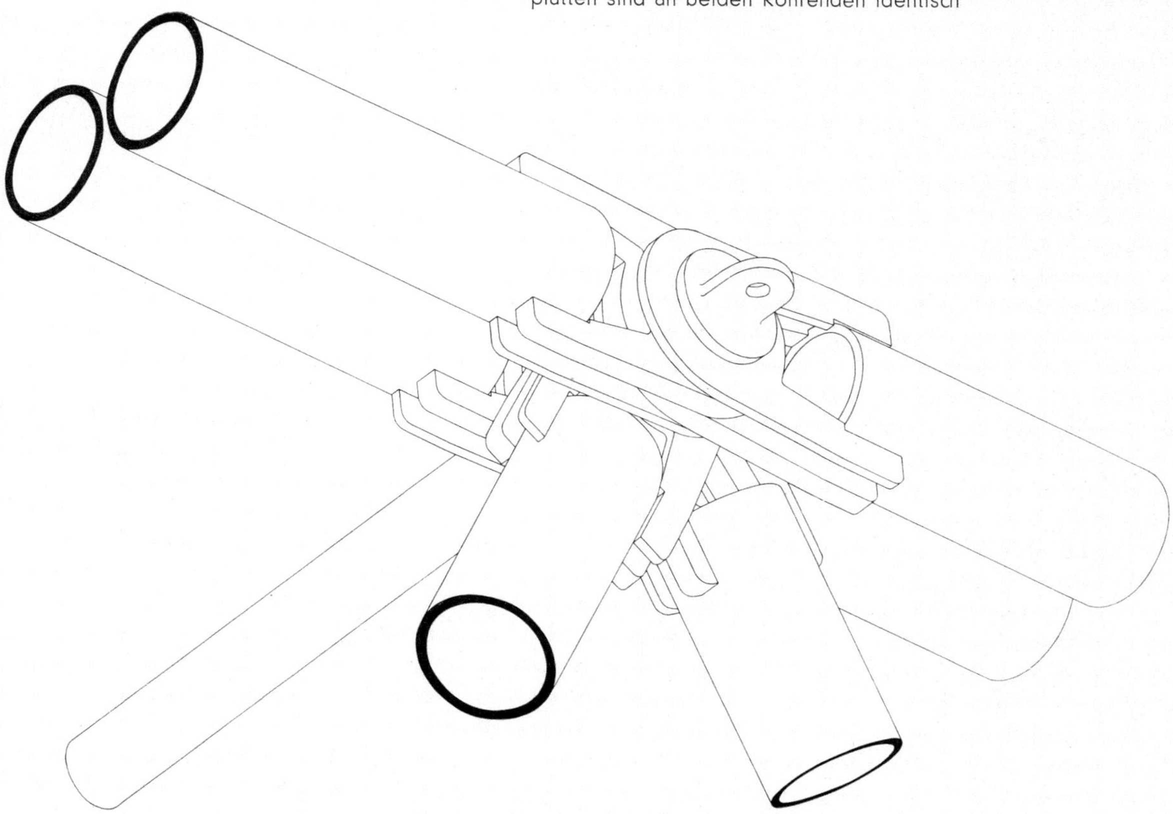

250 Isometrische Ansicht des Knotenpunkts der Mobilar-Struktur

"In 1951 I was commissioned by one of the research departments of the U.S. Air Force to develop a structural system for very large hangars. The basic conditions of this research assignment corresponded perfectively with the principles of industrialized production methods.

...

"It was decided to give the structural members a tubular cross section. The work led gradually to the development of a space frame design, which, however, in application, was equivalent to a two-directional, statical system of stress transmission. This design called for principal members, used for top and bottom chords, and secondary members. Accordingly, two diameters of pipe were selected. The joints between members were formed by means of three-dimensional swivel connectors."

Konrad Wachsmann, *The Turning Point of Building*, op. cit., p. 170, 172

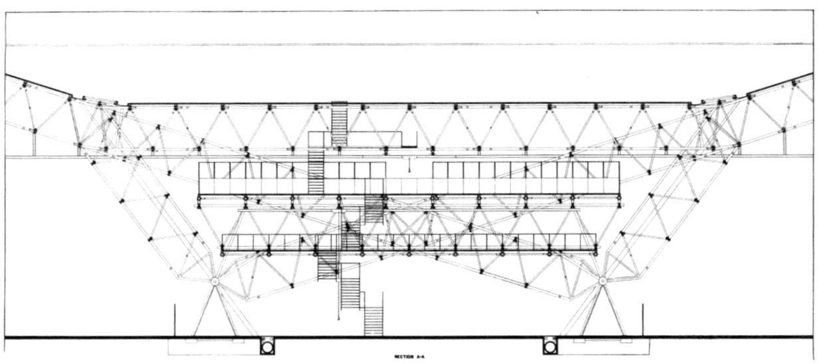

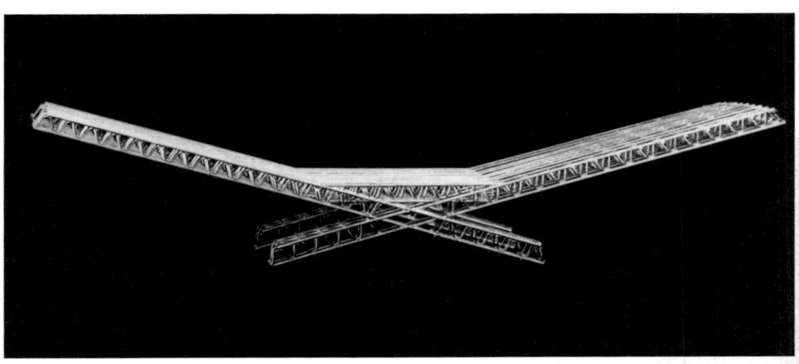

Section through the hangar with the crosswise organised trusstructure and the connectors, supported by triangular tube construction as "feeds"

Model of the of the crosswise organised truss structure

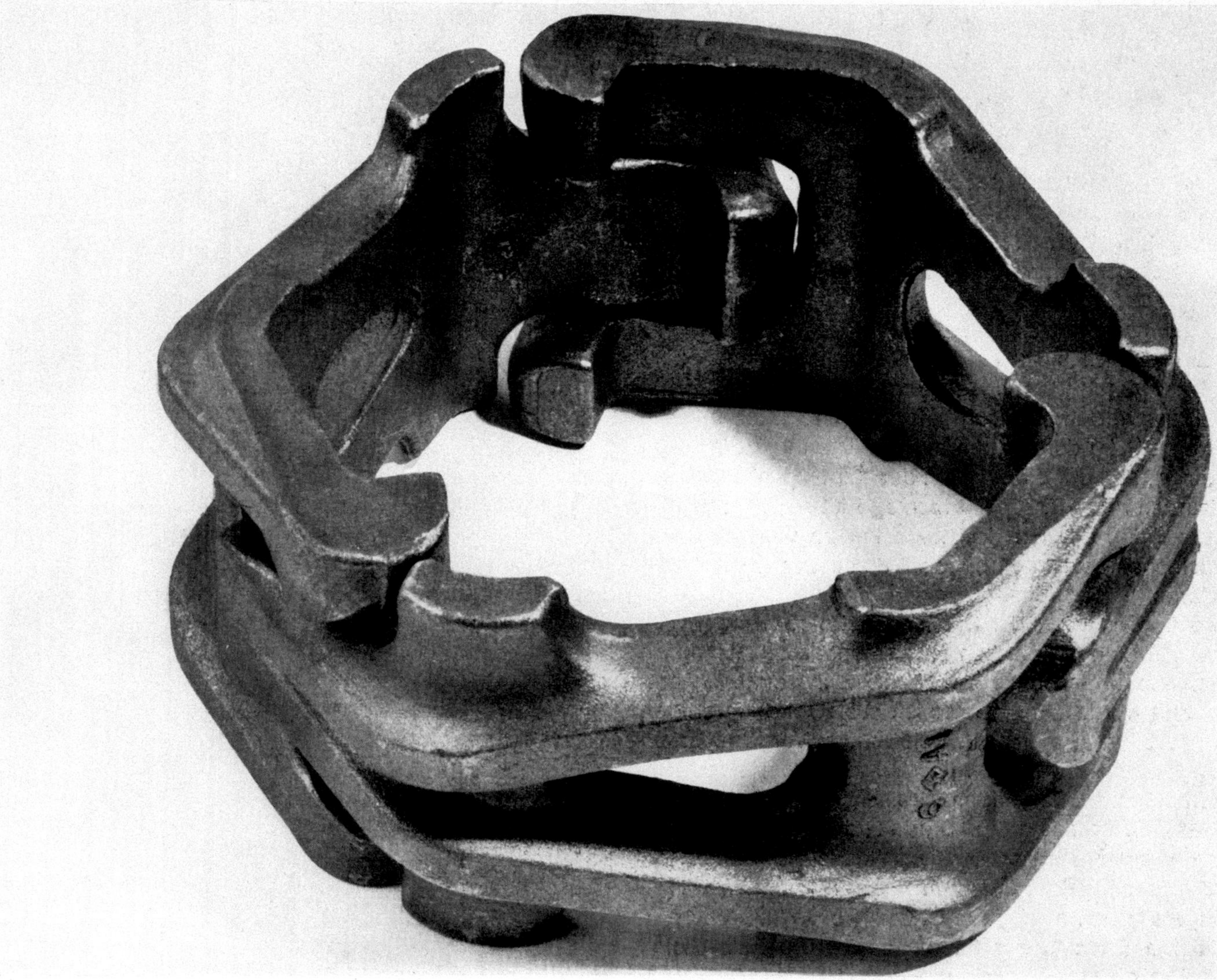

267 Die ineinandergestapelten Elemente der Gliederkette ◀
268 Das einzelne Element dieses Konstruktionsteils ◀

269 Die Position der Teile, wie sie, eine Kette bildend, den Knotenpunkt umschließen

Nodal Joint, the Various Preliminary Studies[1]

The preliminary studies depict the development of the joint's various components: primary pipe and 6 secondary pipes, 3 wedge-shaped elements (yellow), 3 locking elements welded on the primary pipe (blue), 3 chain elements (red), 6 clasps (green) on which up to 3 secondary pipes are connected. At stake in the diagrams, (not true to scale) is a hypothetical thought process completed in drawing based upon existing photographic materials. The succession for the different variations follows a typological and not a chronological order.

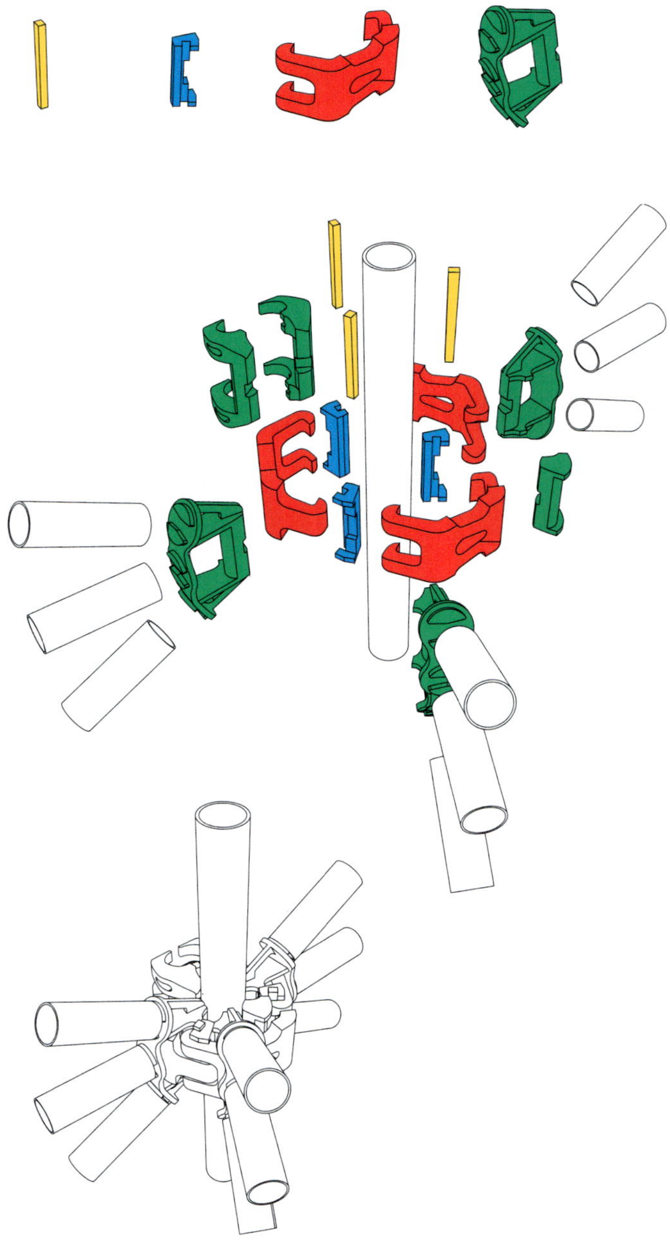

1 Collaboration on the reconstruction of preliminary studies: Hortense Le Coniac, Patrick Heller and Oscar Mather 2017. Reconstructive drawing and video of definitive nodal joint: Lorenzo Fassi and Niccolo Bononi Baraldi supervised by Carlo Nozza (Chair Prof Franz Graf) AAM Mendrisio 2015. Steeve Sabatto provides a comprehensive chronology in: *Architecture industrialisée*, op. cit., p. 178 ff.

USAF joint. Image courtesy of the Aaron Siskind Foundation

Version A: Pin; Flexible Connection

Two flat steel elements whose form recalls Mickey Mouse (blue) ears are welded opposite to the primary pipe. By doubling these "ears," a pliers-like construction is made, which is then used to affix the three ring-shaped elements with one or two countercurves (red). Bolts (yellow) attach these constructs to the pliers-like construction. The boomerang-like secondary pipes are in turn locked into the truss by the ring elements.

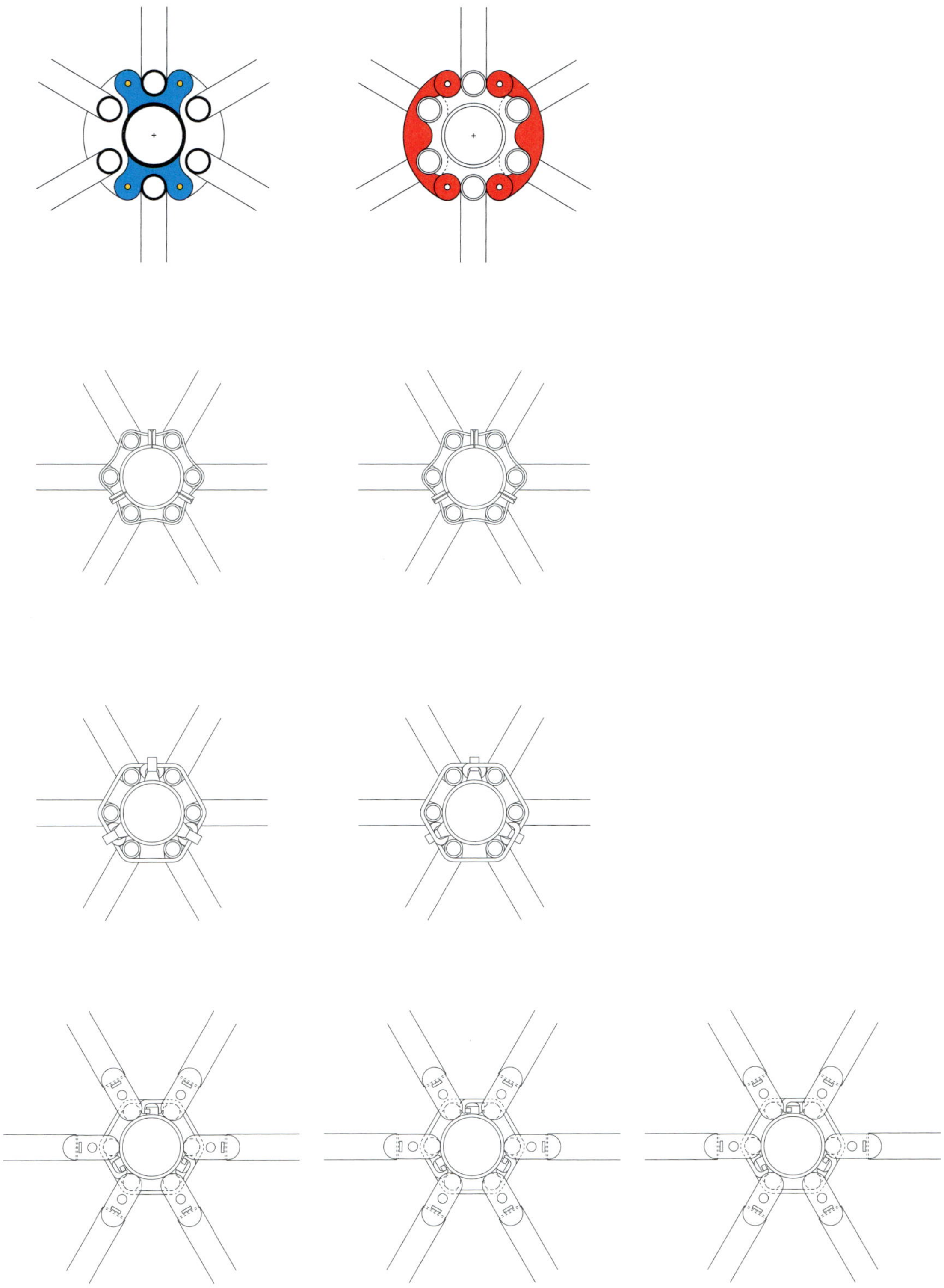

Version B: Screw; Flexible Connection

Three wave-like ring elements (later to become the chain elements, red) are screwed in place on the pipe by a clip (later, the locking element and the pin, yellow and blue). Each ring element encircles two boomerang-like secondary pipe elements (later, the clasps, green).

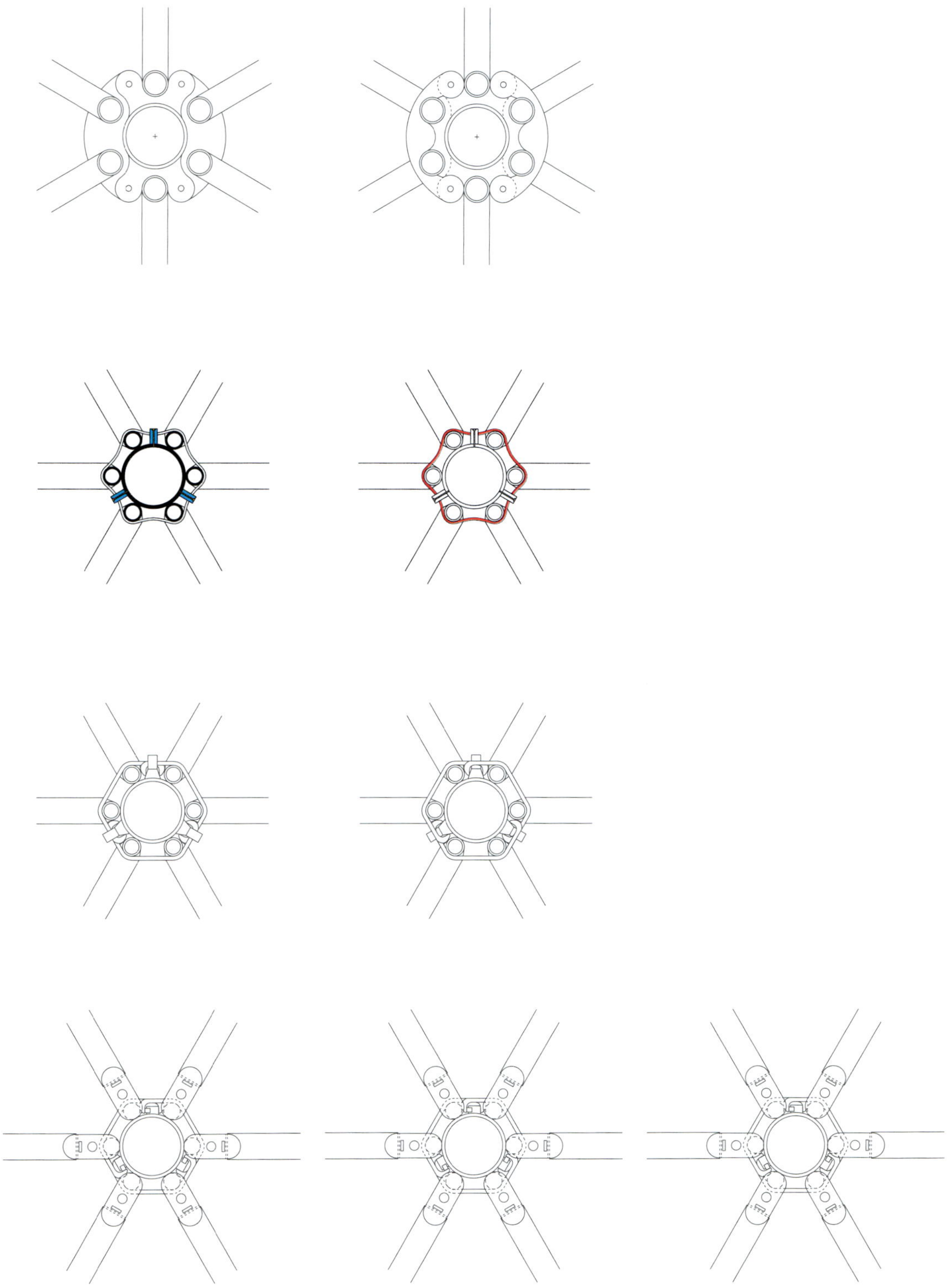

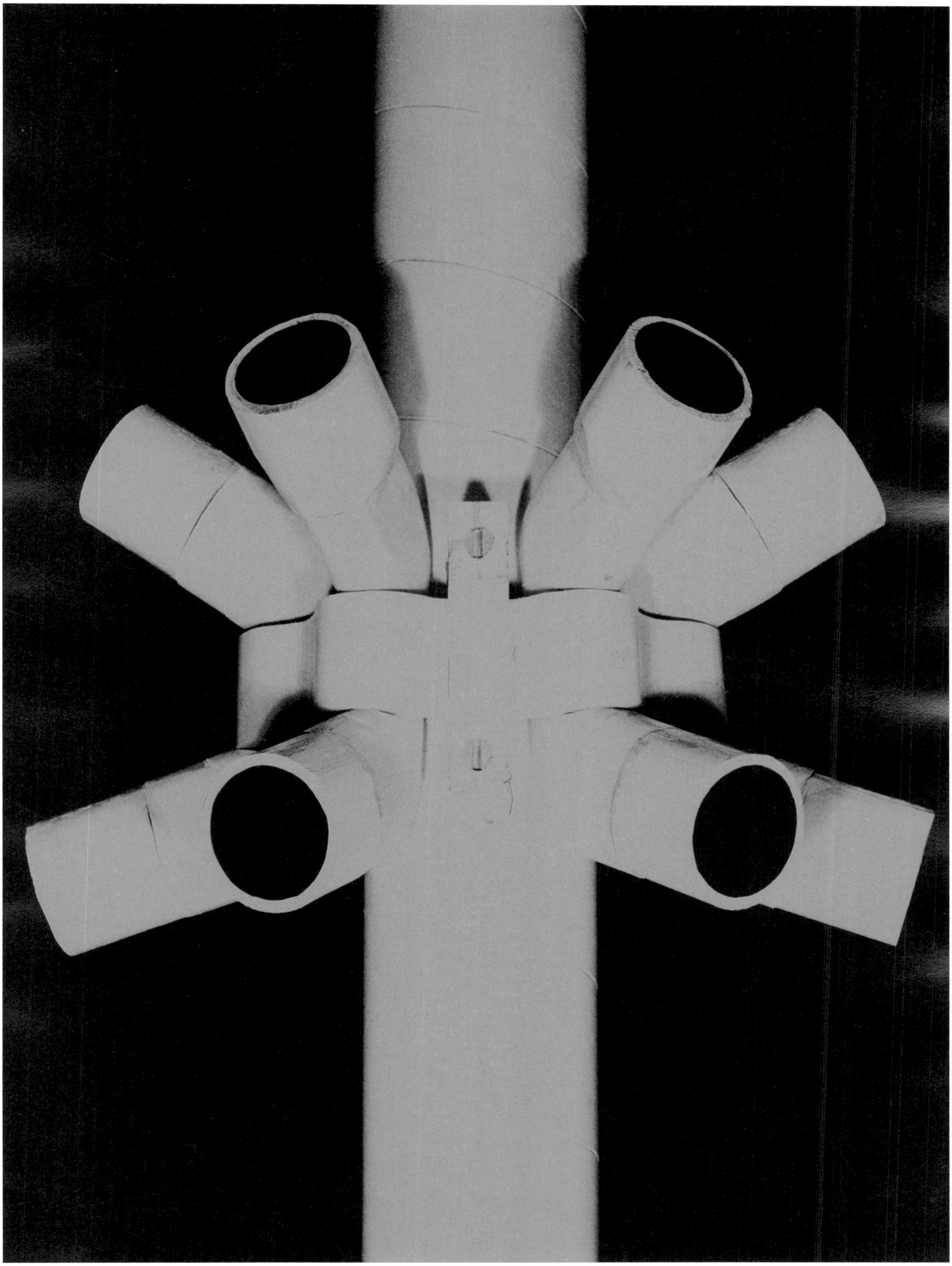

Version C: Clip; Compression and Friction

This is a decisive step with regard to the locking connection of the chain elements (red). A type of hook fits into the bifurcation in the adjacent element (red), and the black clip holds the two components to the locking element (yellow and blue). The "boomerang" has become more sophisticated.

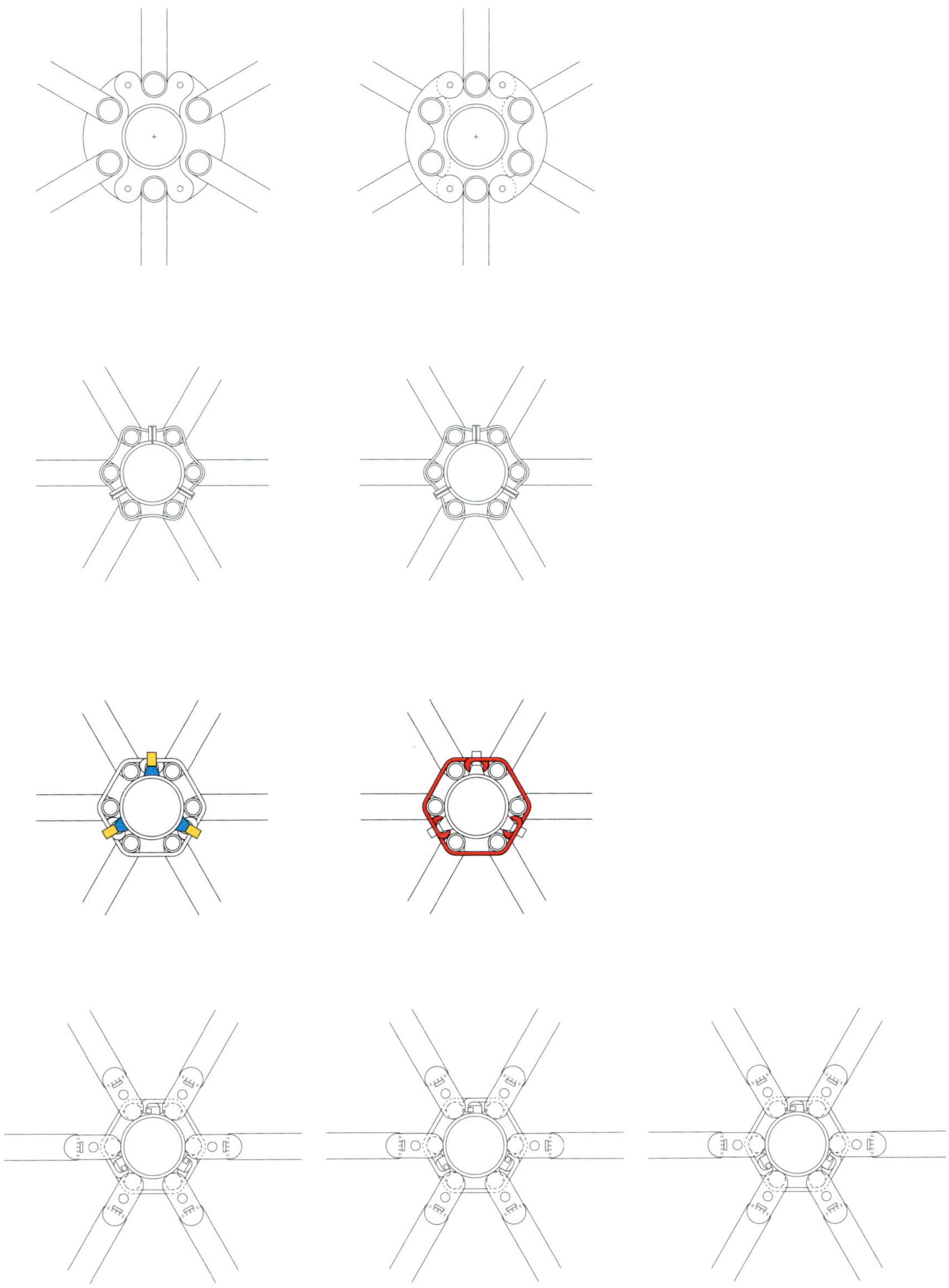

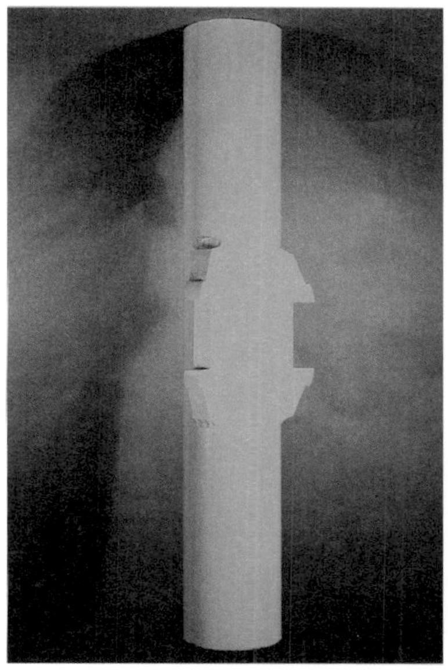
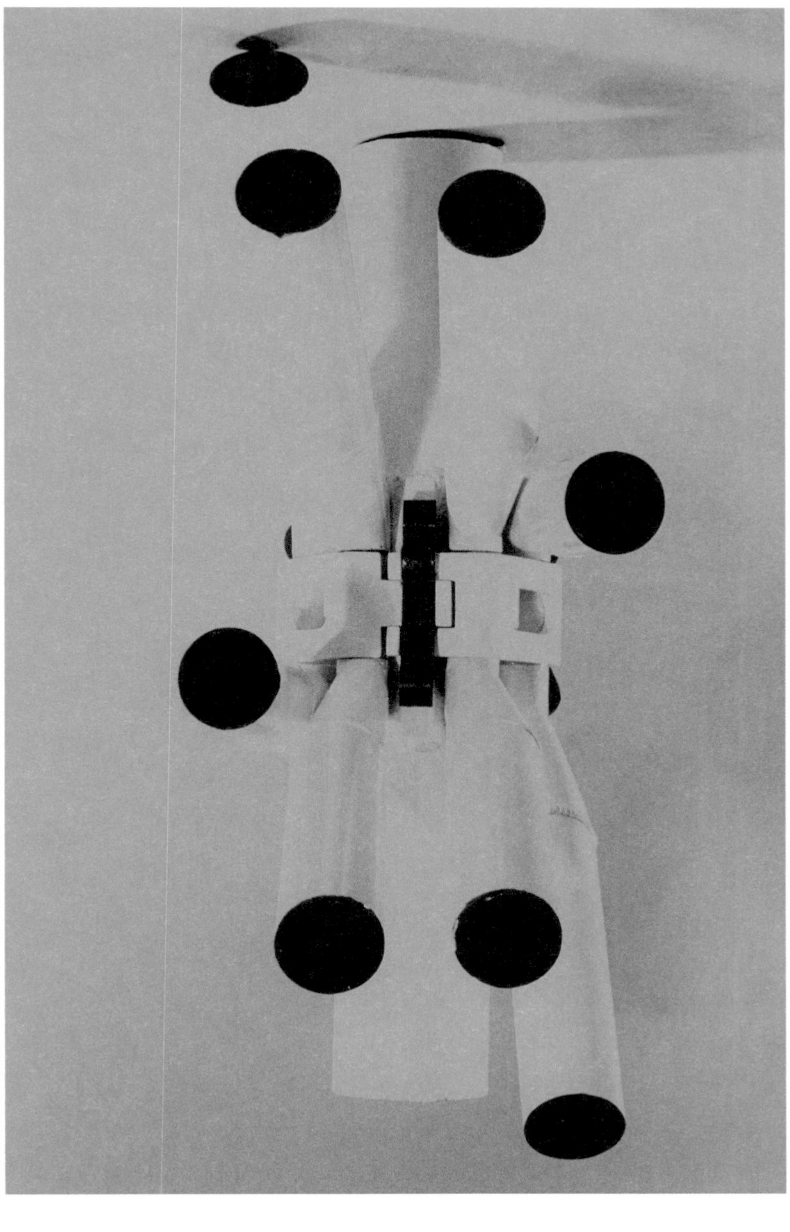
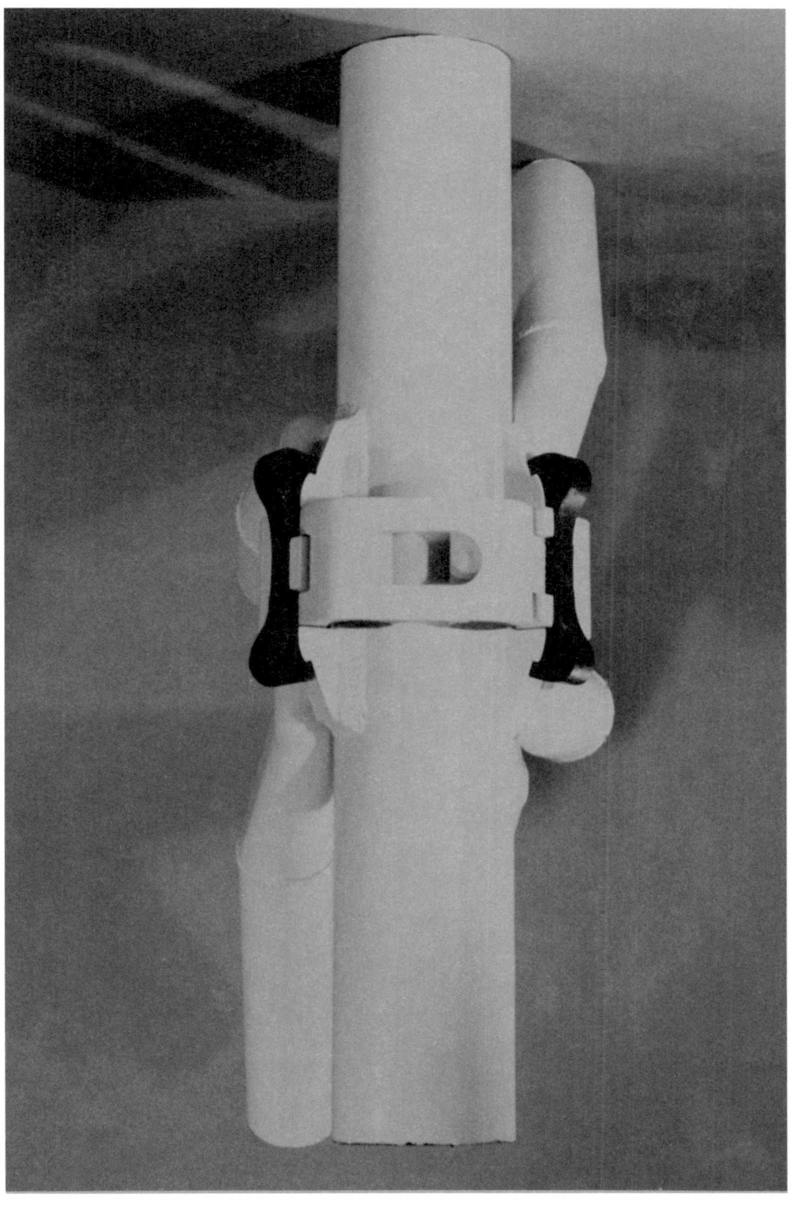

Version D: Wedge, Compression, and Friction

The means of "anchoring" to the ring element and adjacent pipes – thus far a single element – is sub-divided into two elements (green). Instead of the clip, a conical pin (yellow) is driven between the welded locking element (blue) and the wedge-shaped ring element with a hammer. The connection among elements of the joint now consists exclusively of compression, and therefore, of friction. This variation corresponds to a large extent to the definitive solution, which was executed in high quality stainless steel.

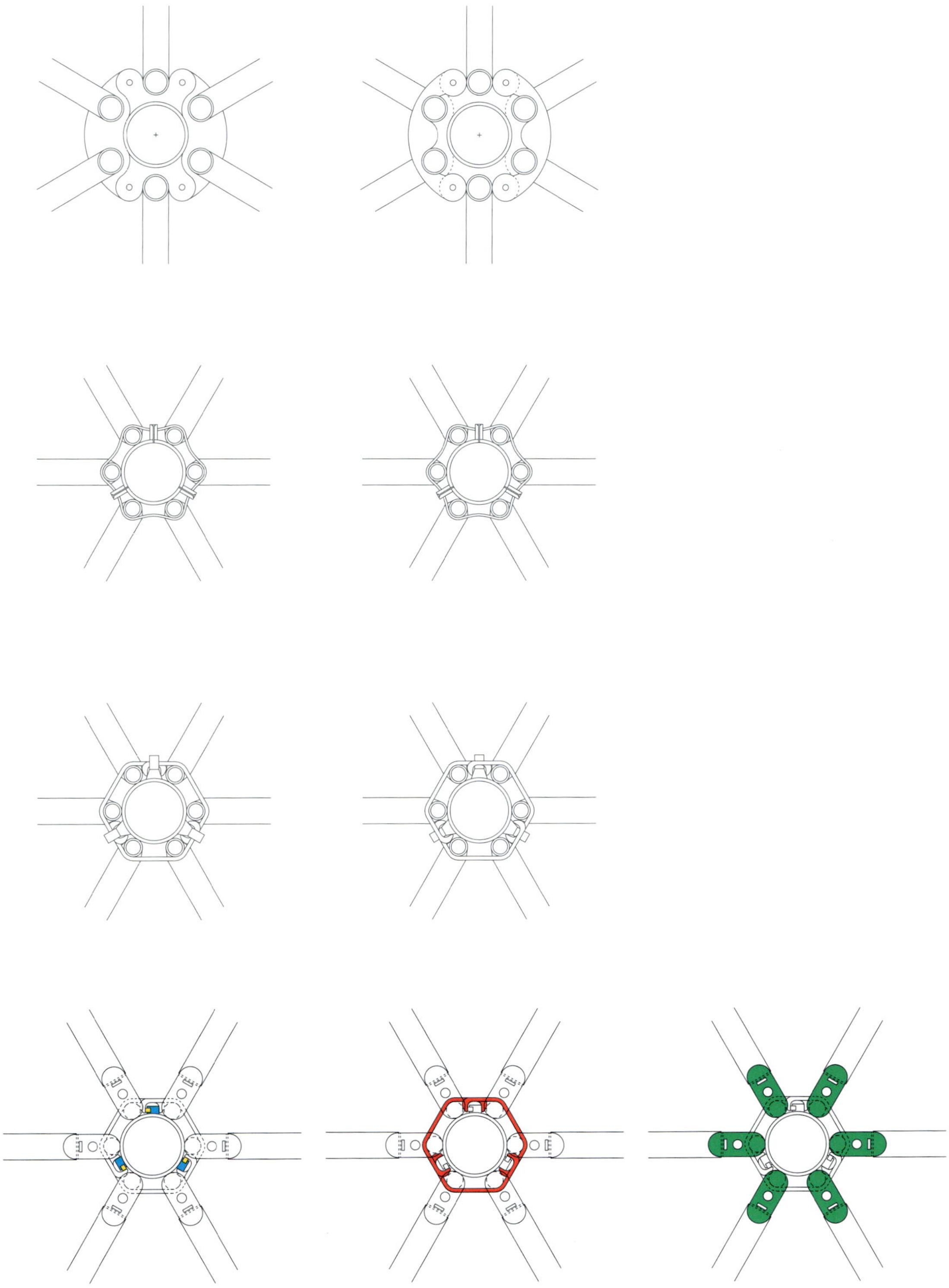

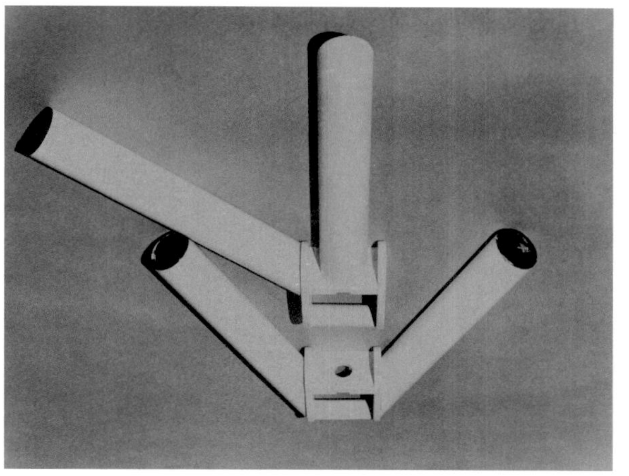

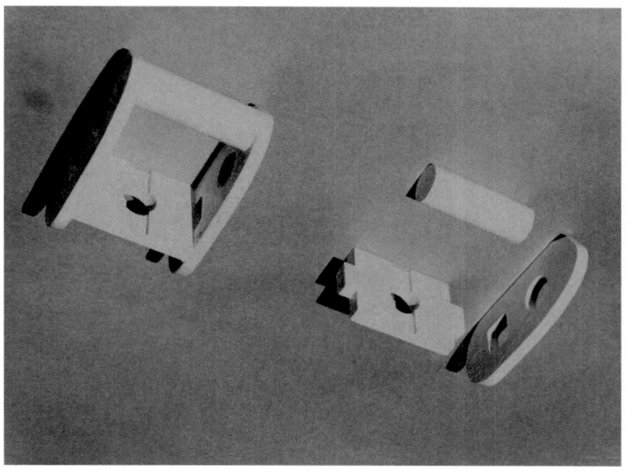

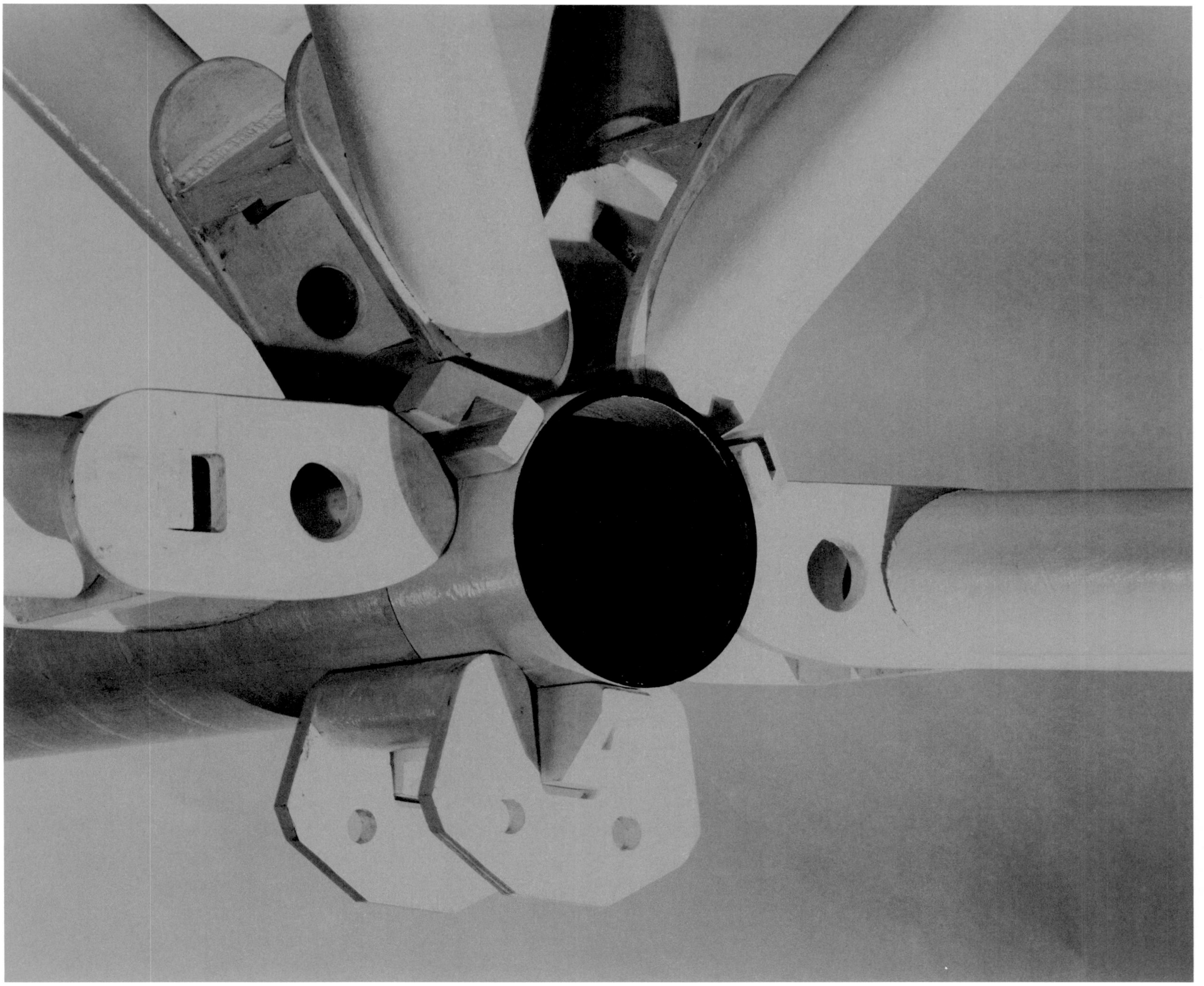

Mock-ups, Akademie der Künste, Berlin, Konrad-Wachsmann-Archiv
Photos Heinz Unger, Zürich

In the archives held by the Berlin Academy of Arts (Akademie der Künste, Berlin, Konrad-Wachsmann-Archiv), there are more than 100 mock-ups of the universal joint in cardboard, wood, metal and plastic. Many of them are witness to the persistent, step-by-step development of a new joinery element, for example the joint used in the USAF. In addition, there are objects that were generated in collaboration with work completed by Fritz Haller at the Institute.[1] Other objects, by contrast, illustrate a playful search for a new basis upon which to develop the topic of juncture and space. Where and when this work was completed remains largely unknown.

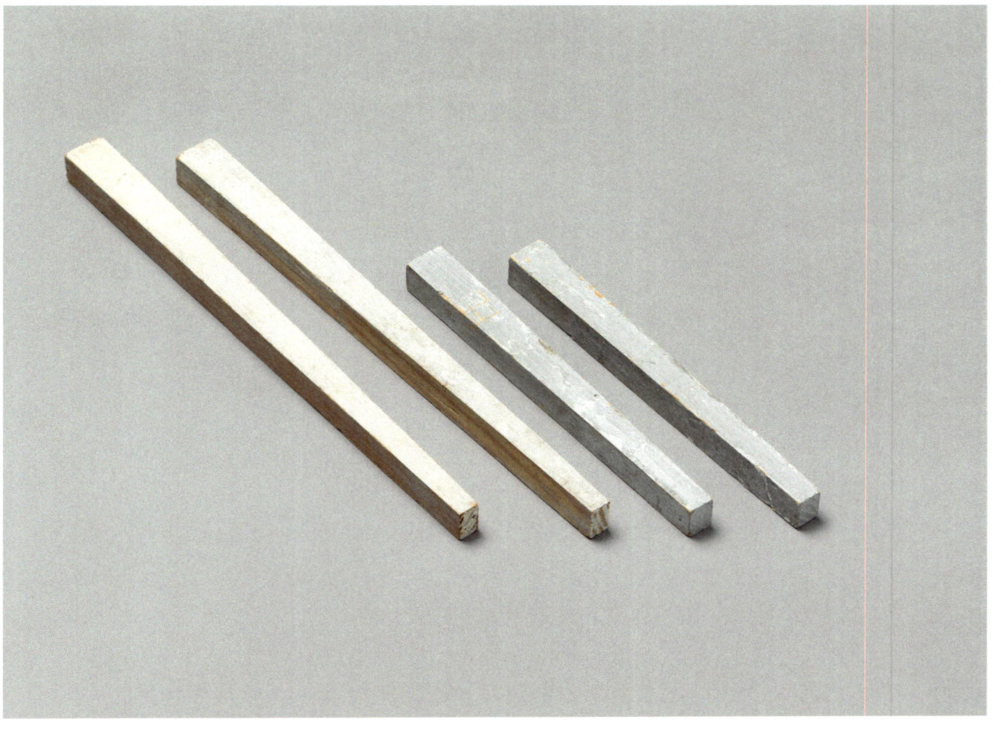

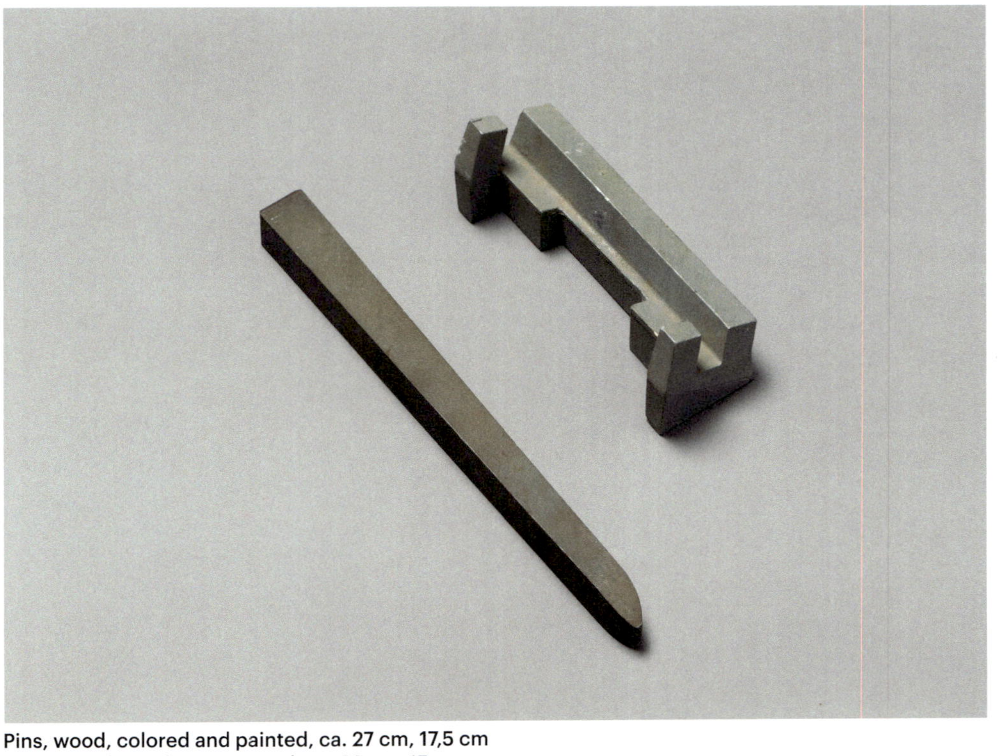

Pins, wood, colored and painted, ca. 27 cm, 17,5 cm
Pin and locking element, metal, ca. 26 cm, 15 cm

1
See Georg Vrachliothis, "Modell, Werkzeug und Metapher. Fritz Hallers Architekturforschung," in: *Fritz Haller*, op. cit., pp. 78ff.

Locking element remnants, metal, ca. 26 cm

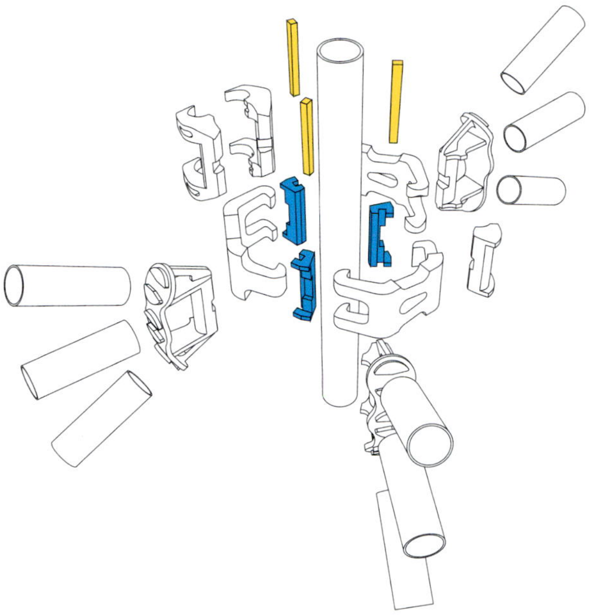

Chain remnants, ca. 48 cm

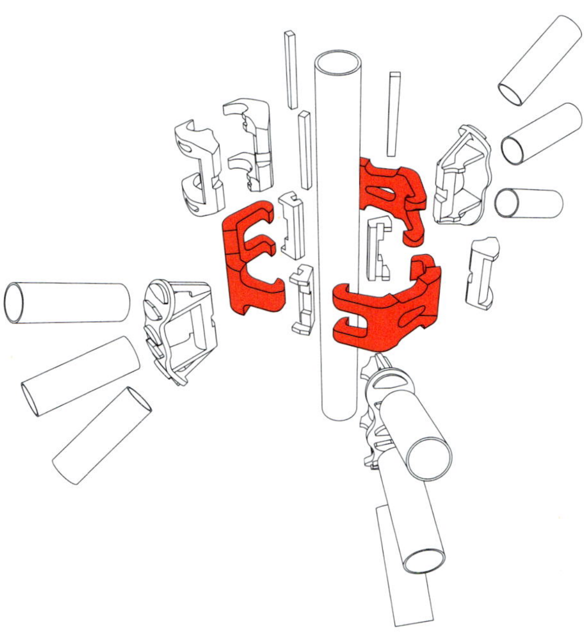

Chain, molded, gray ca. 26 cm
Chain, metal, ca. 26 cm

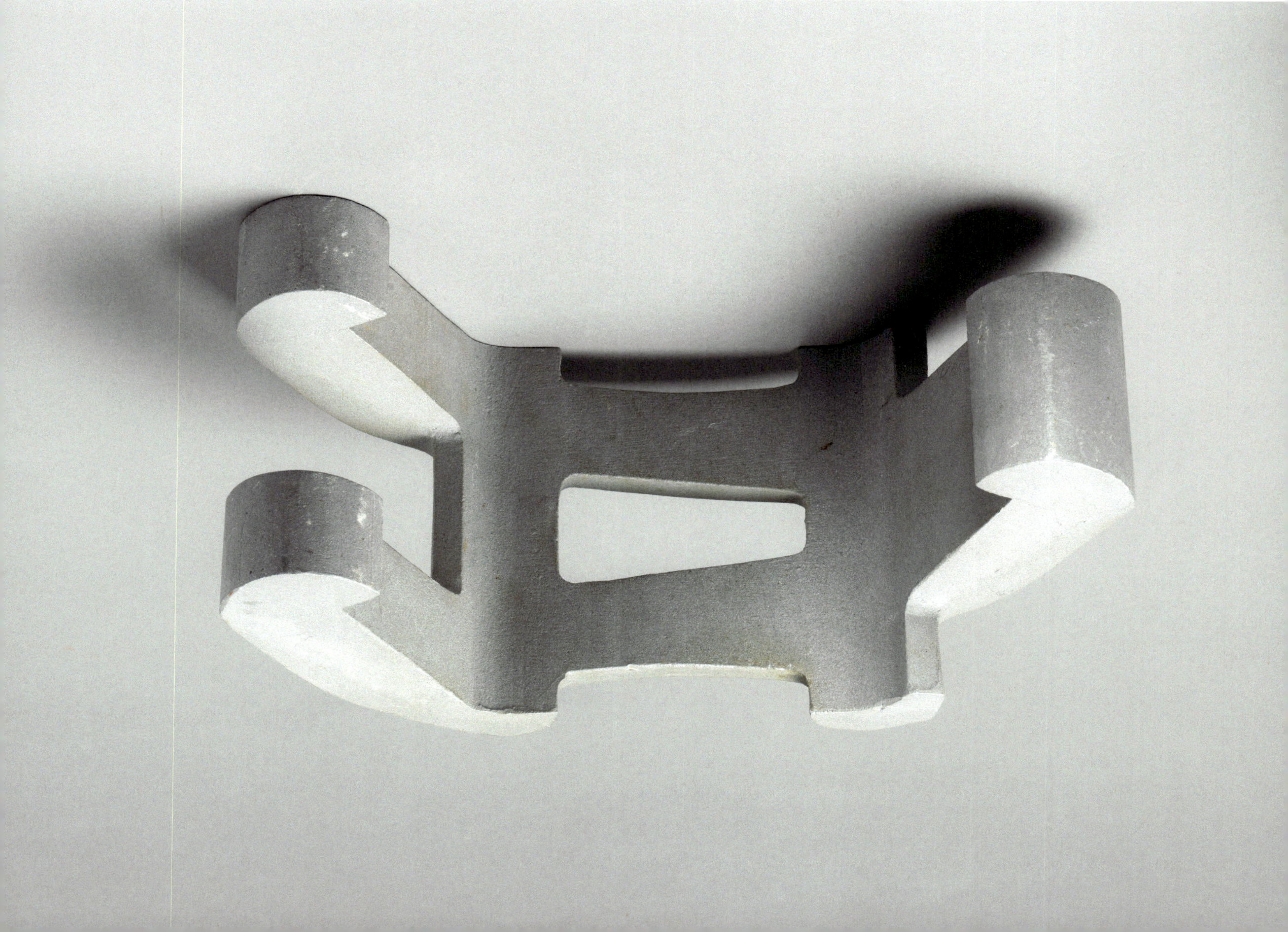

Chain, wood, colored and painted, ca. 27 cm

Clasp, metal, ca. 27 cm

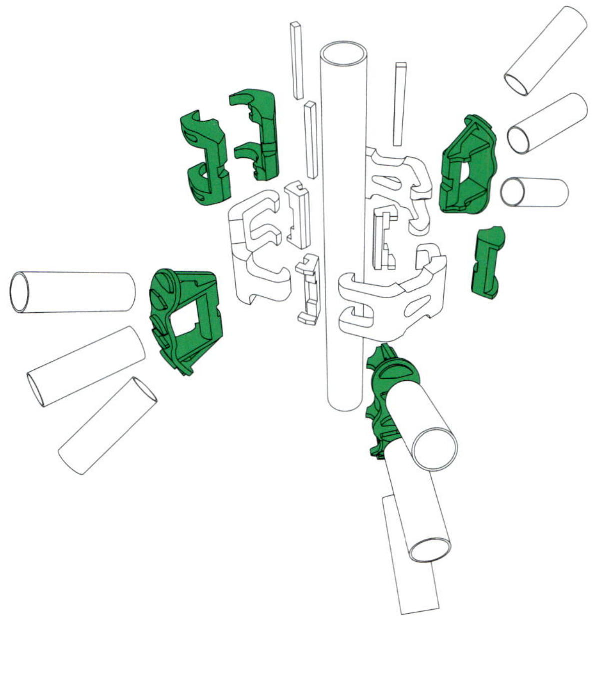

Clasp, wood, colored and painted, ca. 29 cm

Clasp with one tube centered, metal, colored and painted 29,5 cm

Clasp with one tube laterally placed, metal, colored and painted, ca. 35,5 cm

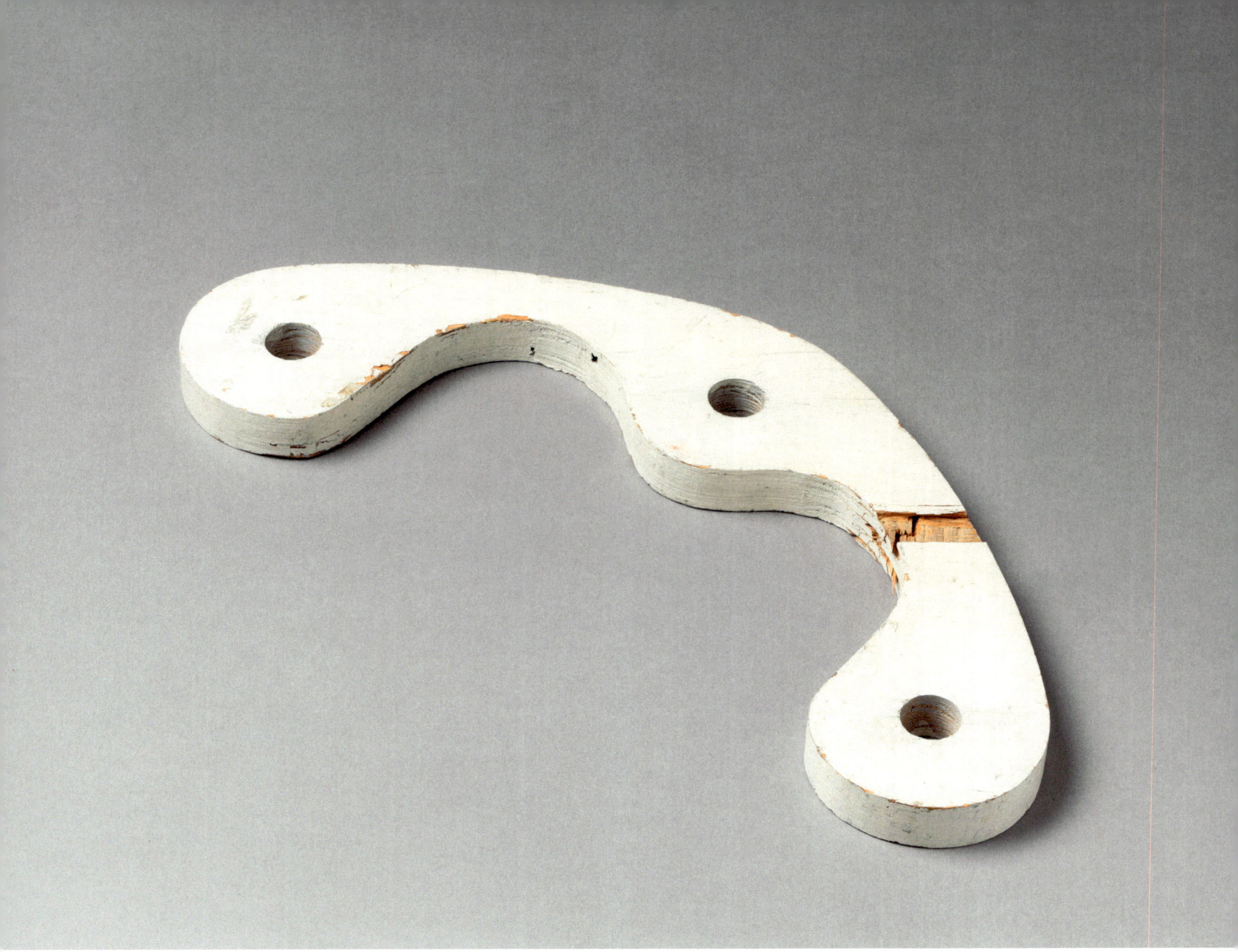

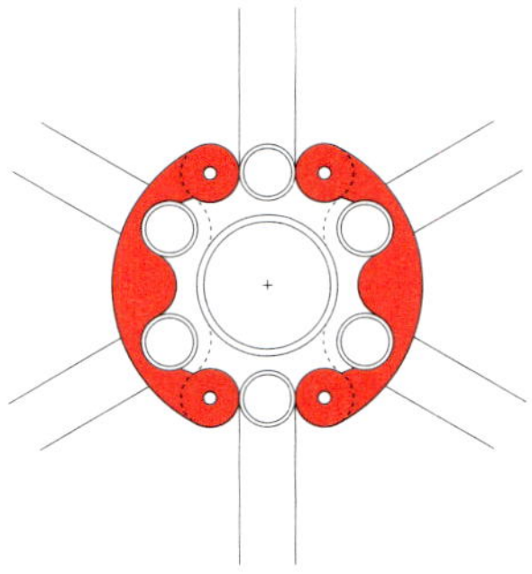

Version a: chain element, wood, colored and painted ca. 20,5 cm
"Boomerang," wood, colored and painted, ca. 44 cm

USAF version b: chain element, wood, colored and painted ca. 33,5 cm

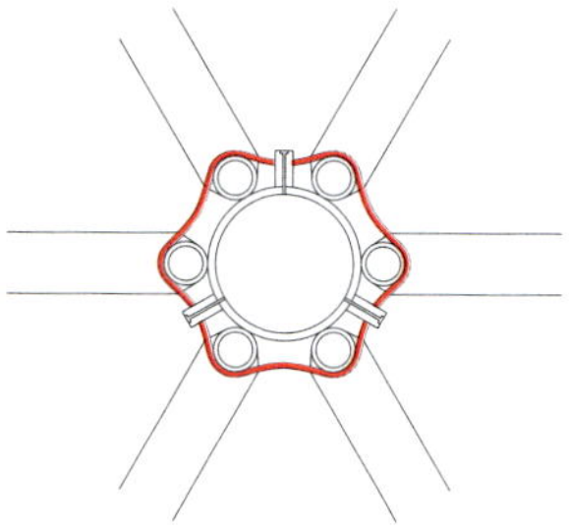

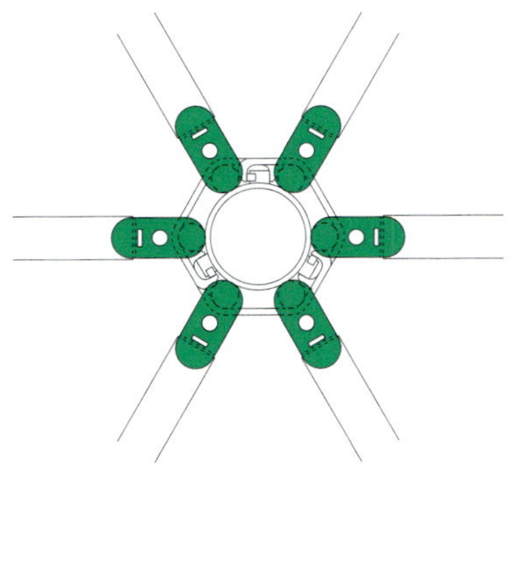

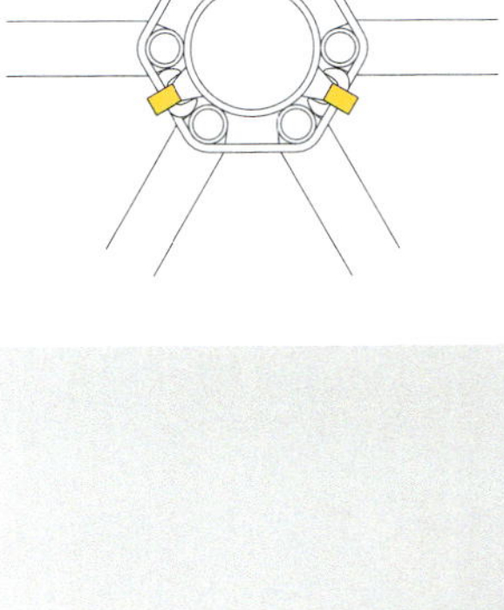

Version c: clip, wood, colored and painted, ca. 19,5 cm

Version d: Clasp, wood, colored and painted, ca. 22,5 cm
Clasp with two tubes, wood, colored, ca. 29,5 cm

Mobilar Structure: Junction of the four tubes, painted wood, length ca. 62,5 cm

Balls glued together, metal, ca. 1,5 cm, 2 cm

Node, metal, ca. 1,5 cm, possibly developed by Fritz Haller

Node, metal with rods ca. 30 cm

Node, metal, wood, ca. 35 cm, possibly developed by Fritz Haller

Scaffolding, metal, ca. 30 cm

Grapevine Structure
1953

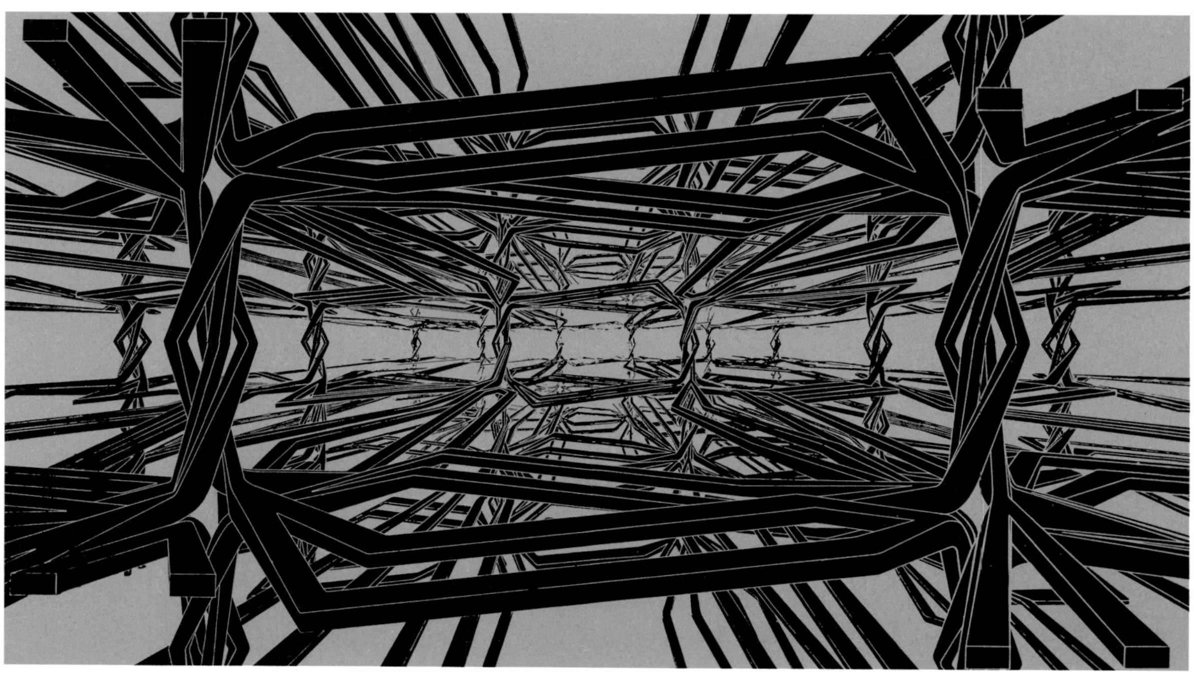

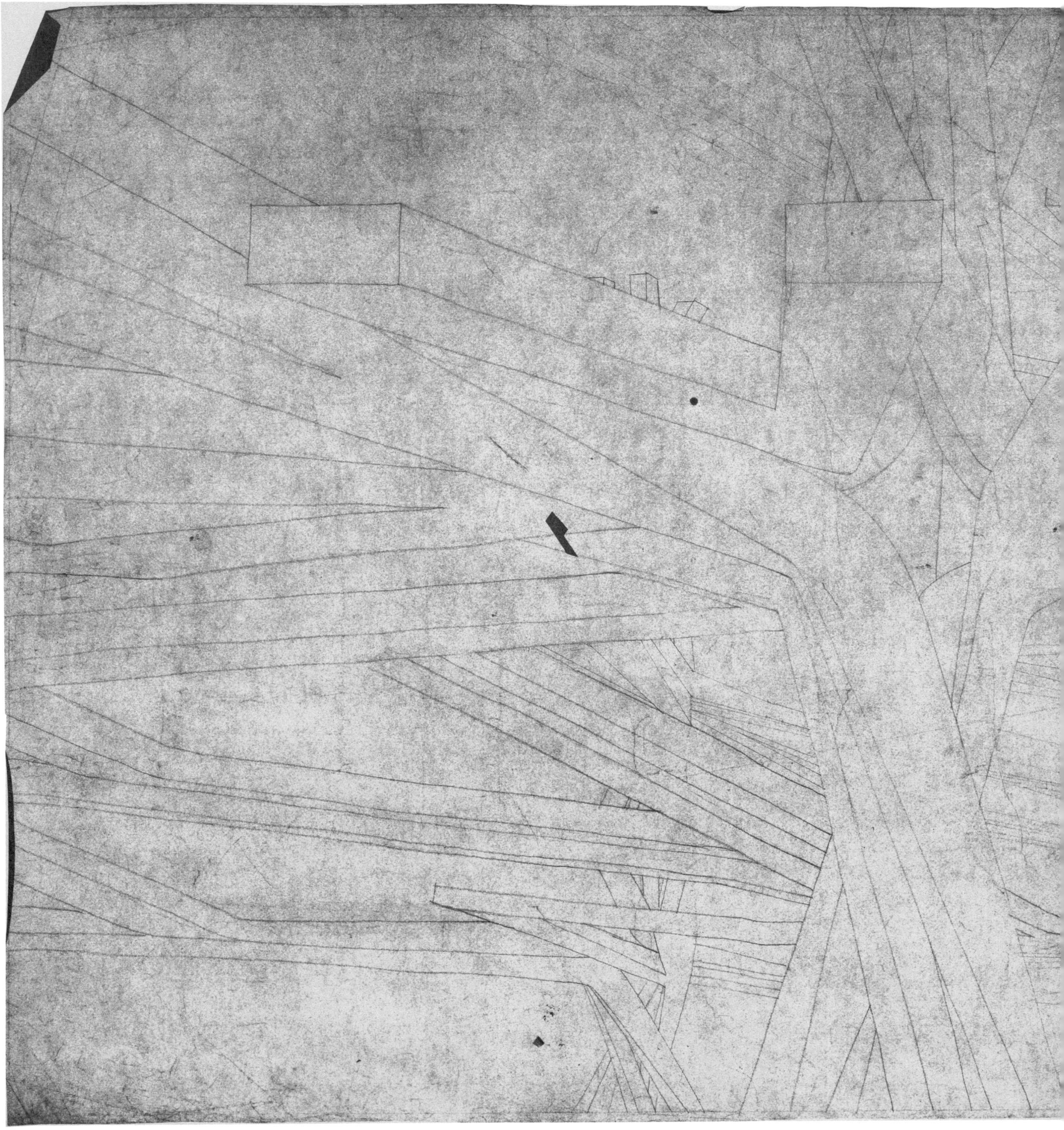

Early drawing of the Grapevine Structure

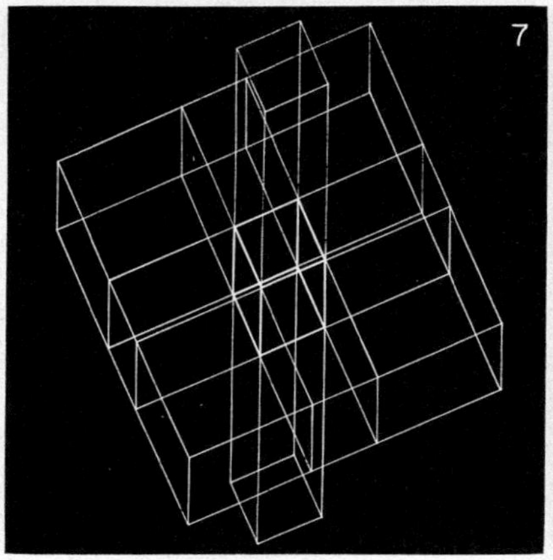
7

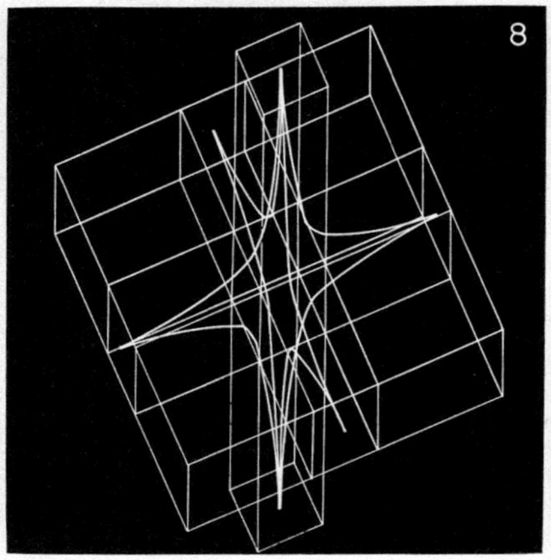
8

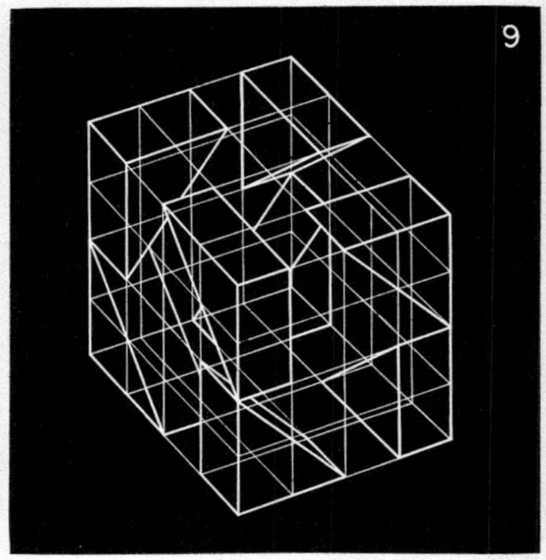
9

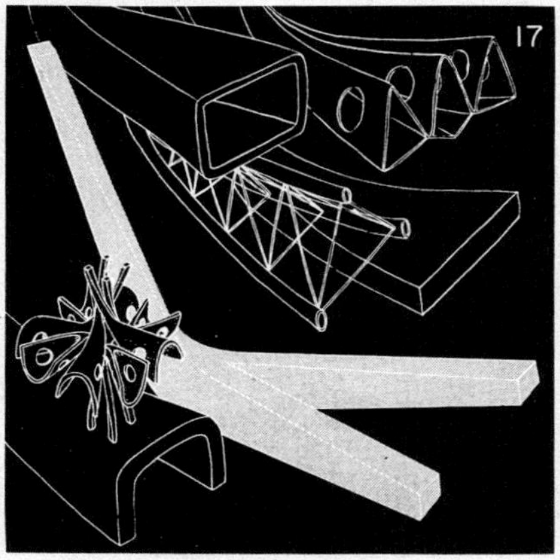
17

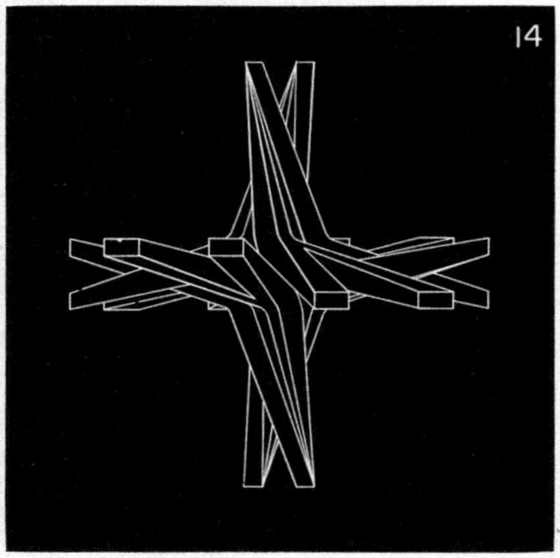
14

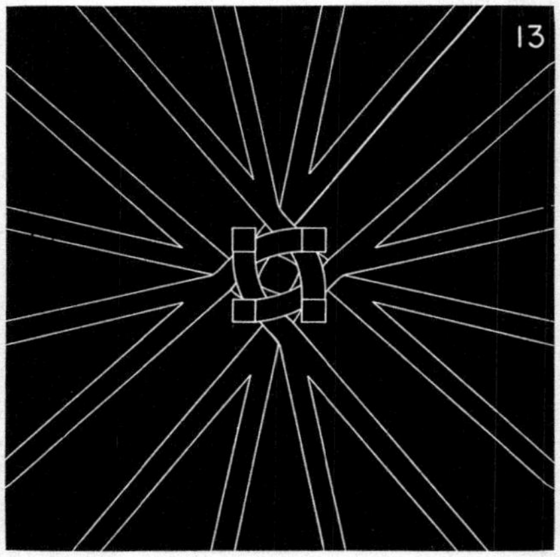
13

301 Beispiele von Vorstudien zur Bestimmung von Konstruktionsprinzip und Einzelelement

7 Die Basis der Analyse, das sechsschenklige Kreuz in der quadratischen Platte
8 Die Durchdringung des inneren Kubus des Kreuzes durch 8 unabhängige Kraftlinien
9 Die Zerlegung des inneren Kubus in 8 dreieckförmige Körper zur Ermittlung des Raumes für das einzelne Standardkonstruktionselement
10 Variationen von Positionen des Kubus in der Bauplatte mit Studien über die räumlichen Ausdehnungsmöglichkeiten des Standardkonstruktionselements
11 Modulare Zerlegung aller Außenflächen zur Bestimmung der zu erreichenden Außenpunkte des Standardkonstruktionselements
15 Das Resultat, ein dreischenkliges, in sich verdrehtes Gebilde
17 Andeutung von Möglichkeiten der Materialanwendung, des strukturellen Aufbaus und Produktionsprozesses des Standardkonstruktionselements als Basis weiterer Forschung
14 Das Konstruktionsschema, ein Doppelpilz
13 Die gleichmäßige Verteilung der Auflagefläche der ca. 4 m großen Bauplatte
21 Die Integration des Bauelements und Installation
20 Schema der Verteilung von vier tragenden Elementen
19 Isometrische Durchdringung von vier übereinanderliegenden Niveaus, in dem die direkte Fortsetzung eines Elements gezeigt ist unter Fortlassung von zwei Pilzkonstruktionen. Man erkennt den spiralförmigen Verlauf der Kräfte in einem gedachten Baukörper
22 Das komplette vorfabrizierte Bauelement mit allen Installationen, Fußboden, Decke, usw.
24 Die geometrische Form des Bauelements
3 Der Montagevorgang. Das Fertigelement wird an dem Ende der Pilzstütze mit dem bereits aufgestellten Element verbunden und hochgekippt. Die Zwischenplatten werden eingehängt
4 Schema der Verlegung der Anschlußpunkte der Fertigelemente an deren Peripherie

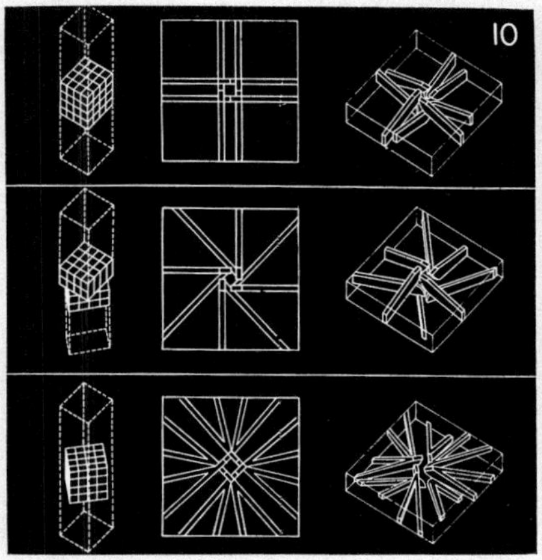
10

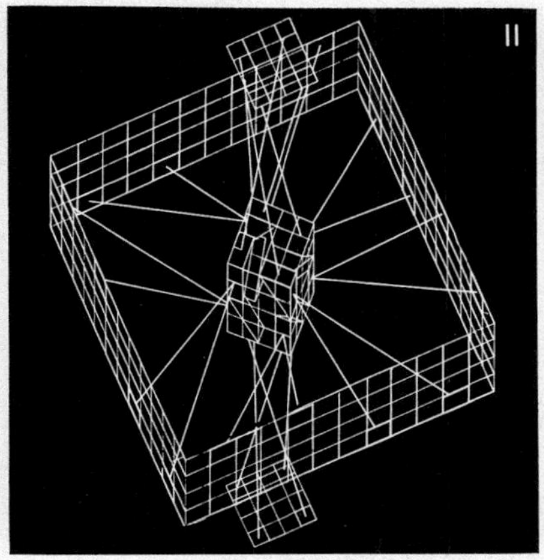
11

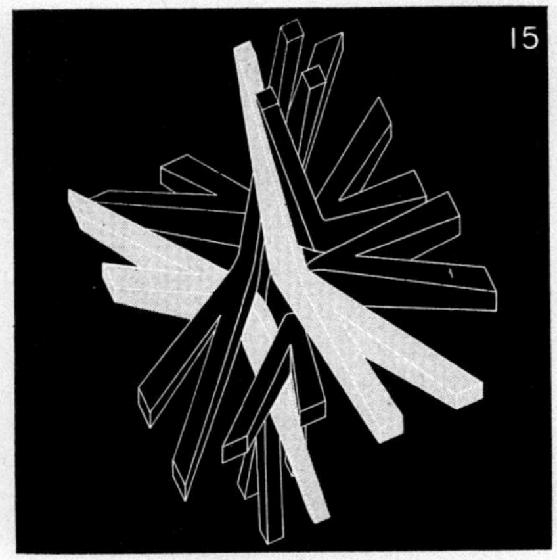
15

21

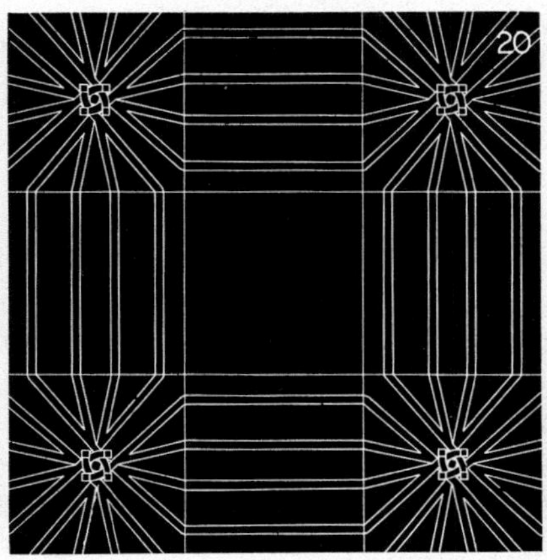
20

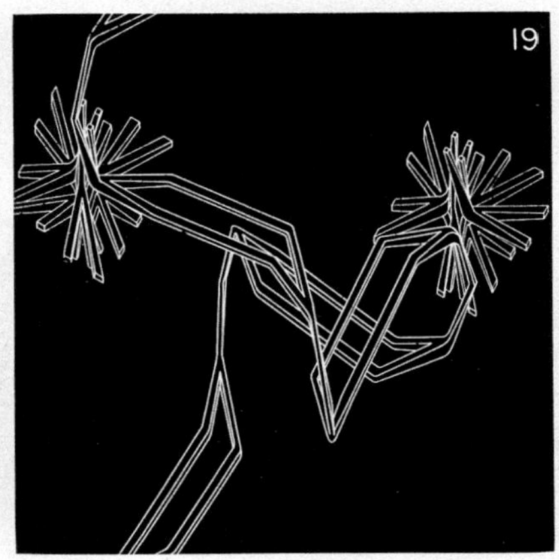
19

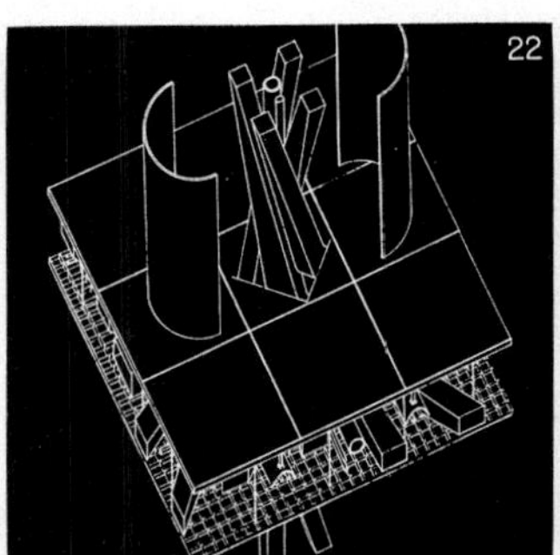
22

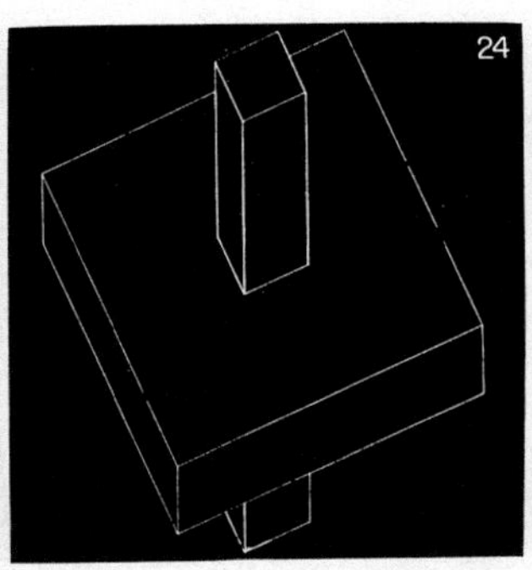
24

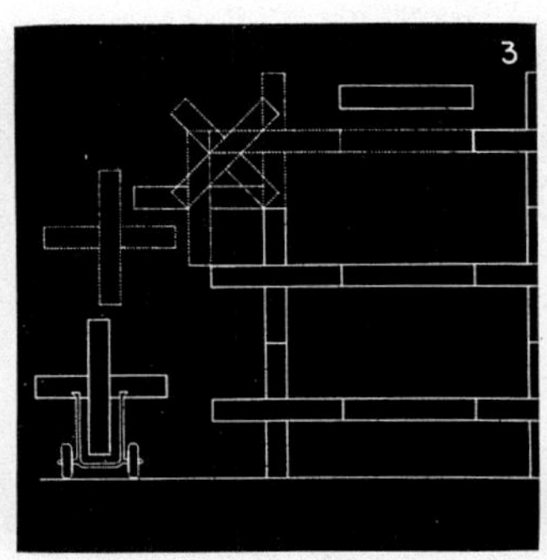
3

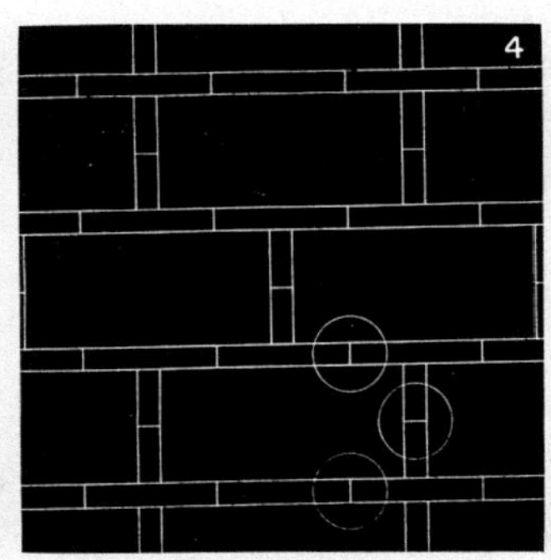
4

Marianne Burkhalter, Christian Sumi

Grapevine Structure[1]

Study of a dynamic structure, development of a universal construction element with students at the Chicago Institute of Design

"This study originated in the winter of 1953 and was intended for further development at a later date. It was a preliminary investigation concerned with the problem of substituting rigid nodes for the points of connection between structural elements, in contact vertically and horizontally, and with the problem of breaking down columns into groups of spatially developed elements jointed midway between two horizontal planes formed by the structural members. The distance between the point of connection of such a structural member and the axis of a group of column elements was to be determined by stress considerations."[2]

With the Grapevine Project, the nodal joint was "spatialized" and became part of a networked structure comparable to a grapevine which, in Marvin Gaye's song "I heard it through the grapevine" is the medium, the bearer of ill tidings. The two mushrooms comprised four bent bars oriented according to rotational symmetry; they "bifurcate" at the horizontal planes of floor and ceiling. The Grapevine's centerpiece is a double mushroom shaped structure, inscribed within a virtual 4×4×4 meter cube. A single construction component generated an entire, networked structure. Konrad Wachsmann called this a "three-legged, wishbonelike member" with "rigid nodes."

"Since each component has the tendency to shift away from the other components, they must be held together with small tension members on each point of joinery and in this sense, they create a tensile structure."[3]

The statics, the path of forces, does not correspond to the structure's geometry, "the individual branches." Near the shaft, every four strands were bundled by tensile members; these pick up the primary forces. The figure of the branching construction thus contradicts the structure's actual force lines; image and statics drift apart and create a classical tectonic construct.

In section, two versions were considered. In the case of the first, the "vines" lay on top of one another, bound together by intermediary horizontals. In the second, the vines are interlocked. This is the more interesting solution since the horizontals are not needed.

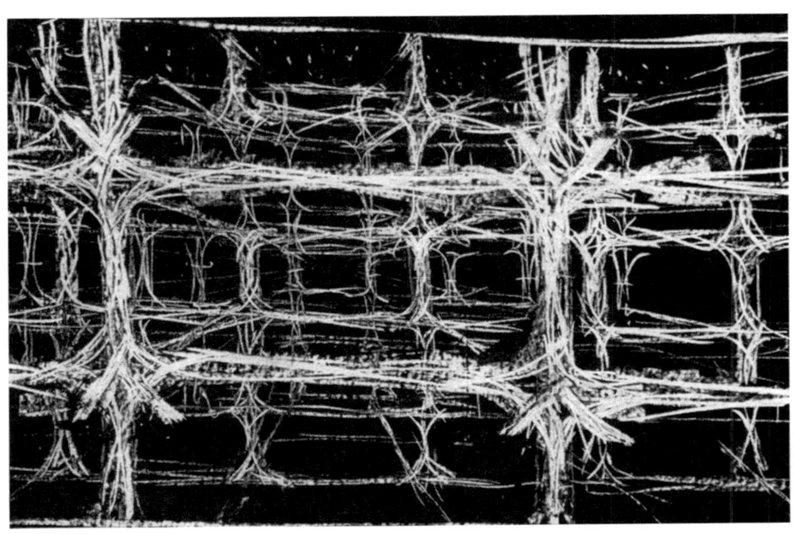

Grapevine: sketch version 1

1
In our office, Oscar Mather has reconstructed the Grapevine Structure in a 3 D model as a first attempt. Pietro Maria Romagnoli, Kathrin Röthlin, Giacoma di Vieste and Besart Krasniqi have built upon this examination by means of drawings and models. Gramazio Kohler Research ETH has completed a comprehensive digital reconstruction.
Fully two exhibitions have dealt with the Grapevine Project in recent years.
John Enright, Connection Points: Konrad Wachsmann Reconsidered, Los Angeles Forum for Architecture and Urban Design, 2010
Barkow Leibinger, Structure Grapevine by Konrad Wachsmann, Princeton University School of Architecture, 2016

2
Konrad Wachsmann, *The Turning Point of Building*, op. cit., p. 194

3
Manuscript, Akademie der Künste, Konrad Wachsmann-Archiv Berlin

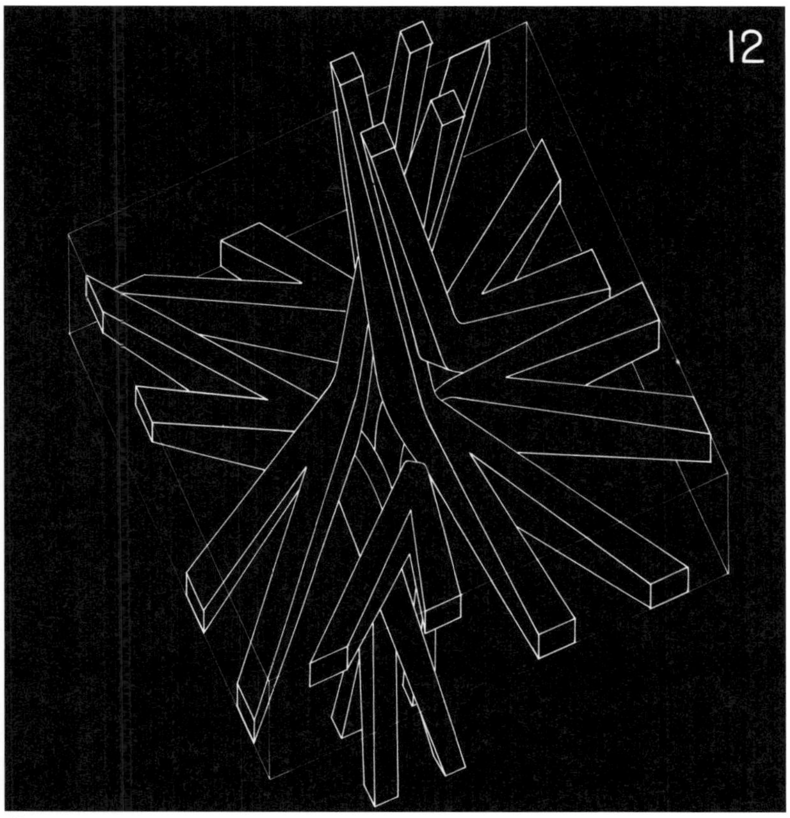

Illustration 12

I heard it through the grapevine
Marvin Gaye 1968

I bet you're wonderin' how I knew
'Bout your plans to make me blue
With some other guy you knew before
Between the two of us guys
You know I loved you more
It took me by surprise I must say
When I found out yesterday
Don't you know that I heard it through the grapevine
Not much longer would you be mine
Oh I heard it through the grapevine
Oh I'm just about to lose my mind

Honey, honey yeah
I heard it through the grapevine
Not much longer would you be mine baby

I know a man ain't supposed to cry
But these tears I can't hold inside
Losin' you would end my life you see
'Cause you mean that much to me
You could have told me yourself
That you loved some one else
Instead I heard it through the grapevine
Not much longer would you be mine
Oh, I heard it through the grapevine
And I'm just about to lose my mind

Honey, honey yeah
I heard it through the grapevine
Not much longer would you be mine, baby

People say believe half of what you see
Son and none of what you hear
But I can't help but be confused
If it's true please tell me dear
Do you plan to let me go
For the other guy you loved before?

Don't you know I heard it through the grapevine
Not much longer would you be mine, baby yeah
I heard it through the grapevine
Just about to lose my mind
Honey, honey, yeah
I heard it through the grapevine,
Not much longer would you be mine, baby yeah

Honey, honey, yeah
I heard it through the grapevine,
Not much longer would you be mine, baby yeah yeah
I heard it through the grapevine,
Not much longer would you be mine, baby yeah yeah

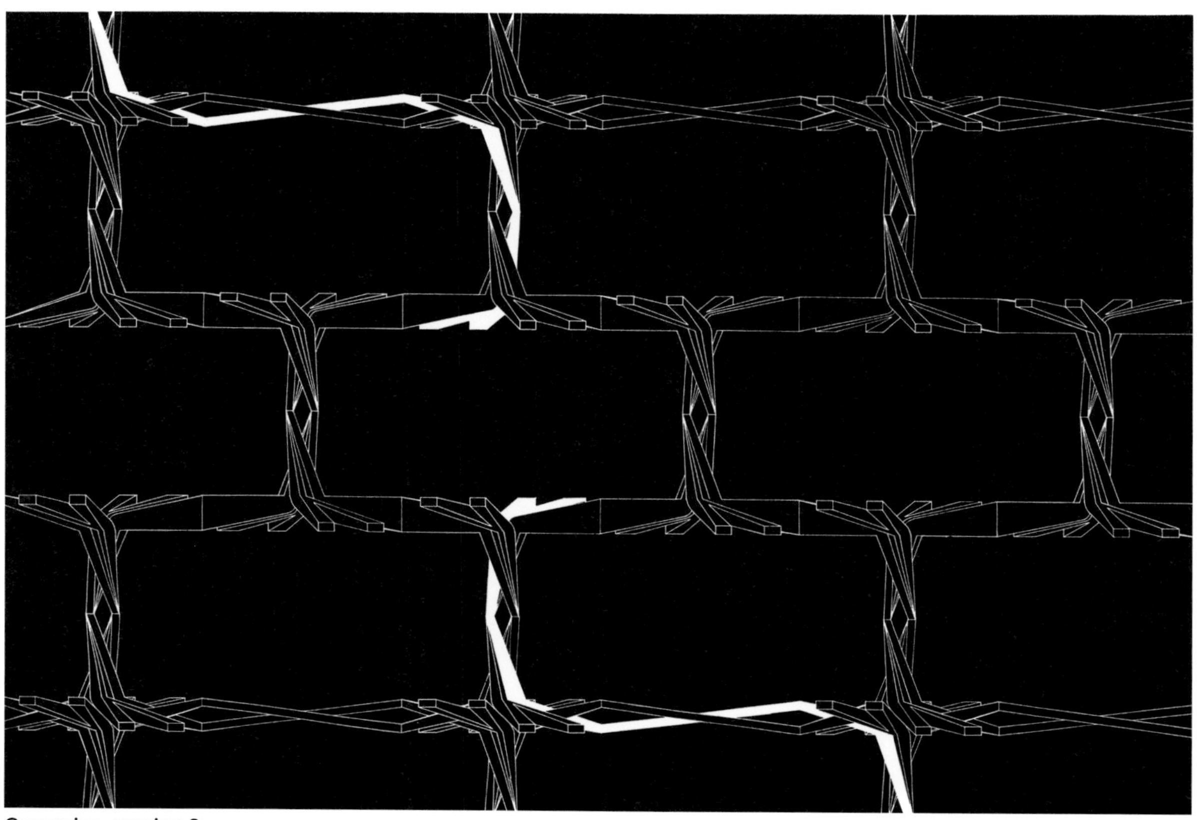

Grapevine: version 2

Revealingly, the geometric considerations and manipulations are presented and summarized in a synoptic manner by Wachsmann, particularly in illustration 10.[1] In the caption, Wachsman writes: "*Variations on the position of the cube within the plate together with studies of possible ways of extending the standard structural element in space.*" The following is an attempt to understand and describe the three variations.

burkhalter sumi architekten: reconstruction of the Grapevine Structure

Variation a: cruciform organization of two bars that run parallel to each other respectively. These cross at their middle in a rotation-like intersection, lying above or beneath each other, extending above or beneath, like "Hebestabwerke" (stick-built frameworks).[2]

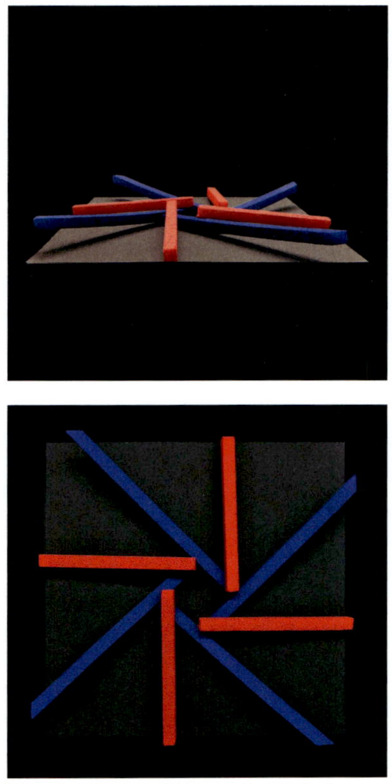

Variation b: is a 45° rotation (relative to the cube) of the windmill-like reduced figure of variation a but still maintaining the original figure. It produces two overlapped "windmills."

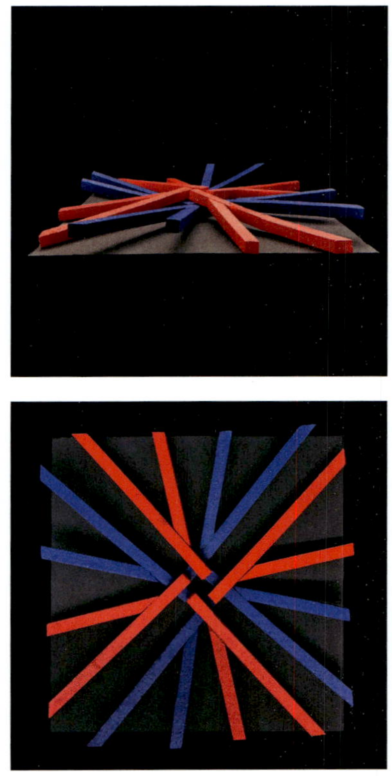

Variation c: the figure is an extension of variation a, recognizable in the parallel, cruciform organization of the bars. These are complimented with branching secondary bars at 30°. In addition, the cube is rotated 45° and the "radiating" members are adjusted and trimmed. The figure is the foundation of a later v-shaped basis of the three-angle standard element (wishbone).

Variation c is a preform of the definitive solution depicted in illustration 13. The newly introduced vertical bar slopes forward as an extension of the "foot's" primary bar. In this way, the four sloping bars are intertwined through rotation (first intertwining), then bent counterclockwise towards the middle (second intertwining) and finally twisted internally at 45° (torsion, third intertwining).

Both integrally overlapped "triangular configurations" thus complete a full 360° rotation. At the center of the drawing is a potential tension connection, indicated with four lines, which holds each of the four standard elements together.

1
Konrad Wachsmann, *The Turning Point of Building*, op. cit., p. 196f.

2
See for instance: Udo Thönnissen, *Hebelstabwerke. Tradition und Innovation*, gta Verlag, Zürich

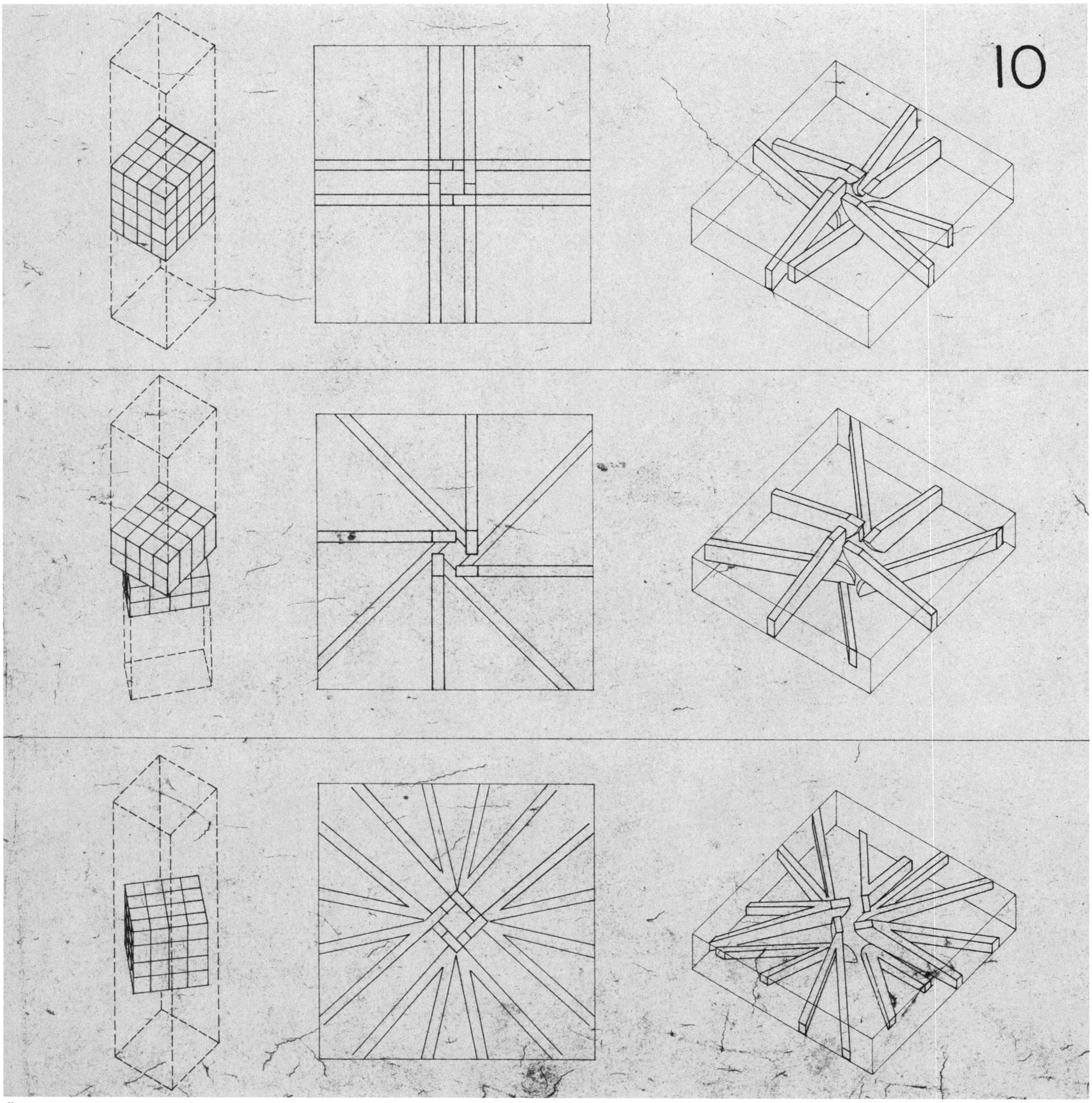

Illustration 10

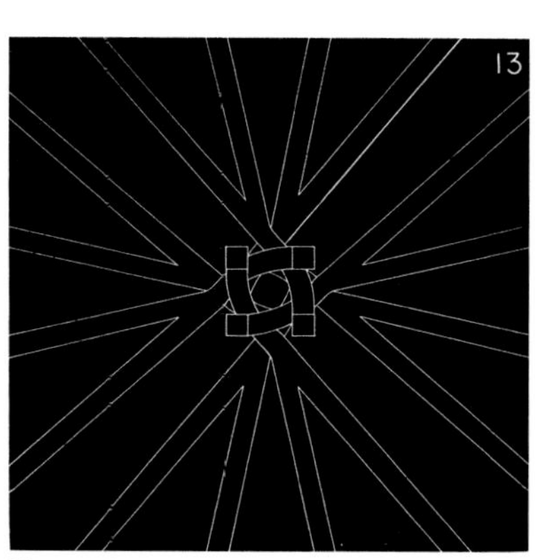

Illustration 13

In his overview, Wachsmann suggests varied ways of executing the "wishbone-like configuration" in illustration 17:

0 The wishbone
1 as a bent tapering sheet metal element (evocative of Jean Prouvé)
2 as a U-element open at its base and a square pipe that tapers at its top
3 as a truss-like pipe construction (three pipes) that taper to their top
4 as a flat, tapering plane that slopes upwards
5 as a folded element consisting of three triangles and sloping upwards.

In the caption for illustration 17, the text also states: "*Suggested utilization of material, structural assembly and production process for the standard structural element as a basis for future research.*"[1] The grapevine project is the "basis for future research," a concept that can be developed case by case depending on material (concrete, steel, wood, plastic, etc) and fastening technology (screws, rivets, shearing, casting, etc). It is perhaps also not thought through "to its conclusion" and is thus an "open" project.

1
Konrad Wachsmann, *The Turning Point of Building*, op. cit., p. 196f.

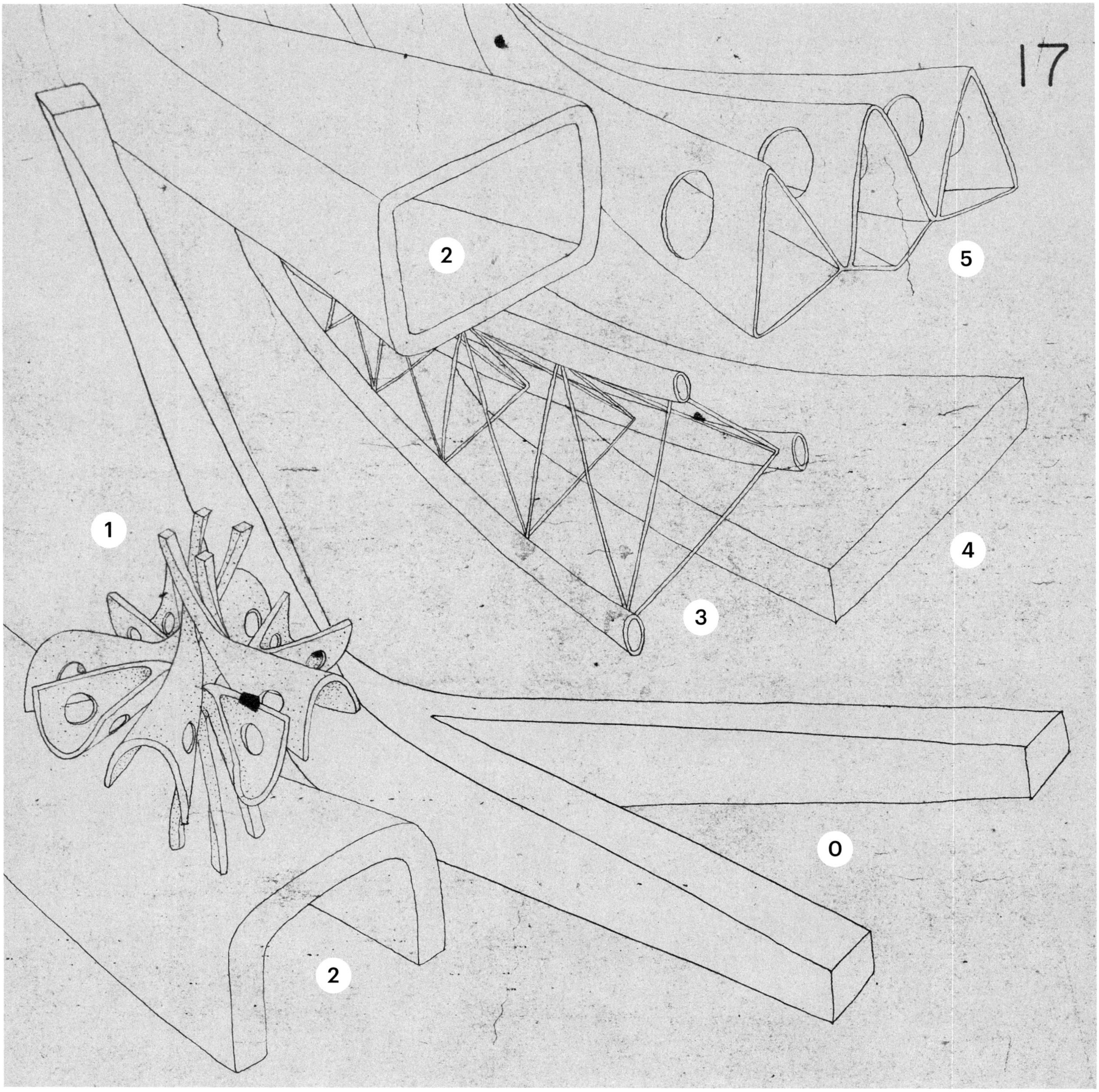

Illustration 17

The Grapevine Structure as a Prefabricated, Stick-like Wood Construction at the Biennale Venice 2018[1]

Tectonics is “the art of combining rigid, stick-like members to form a system that is internally coherent.” (Kunst des Zusammenfügens starrer, stabförmig gestalteter Teile zu einem unverrückbaren System.)[2]

The aim is a clear, experiential, powerful tectonic which actualizes and depicts Wachsmann’s abstract concept in built reality. The individual elements consist of “stick-like members” in Semper’s sense. The basis, the character of the construction “is given” by illustration 10 of the overview.

In contrast to the definitive concept shown in illustration 13, the sloped element, bent towards its center and shifted 45°, is replaced by a straight bar rotated 45°. In this way, the four rotationally disposed bars touch or intertwine in their upper and lower thirds, and lock themselves in an “internally coherent system.” Instead of the tension elements that Wachsmann sketched but never further described for the connection among the four strands (illustration 13), the construction uses a classical cabinetry solution, hopefully in Wachsmann’s spirit. Wachsmann was trained as a cabinetmaker and worked as an architect for the timber construction company Christoph and Umack in Niesky in the late 1920s where he built the famous summer house for Albert Einstein, among other projects.[3]

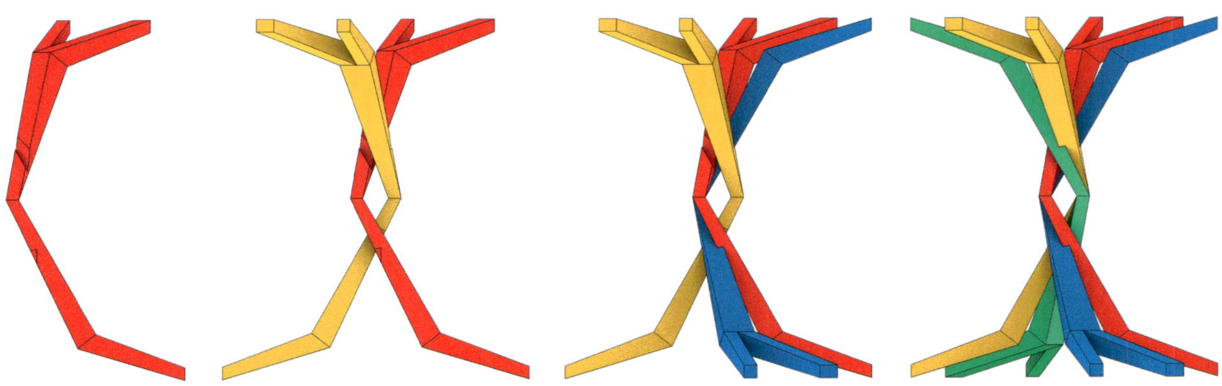

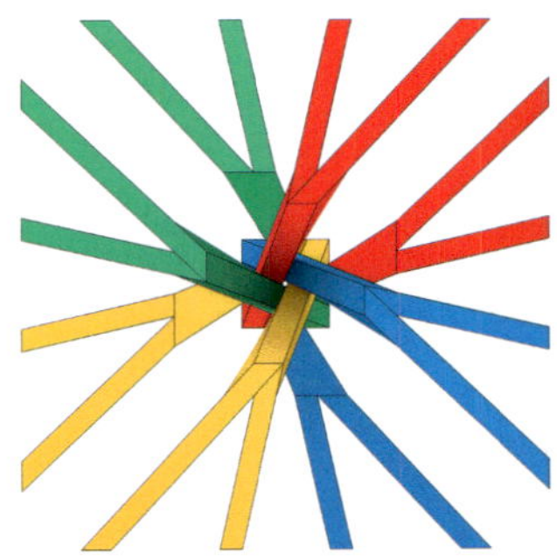

1
Together with Gramazio Kohler Research ETH Zürich

2
Gottfried Semper, *Der Stil in den technischen und tektonischen Künsten oder Praktische Ästhetik*, op. cit.

3
See Holzhausbau, op. cit. p. 68 ff

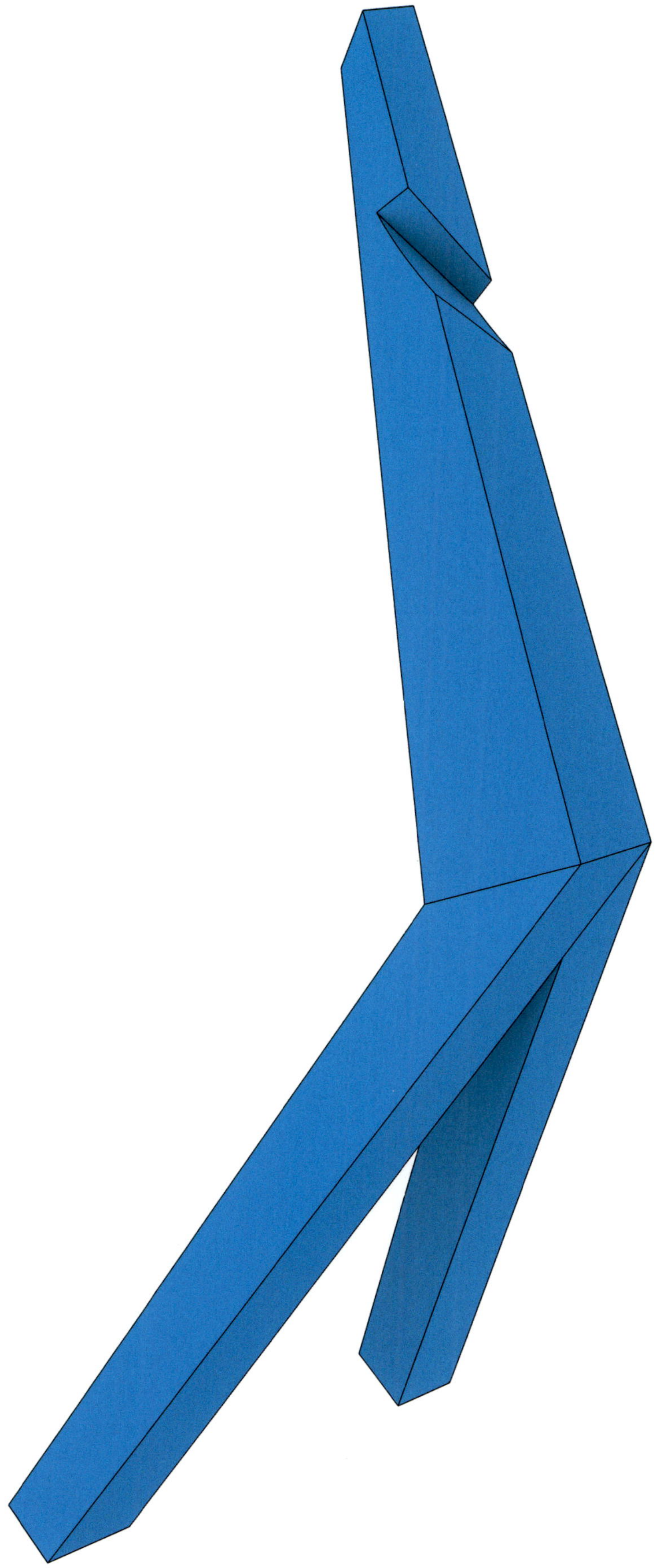

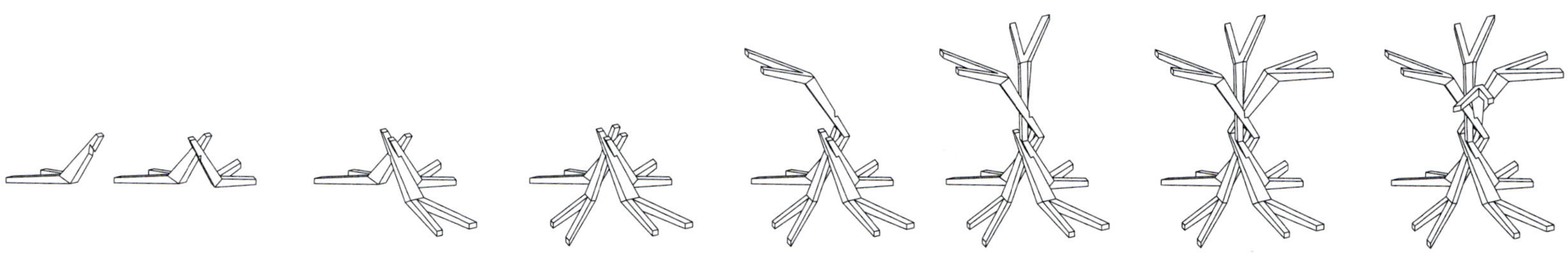

Joints and montage of the Grapevine

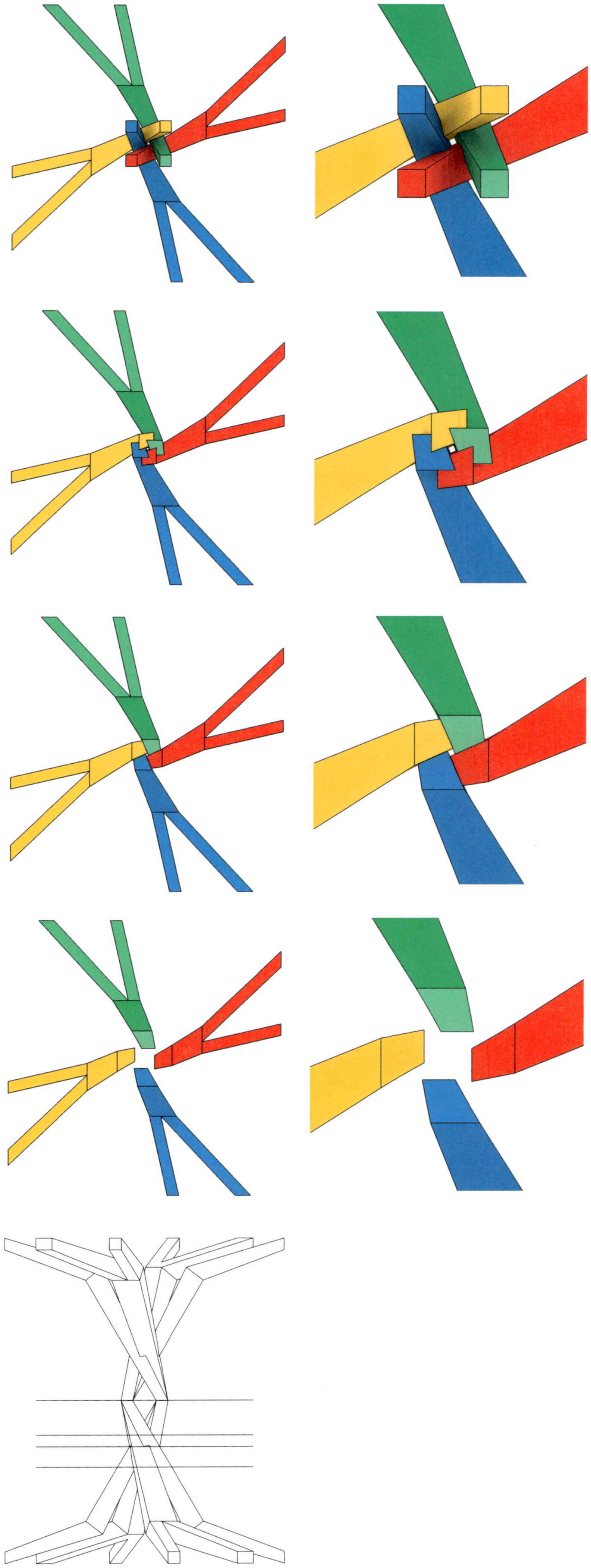

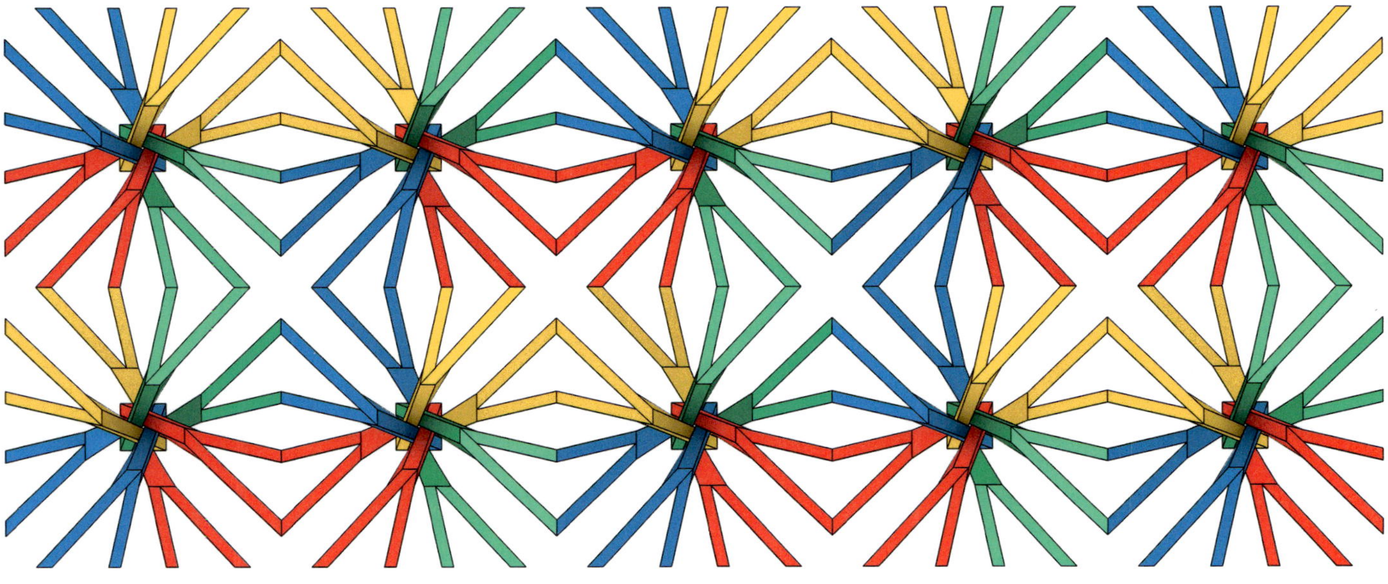

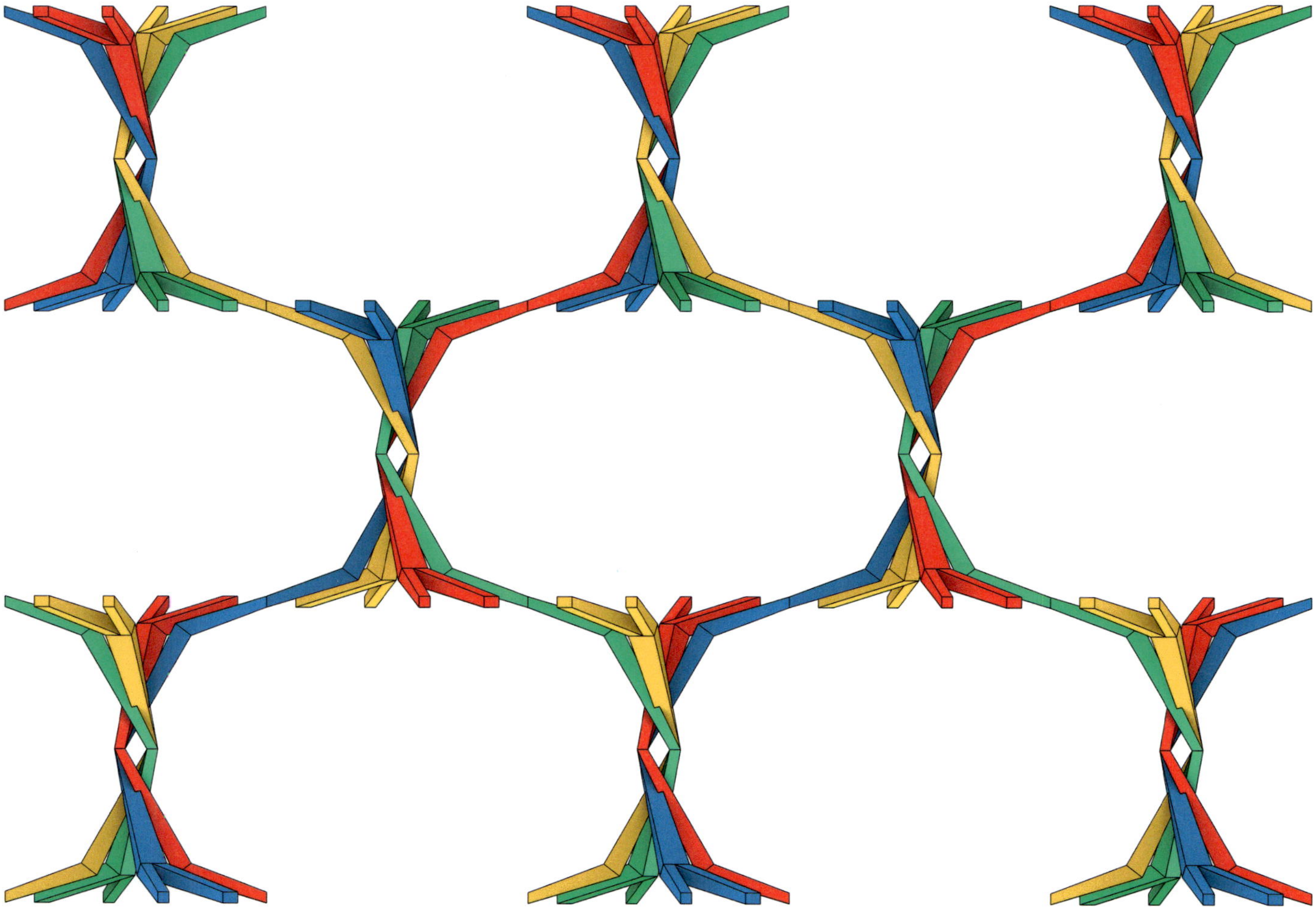

Joints and montage of the Grapevine

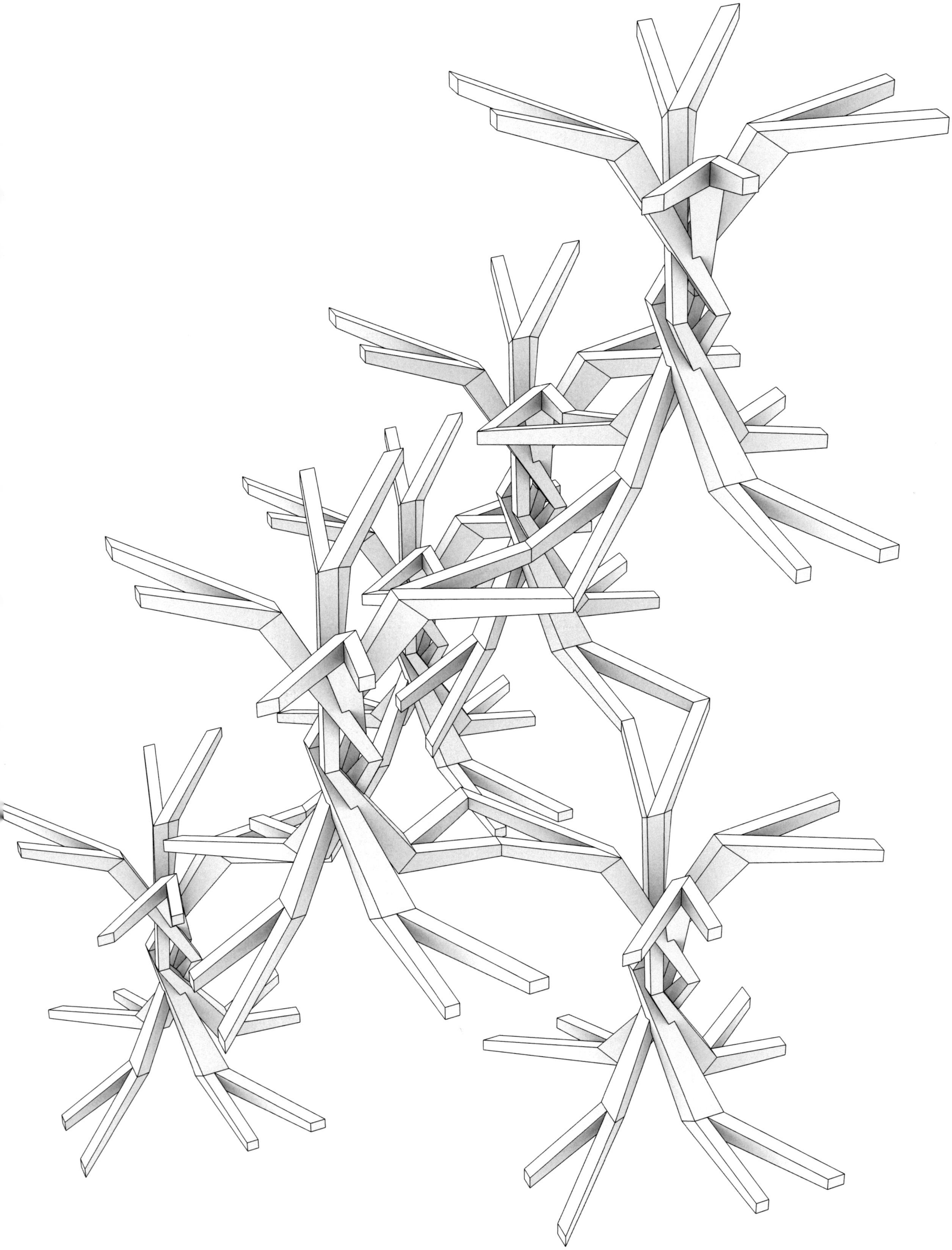

Grapevine Structure

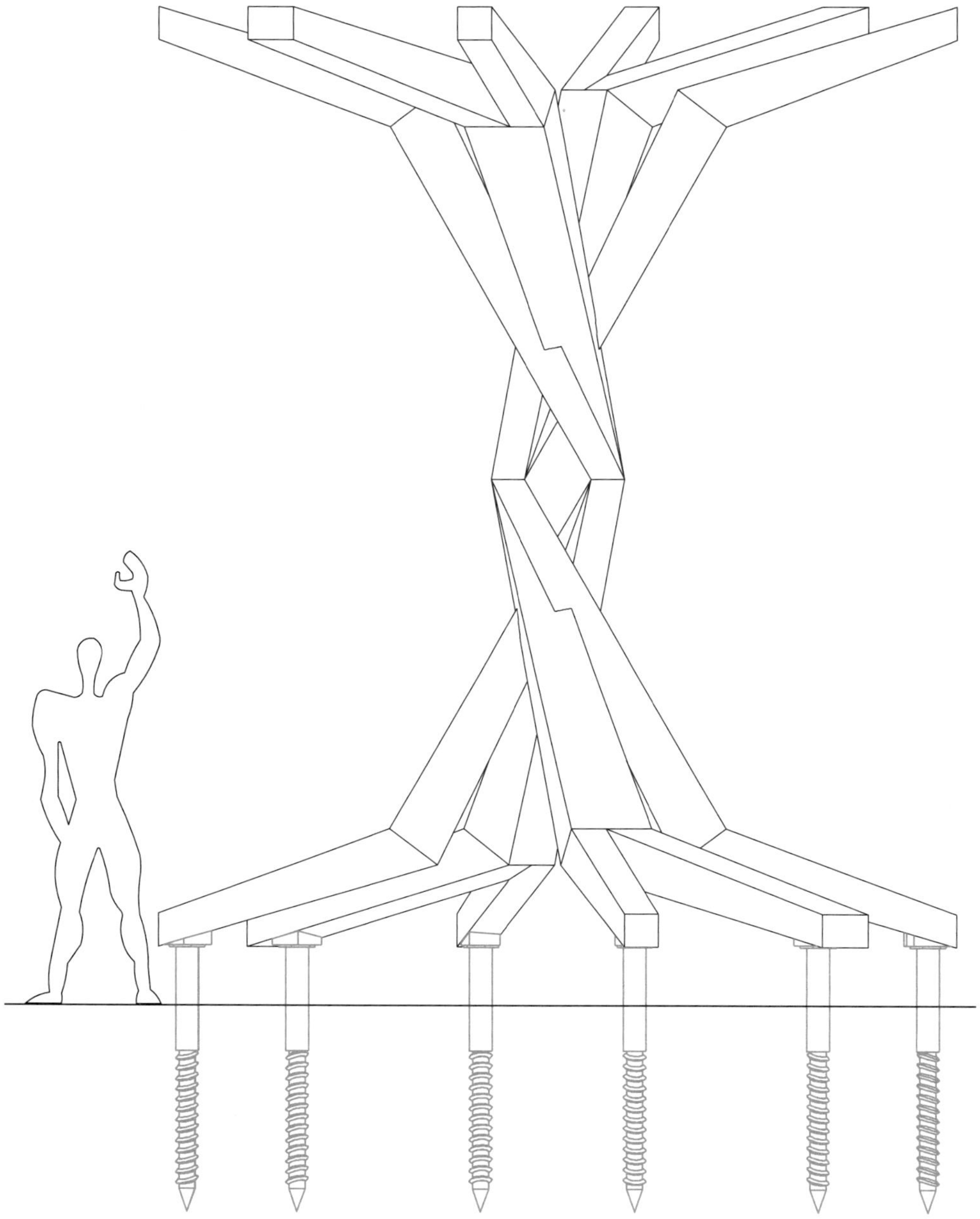

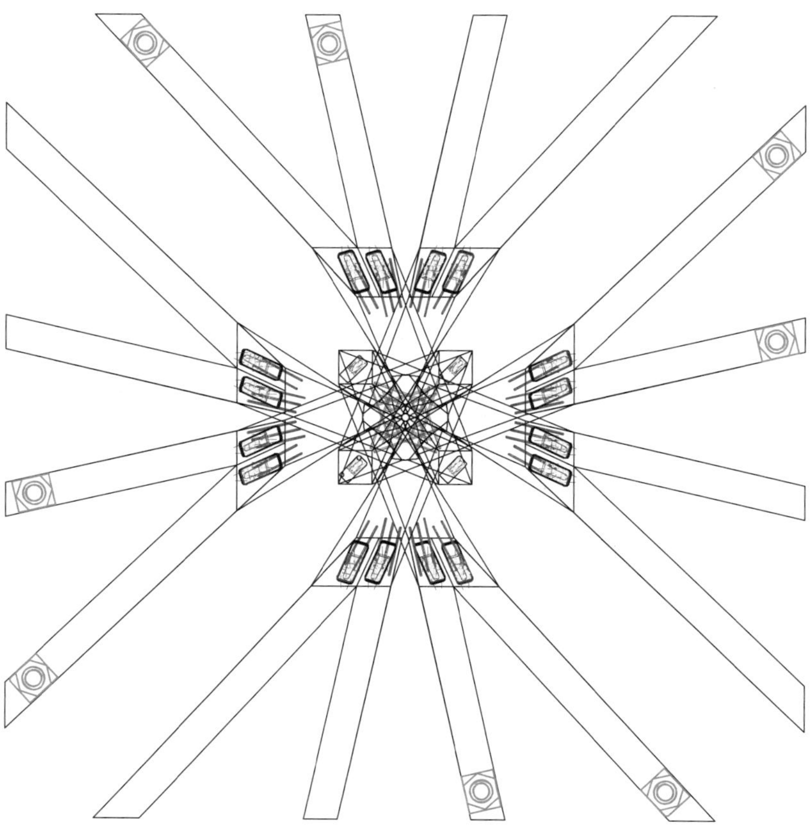

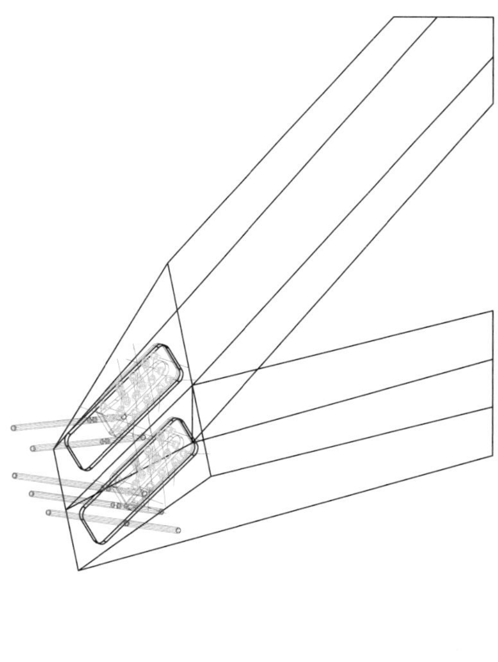

Erne Holzbau: Construction of the Grapevine

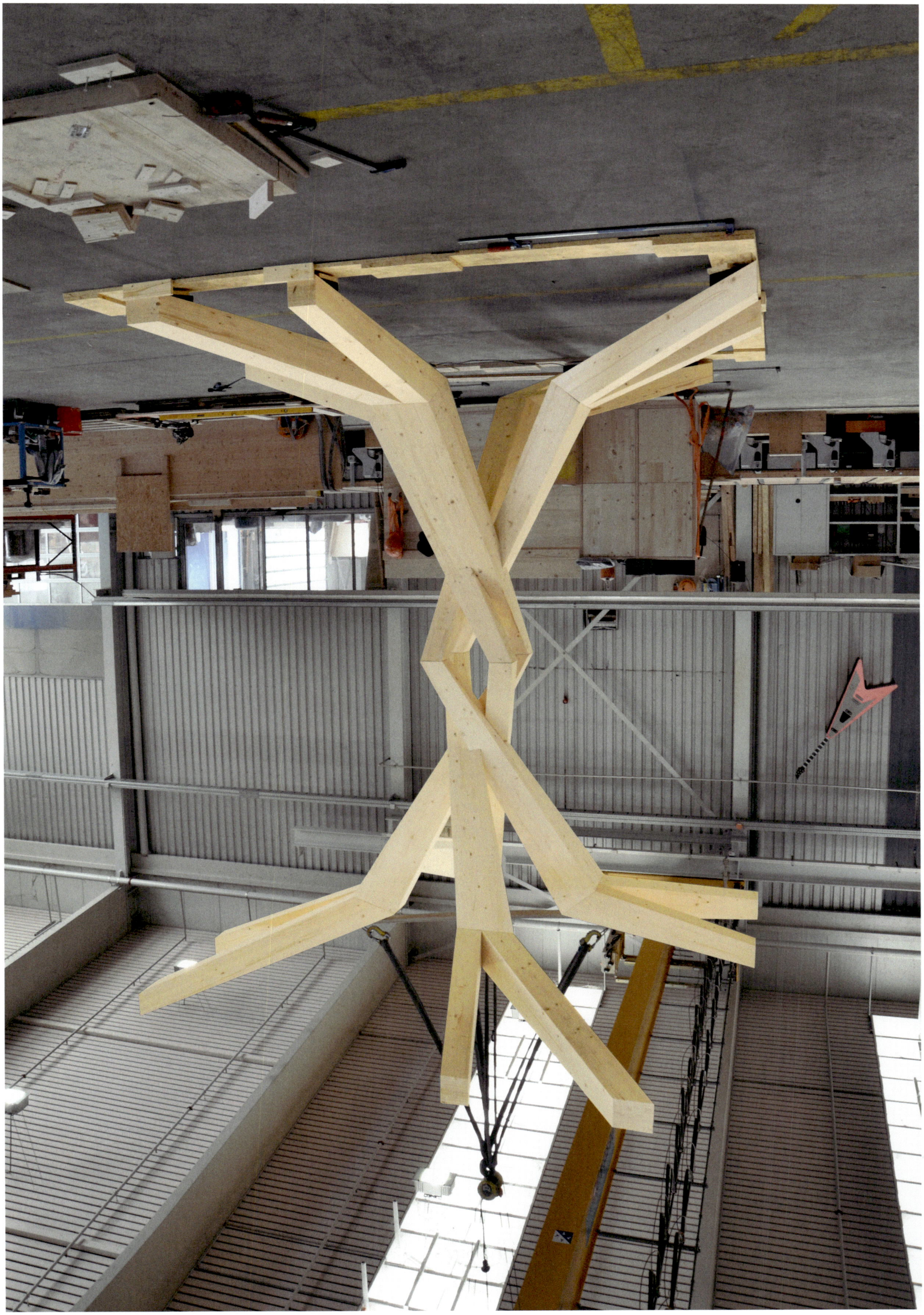

Erne Holzbau: Construction of the Grapevine

Neuronal cell bodies, spine covered dendrites (thick knobby processes) and fine axonal fibers. Scale: 0.01 mm

The Architecture of Thinking

New ideas often come to mind through unexpected coincidences. This certainly was the case at the birth of the present digression, which juxtaposes the architecture of buildings with the architecture of the brain.
The unforeseen was triggered by Konrad Wachsmann's book "Wendepunkt im Bauen"[1] and Javier DeFelipe's "Butterflies of the Soul,"[2] which unexpectedly caught our attention on the coffee table in front of us. In the eyes of the architects Marianne Burkhalter and Christian Sumi, Wachsmann's grapevine structures appeared similar to the brain networks as seen through the microscope by the Spanish anatomist Santiago Ramon y Cajal (1852–1934). The resemblance appeared most striking in the rind around the forebrain. To most of us this two millimeter thick sheet which occupies seventy percent of our brain mass is known as gray matter and is set apart from the underlying white matter.
Observations by neurologists and neuroscientists over the last 150 years have shown that the cortex is the major source of intelligent behavior. In the words of David Hubel and Torsten Wiesel: "Without a cortex a man is almost a vegetable, speechless, sightless, and senseless."[3] The cortex is arguably the most complex structure known to mankind and is considered the pinnacle of brain evolution.

Gray matter is made of nerve cells or neurons, whose glorious trees of dendritic branches and long, thin nerve fibers, referred to as axons, were first and most faithfully depicted by Cajal (Figure 1).[4] Cajal drew these images with great mastery by looking through a microscope at sections stained by the "reazione nera," invented by the Italian physician Camillo Golgi (1843–1926), and tracing neurons through a Camera Lucida with pencil or Indian ink on cardboard or paper. To the architects the neurons, with their prominent single apical dendritic branch and their hula skirts of basal dendritic processes, looked like skeletons of tetrahedrons, resembling the kinked three-legged wishbone beams Wachsmann envisioned for his designs. But unlike wishbones, the dendritic trees of cortical neurons are more complex, varying in geometry and individual branches ramified by purpose but no readily apparent logic. In contrast, Wachsmann's structures are constructed from a set of four interlocking wishbones arranged in regularly spaced load-bearing four meter high columns with horizontally extending beams. The cortical network is of course smaller by orders of magnitude. To give a sense of scale, a 1×1×1 millimeter cube of human cortex contains 190 thousand neurons and four hundred meters of dendrite. Although some apical dendrites are often bundled into columns, the distribution across the two dimensional cortical sheet shows neither a perfectly hexagonal nor a square lattice pattern.

In Wachsmann's constructs, wishbones are conceived as separate, intertwined elements that touch each other for local structural stability and serial usage to support expansive structures. Static stability is presumably a lesser concern for the cortical network, but how it is achieved may differ from Wachsmann's designs. From Cajal's drawings it is not obvious whether the cortex is built from individual neurons or whether the neural network represents a single rhizome of fused elements. The debate was settled in an acrimonious battle between the two Nobel Laureates, Camillo Golgi and Ramon y Cajal. Cajal's winning insight was that neurons are interconnected through synaptic junctions typically formed at the tips of axons. In contrast, the dendritic trees of different cortical neurons remain separate.

Thus, any possible static support for the cortical network may derive from synaptic connections, not from contacts of "dendritic wishbones." There are as many synaptic contacts in the cortical network as there are stars in the sky. Although difficult to imagine how, there are about 650 million synapses piled into a 1×1×1 millimeter cube of human cortex. And even more bewildering is that each synapse is part of a four kilometer long web of axons. One wonders how all this material even fits into this tiny space, led alone delivers messages to specific addresses through the thicket of the neural forest (Figures 2, 3), without ending the conversation in

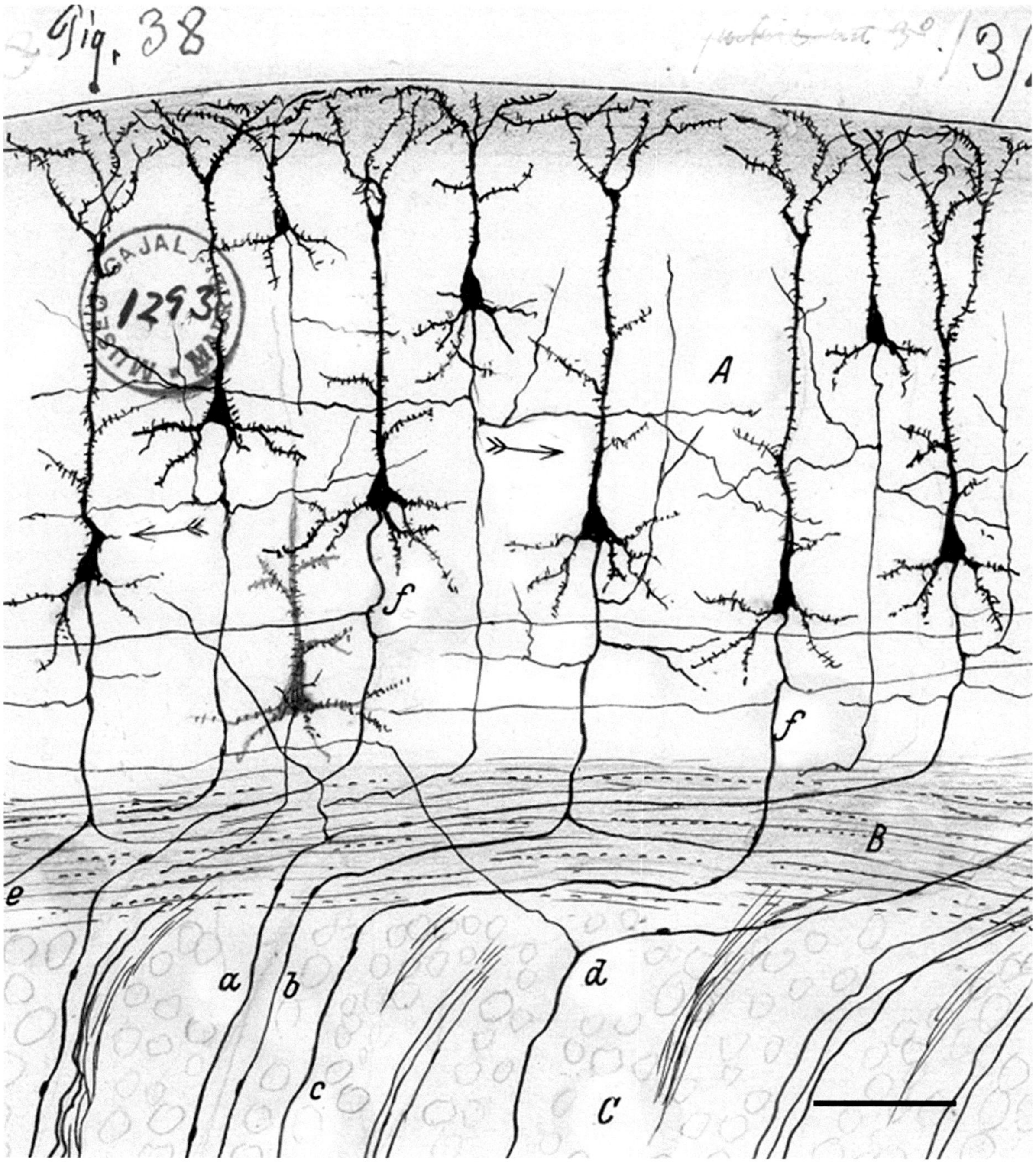

Figure 1: Neural network of the human cortex drawn through the microscope by Ramon y Cajal in 1935.[4] The drawing (Courtesy of the Cajal Institute-CSIC, Madrid, Spain) shows a small number of silver-stained pyramidal neurons with a triangular-shaped cell body, spine covered apical and basal dendrites and thin axons. The upper half of the image shows the gray matter. It contains cell bodies, dendrites and axons. The lower half of the image depicts white matter, which contains horizontal and vertical incoming and outgoing axons. The arrows indicate the direction of synaptic signaling between select pairs of neurons. The surface of the brain is towards the top of the image. Scale: 0.1 mm

Babylonian confusion. Clearly the initial impression that cortical architecture bears similarities to Wachsmann's grapevine structure was misleading. We are left with the conclusion that Wachsmann's lattice structures are unique to buildings we live in and are constructed from structural and geometric principles distinct from those applied in the construction of brain networks.

Embedded concepts

Although the stylistic similarities in the architectures of Wachsmann's grapevine design and the cortical brain network are eye-catching, they do not generalize to common design principles. However there are notable exceptions where nature converges with the built world. For example, both worlds are ruled by the pressures for conserving space. Brain size is of course limited by the cranium in which it is contained. At the most practical level, though, brain size is limited by the size of the birth canal. Spatial economy also applies to internal components of the brain. An obvious example is the separation of gray and white matter (Figure 1). Much the same as directing long distance traffic through beltways around cities or bundling cables and plumbing in chutes of buildings, the brain keeps axons for fast transmission between remote points in the white matter and reserves gray matter for local synaptic communications between nearby neurons. For optimizing the speed of communication between different parts of the brain minimizing cable length is important. One of the ways the brain has accomplished this is by topographic mapping. This means that inputs from nearby points of the sensory surface (e.g. retina, skin, etc.) contact nearby points in the brain in orderly fashion. For example touch sensations from the lip are mapped closer to inputs from the nose than inputs from the eyelid. Perhaps even more remarkably, within these topographic maps the brain has nested clusters of neurons that respond to similar sensory modalities (e.g. orientation of visual objects, visual object motion, color, touch, vibration, etc.) in functionally similar modules. Adopting such fine scale partitioning schemes saves space and speeds up information processing. Without this orderly, dense packing, the brain would be several times larger; computations would be slower and energetically more costly.

Finally, the brain famously coordinates ongoing sensory inputs from all sensory organs with previously stored experiences and produces appropriate motor behaviors including interpretations of the world around us. What principle of cortical connectivity optimizes the workflow across the one hundred and eighty different functionally specialized cortical areas required to accomplish these tasks? How does the cortex effortlessly coordinate the processing of countless sensations, perform spatial coordinate transformations between independently moving eyes, the head and body, and generate behaviorally relevant motor sequences involving multiple muscles when we cross a busy street on foot? The challenge is very familiar to architects searching for optimal solutions for accommodating multiple diverse functions on a small plot of real-estate. The cortex has solved the puzzle by applying a remarkably simple rule, whereby it weighs the strength of its connections by their length. Long connections are weaker than shorter ones but weaken at a slower rate than expected from a geometric decay. The regime may reflect the metabolic costs of long transmission lines; it optimizes wire length and determines the spatial layout of cortical areas. Thus, similar to human-made constructions, the cortical architecture is embedded in the structure of its constituent elements.

To architects this insight sounds trivial and must appear to side-step the question of how anatomical constraints on connectivity influence the spatial layout of maps for different functions on the cortical sheet. Two eminent neuroscientists, Rodney Douglas and Kevan Martin, disagree. They propose that the cortical sheet in both hemispheres has an axial organization that reflects a "behavioral architecture." Specifically, neurons in areas at the center of the sheet deal with sensations from the body such as the skin and internal organs and activate purposeful sequences of motor actions.

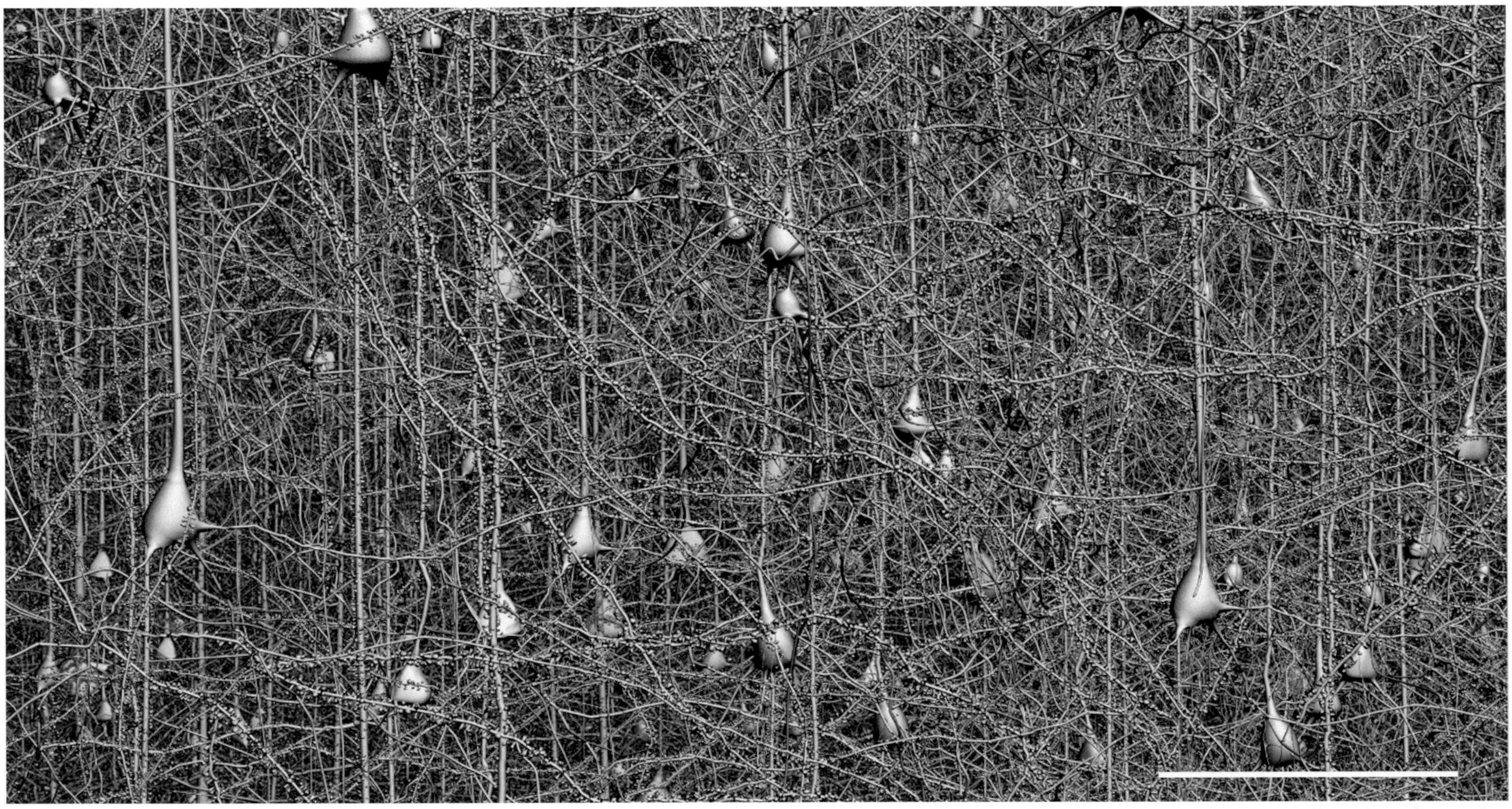

Figure 2: Computer generated image to illustrate the complexity of the cerebral cortex, which resembles a neuronal forest. The image shows a small number of pyramidal neurons and an extremely high density of dendrites and axons. Notice that dendrites are thick processes and are covered with spines. In contrast, axons are thin and contain varicosities, which represent synaptic specializations at points of contacts between neurons. The image was taken from the video "Bosque Neuronal" (Cajal Blue Brain Project) created by (in alphabetical order) Sofia Bayona, Ruth Benavides-Piccione, Juan Pedro Brito, Eva Cortés, Javier DeFelipe, José Miguel Espadero, Susana Mata, Luis Pastor, Ángel Rodriguez and Luis Miguel Serrano. The surface of the brain is towards the top of the image. Scale: 0.1 mm

Figure 3: High magnification extract of Figure 2, showing neuronal cell bodies, spine covered dendrites (thick knobby processes) and fine axonal fibers. Scale: 0.01 mm

By contrast, areas in the southern quadrant process visual and auditory inputs which are telegraphed from the distance. The northern quadrant contains areas representing past experiences and creates plans of future goals. Areas in the east encode information relevant for object identification whereas areas in the west provide information about the agent's present location and how to get back home.

Dynamic connections

Wachsmann remained vague how grapevine structures are interconnected. In his drawings, models and descriptions, he envisioned that two pairs of mirror symmetric wishbones would be arranged in a regularly spaced grid in which four intertwined elements are tension members of loadbearing shafts held together by friction. While such traction assemblies provide stiffness, the netlike overall structure is not completely rigid but maintains a modest amount of flexibility. Maybe this was exactly Wachsmann's intention; enabling grapevine structures to flexibly adapt, albeit modestly, to outside forces.
As displayed in Wachsmann's illustrations, the structure resembles a fabric, although stiffer and less elastic. Designing deformable structures may not have been Wachsmann's main goal. But the experimentation with hexagonal and decagonal hinge assemblies shows his interest in dynamic structures as well as his fascination in exploring multiple dimensions of space for articulating and conjoining constructive elements. Although the hinge assemblies could be folded like origami art into many different configurations, the hinges' fixed axes constrained the architectural freedom of his designs.
Cortical networks are built from squishy cells, which of course allows for a broader range of topologies than in structures made of rigid wood, steel and bricks. An important benefit of the pliable construction material is that brain networks are highly adaptable to changing experiences. Due to the living material, we are able to learn, form new memories and break old ones.
In the healthy brain this is achieved, roughly speaking, with the same stock of neurons with which we are born. What changes throughout life is the number and strengths of excitatory and inhibitory synaptic connections. This involves structural alteration as well as modifications in the electrochemical conduction along nerve fibers and the chemical signaling across synaptic junctions. Unlike the connections in Wachsmann's structures, cortical connections are formed and broken continuously, impacting neuronal computations with little effect on the overall structure of the network or the overall shape of the brain. The structural changes can be observed by microscope and imaging optically tagged synaptic contacts between axons and dendritic spines in the living brain. While an astounding seven percent of cortical synapses are formed and eliminated each week in an ongoing process, the overall density of synapses remains stable. What this means is that throughout life the cortical network is dynamic and continuously explores new connections with new partners, thereby finding optimal solutions for neuronal computations for coping with life in an ever-changing world.

Adaptive solutions require changes in circuits which transform inputs into outputs. This involves the transmission of impulses across chains of neurons. Such chains of cortical neurons were depicted for the first time by one of Cajal's pupils, Lorente de No in 1938.[5]
He proposed that the whole process of impulse transformation is performed in cortical columns thinner than the width of a hair, which he called "elementary units" (Figure 3). In each vertical unit a select group of neurons receives synaptic input from a distant source. Other neurons lack such input, but receive inputs from neurons which do and send output to distant targets. In effect vertical chains of neurons were conceived of as units which amplify weak outside inputs in persistent, reverberating patterns of neuronal activity.
A refined, updated version of Lorente de No's vertical chain involving excitatory and inhibitory connections is known today as a "canonical circuit."
There is intense interest in understanding the connectional logic within this circuit whose nearly identical copies

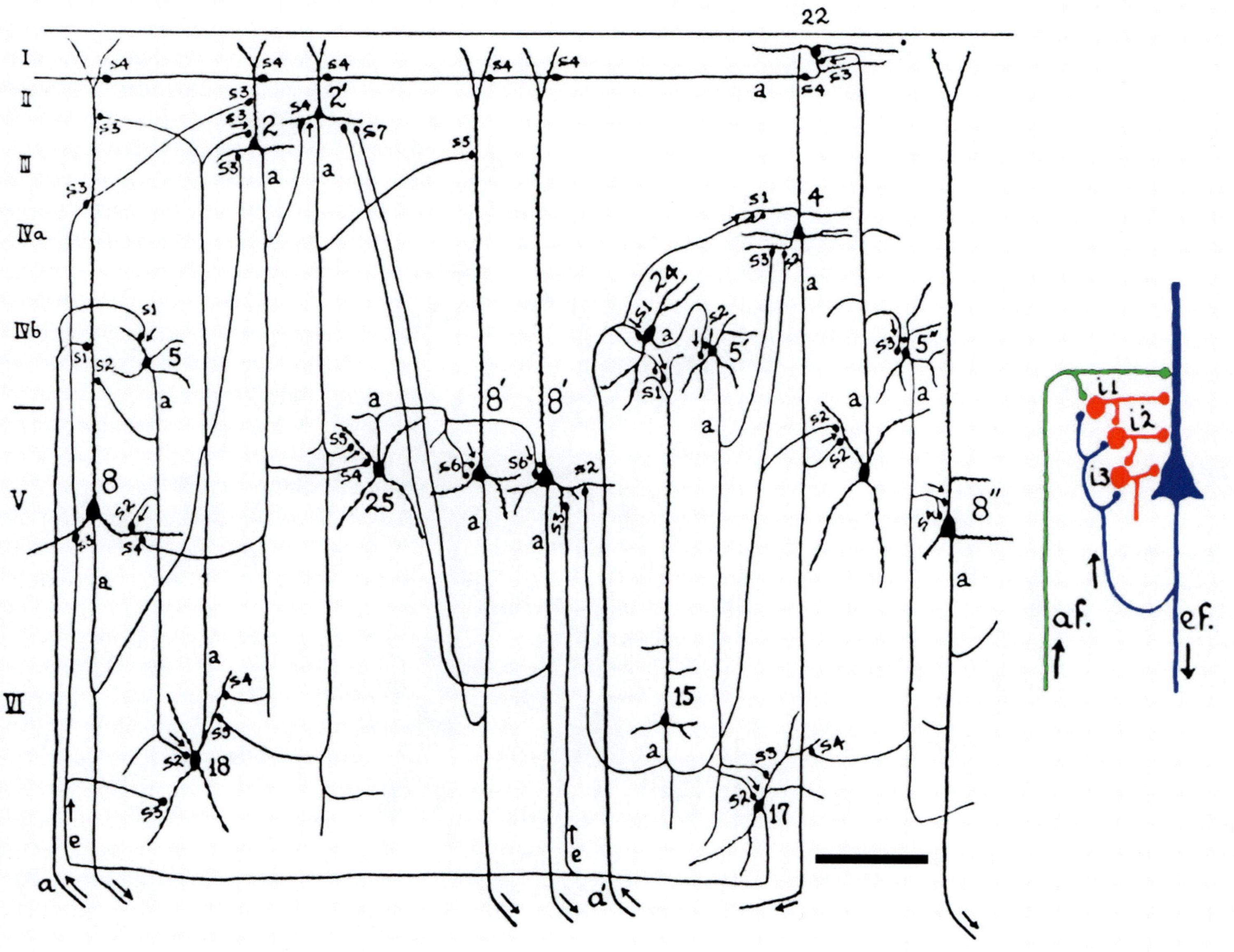

Figure 4: Elementary cortical circuit. The microscopic image shows silver stained neurons and their connections drawn by Lorente de No (1938)[5]. Notice that each neuron is a separate element of an interconnected chain. Lorente de No discovered order in the chain of connections, which he interpreted in terms of the flow (arrows) of information through a circuit within gray matter. For example, input from axon (a) goes to cell (5), whose output axon (a) contacts cell (8), which sends output (α) into white matter. Through recordings of electrical impulses, we now know that the circuit amplifies the stimulatory input from (a). Signal amplification is just one of many operations of cortical computation. Another is impulse inhibition. A circuit for self-inhibition is shown on the far right side. Here, the stimulatory pyramidal cell's (blue) output (ef) is fed through a side branch to inhibitory cells (red, i1, i2, i3) whose stimulation reduces the output (ef) of the pyramidal cell. Scale: 0.1 mm

are repeated across cortical areas with diverse functional specializations such as, for example, hearing, speech production and speech comprehension. If the proposed iterated uniformity of cortex is correct and indeed shows that canonical computations are performed on a wide range of inputs, we may conclude that the functional diversity of cortical areas results from the specificity of the network of long-range connections.

Constructing the structure

Wachsmann left no instructions on how to assemble his grapevine structures. But given the standardized parts list and geometric simplicity of the wishbone elements, it is reasonable to assume that traditional ground-based construction equipment would do the job. Unlike building human-designed architectures which are fabricated by equipment standing on the ground, construction of the cortical network is decoupled from the ground. It uses coordinate frames tied to local landmarks within the cortex and in this regard resembles the architectural fabrication by flying machines introduced by Gramazio Kohler.

Told in the simplest terms, building cortical gray matter is a straightforward affair. In the embryonic brain, neurons are born at an astounding rate of a half a million cells per minute sustained over the first three months post conception. After this frantic early period, cell proliferation comes to an end and neurons migrate from their diverse birthplaces to settle in different layers of the cortical sheet. It is a process that is not fundamentally different from procuring the building material from the supplier and the handiwork of the bricklayer in building the walls. The basic cortical sheet is fully established at birth. Outgrowth of axons and dendrites begins in the last trimester of gestation, then continues postnatally until the network has acquired its final configuration at around puberty when gray and white matters have attained their mature structure. Wiring the cortex involves directed growth of axons, instructed by a map of molecular cues encoded in the genome and expressed in a temporal hierarchy. Despite the detailed blueprint evolved by natural selection, the target innervation is sloppy. Because of that, the final wiring is achieved gradually by eliminating excessive or imprecise connections. This involves an active process that makes use of the neurons' ability to exchange electrical signals. An easy way to think about it is captured by the catchphrase "whoever fires together, wires together." Only the future will show whether activity-dependent construction will become an option in architecture.

While activity-dependent construction provides adaptive advantages, it carries the risk that two structures may not be identical and unduly shaped by unforeseen events during assembly. The risks (or advantages) of individuality are illustrated by the effects of bandaging an eye during infancy. Even a few days of unilateral visual deprivation is long enough to permanently alter the structure of the visual cortical network and render the eye legally blind. Interestingly, the dramatic impact is confined to a sensitive period during the first few years of life. Covering the eye in the adult has no effect on the visual cortex and on vision. Thus, normal activity is necessary to maintain the developing cortical network; once it has acquired its final form, stability is favored. At this stage, more subtle forms of learning and memory replace the early largescale plasticity, which enable the effortless acquisition of language and speech during early childhood, a skill which in adults requires years of practice and may never reach perfection. In both phases of life, though, intelligent behavior emerges only by interactions between the active body and the brain.

Zooming out

The collision of minds with diverse backgrounds has led us from Wachsmann's grapevine structures into the jungle of brain networks. What motivated Marianne, Christian and me to take the trip was not the pursuit of neuroarchitecture or the engineering of evidence-based design, but the stylistic similarity of the architecture in the built environment and that used for thinking. The farther along the path we traveled, the clearer it became that the worlds of architecture and the brain differed in construction and purpose. At the end of the trip it is fair to ask, was it worth it? For the explorer for whom the joy of knowing is limitless, the answer is yes, because it offered the possibility for discovering something new and eye-opening. Outcomes of experiments are not always predictable. Taking trips focuses attention, broadens perspectives and brings clarity. For the same reasons, we visit art exhibitions, attend concerts or travel across the ocean in search for the resistance that unlocks a tiny burst of energy for reaching beyond the horizon and discovering the unknown.

Acknowledgments

We would like to thank the Instituto Cajal (Spanish National Research Council, CSIC) for the permission to reproduce an original drawing of Cajal that forms part of the Cajal Legacy. © CSIC. Many thanks also to Professor Javier DeFelipe (Universidad Politecnica de Madrid, Spain; Instituto Cajal, Madrid, Spain) and the Cajal Blue Brain Project (UPM-CSIC) for the generosity to reproduce a computer generated image of the cerebral cortical network.

1
Konrad Wachsmann, *Wendepunkt im Bauen*, Krausskopf-Verlag, Wiesbaden 1959.

2
J. DeFelipe, *Cajal's Butterflies of the Soul,* Oxford University Press 2010.

3
D.H. Hubel and T.N. Wiesel, T.N. (1979) *Brain mechanisms of vision*, Sci. Am. 241, 1979, pp. 130–144.

4
S.R. Cajal, *Die Neuronenlehre* (Translated by D. Miskolczy), *Handbuch der Neurologie, Vol. 1*, O. Bumke and O. Foerster (eds), Springer, Berlin 1935, pp. 887–994.

5
Rafael Lorente de Nó, Cerebral cortex: Architecture, intracortical connection, motor projections, in: *Physiology of the Nervous System*, J.F. Fulton (ed.), 2nd edition, Oxford University Press, London 1938, pp. 174–313.

The Location Orientation Manipulator at Wachsmann's Institute for Building Research at the University of Southern California with study models by Fritz Haller

LOM: Location Orientation Manipulator 1969

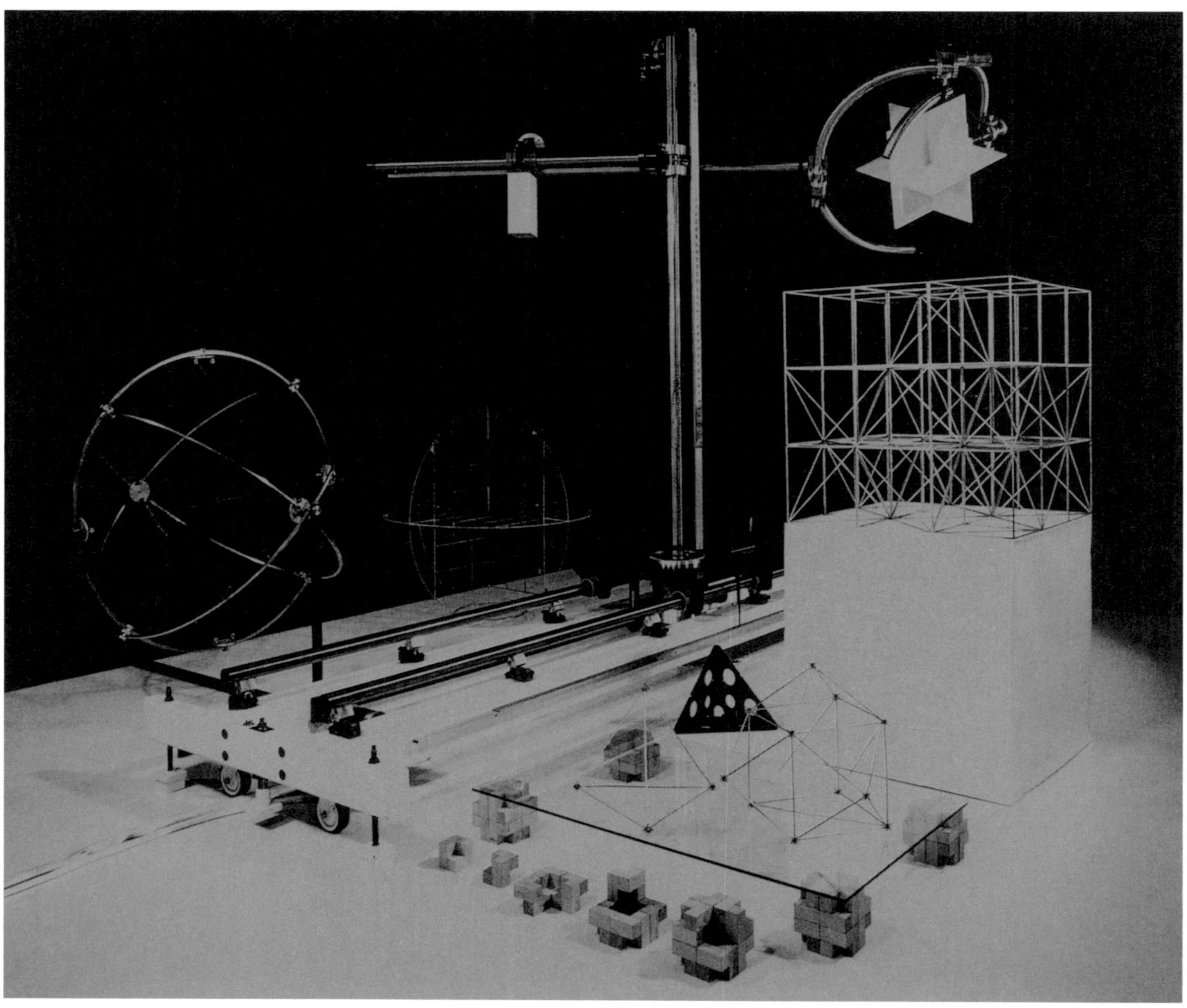

In 1969, Konrad Wachsmann developed the Location Orientation Manipulator (LOM) at the University of Southern California together with his doctoral students John Bollinger and Xavier Mendoza.[1] It was a project that received far less attention than his iconic hangar structures for the Atlas Aircraft Corporation or the study project at the Institute of Design in Chicago that we know as the Grapevine Structure.

Yet the LOM addressed the criticism Konrad Wachsmann formulated in his seminal book *The Turning Point of Building*: directed towards what he called "seemingly modern buildings,"[2] (TiB S.49) his motivation was not so much the critique of the finished project but rather, its construction process, a process that had changed very little over time. For Wachsmann, the building site was all too often "disorder and confusion"[3] ("aus dem verwirrenden Durcheinander einer eingerüsteten, unorganisierten und von Abfall entstellten Baustelle erwächst", TiB 49 "out of the disorder and confusion of a scaffolded, ill-organized and waste-encumbered site") that stood in stark contrast to the precision and control of the modern factories he celebrates in chapter two of *The Turning Point of Building*.

When the book was published in 1959, his solution to the problem was pre-fabrication, seriality and simplicity. His conception of industrially-produced elements and modules with their geometric rigor and ingenious connection systems only required the material-agnostic assembler on site. Still, industry was one-step ahead. The same year in which the book was published, General Motors installed the prototype of the very first industrial robot on an assembly line. Thousands of Unimates were to follow throughout the sixties, initiating the biggest revolution of the sector since Henry Ford invented the moving assembly line.
Eager to understand and employ the contemporary "resources of the times"[4] (TiB 232), Konrad Wachsmann's Location Orientation Manipulator continued his ambition of introducing the logic of industrial processes into architecture and the building sector. It was the next step, a functioning prototype of a machine that allowed the repetition of recorded sequences of movements to place elements in space through the mechanical representation of kinematics. "The objective of this study is to develop the equations of motion necessary to describe object manipulation with our machine, the LOM; and to develop a computer simulation program based on these equations."[5] It was by definition Wachsmann's take on the robot.

The LOM can be easily read as the next generation assembler in the factory as well as on site, and thus, as an important precursor to robotic automation in the building sector. It extends industrial logic to include the assembly process while aligning with Wachsmann's praise of mass-produced standard elements based on accurate repetition and high output. Large-scale structures such as the Atlas Aircraft Corporation hangar space frames built up from tetrahedrons are the perfect example to illustrate the capacity of a robotic assembly process.

At the same time, Konrad Wachsmann considered the invention of new tools to be an expression of our human culture. He embraced technology as a progressive field, constantly updating the "resources of the times." Consequently, his main objective was "liberation from the dogma of convention"[6] (WiP 232); as a passionate theater-goer, he also made sure not to forget philosophy and art when discussing science and technology. Yet seen from today's perspective, the structures, which Wachsmann based on uniform tetrahedrons, capture the Zeitgeist of post-war structuralism; among them, the Mero System is another prominent and economically successful system. While still common today, the repetitive assembly of identical parts has become a convention of the past.

Nowadays, the "resources of the times" are computation, sensing, digital control and – still – industrial robotic arms. However, the latter no longer manipulate, orient and place identical objects in space. Routines can change thanks to computation and elements can be unique while sharing similarities. Architectural structures assembled by industrial robots can thus be differentiated and spatially complex. Computational control and simulation extends conventional wisdom in structural capacities, and the hybridization of robotics and 3D printing is rapidly changing our understanding of toolmaking and manufacturing. The unique has been rationalized, the non-standard has replaced the standard as paradigm.

Konrad Wachsmann's call for interdisciplinary research was visionary, as was his overarching ambition to bring together science, technology, art, culture, architecture and construction. His abilities to read the potential of new developments outside the architectural discourse and to translate his understanding into novel construction processes and architectural concepts remain highly relevant for the contemporary architect facing both rapid digital development and a conservative construction sector.

An epilogue on enigmatic rationality

Stored away in boxes, the LOM went missing after a few public displays. What remained were a video, photographs and accurate descriptions in the doctoral theses of John Bollinger and Xavier Mendoza. Wachsmann himself kept remarkably silent about their pioneering work, leaving much room for future speculation. While keen to understand the present state of the art, he must have felt the limitations of being a visionary.[7] Here, at the threshold of rationality, the LOM establishes an intriguing link to the Grapevine Structure. This puzzling proposal for a structural system consists of interweaving, space-defining columns and trusses with no apparent need for joints surprises. Its unusual focus on expressive perspectival drawings comes at the expense of the focus on connections. Its prominent presentation in *The Turning Point of Building*, although clearly beyond the industrial production standards of his time, only adds to the quest for meaningful connections. Did the Grapevine Structure, with its departure from rectilinear constructs and its emphasis on complex configurations of elements in space, motivate the development of the Location Orientiation Manipulator as a tool to execute the required spatial and rotational operations?[8] Departing from the logic of industrial repetitive tasks, it would have been a very accurate proposition for robotic construction – anticipating contemporary research in robotic additive assemblies of custom structures.

1
Konrad Wachsmann had initiated a doctoral programme at USC in building science.

2
Konrad Wachsmann, *The Turning Point of Building*, Reinhold, New York 1961, trans. Thomas E. Burton.

3
ibid.

4
ibid.

5
John Bollinger on the mathematical model of the LOM, Konrad Wachsmann Archiv, Berlin, in Bock, Thomas, Lauer, Willi Victor Location Orientation Manipulator by Konrad Wachsmann, John Bollinger, and Xavier Mendoza, Conference Proceedings to the 27th International Symposium on Automation and Robotics in Construction (ISARC 2010).

6
Konrad Wachsmann, *The Turning Point of Building*, op. cit.

7
"Die Zahl der technischen Mittel ist so groß, daß sie ein Mensch allein nicht mehr überschauen kann. Die Möglichkeiten, welche die Maschine schafft, unterscheiden sich von jenen des Handwerks vollständig – und wir kennen diese Möglichkeiten erst zum Teil," Franz Füeg, Review on *The Turning Point of Building*, in: *Bauen + Wohnen*, 14, 1960, issue 10, p. 18.

8
comp.: Antoin Picon, 'Robots and Architecture', in: AD, 229, May/June 2014, p. 59.

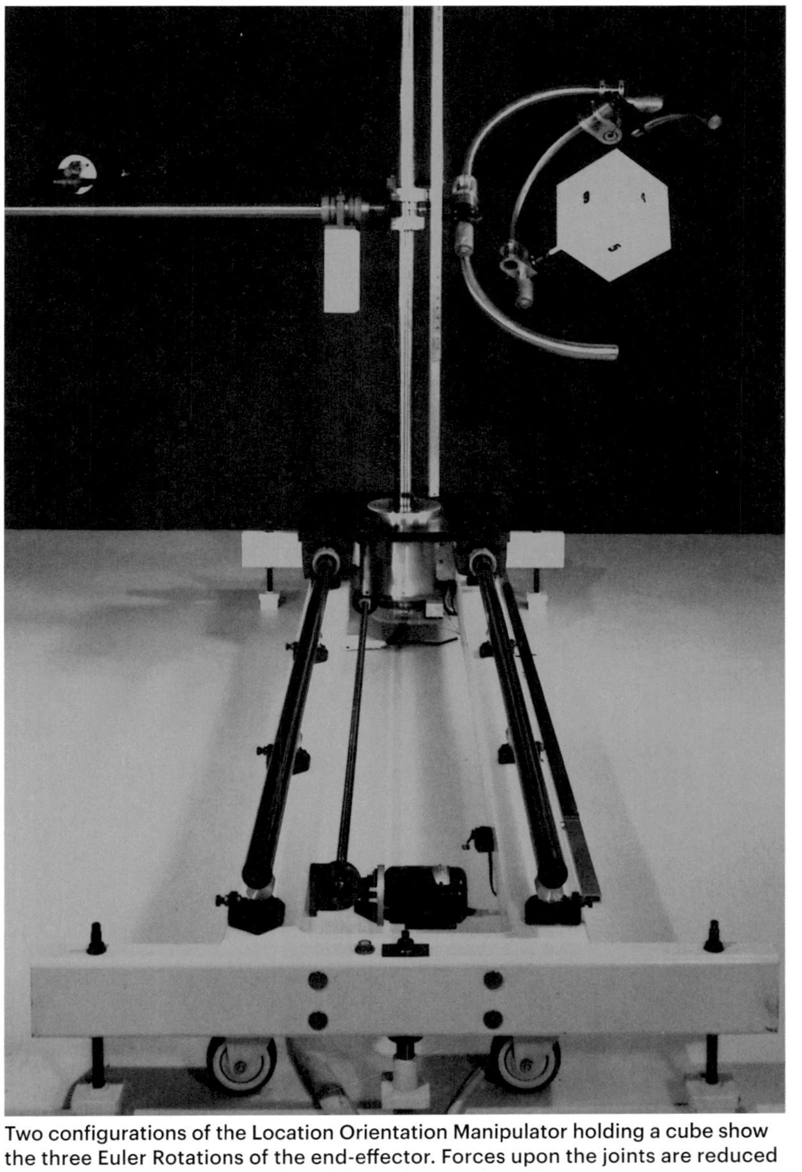

Two configurations of the Location Orientation Manipulator holding a cube show the three Euler Rotations of the end-effector. Forces upon the joints are reduced by dynamic counterweights that slide on the metal profiles

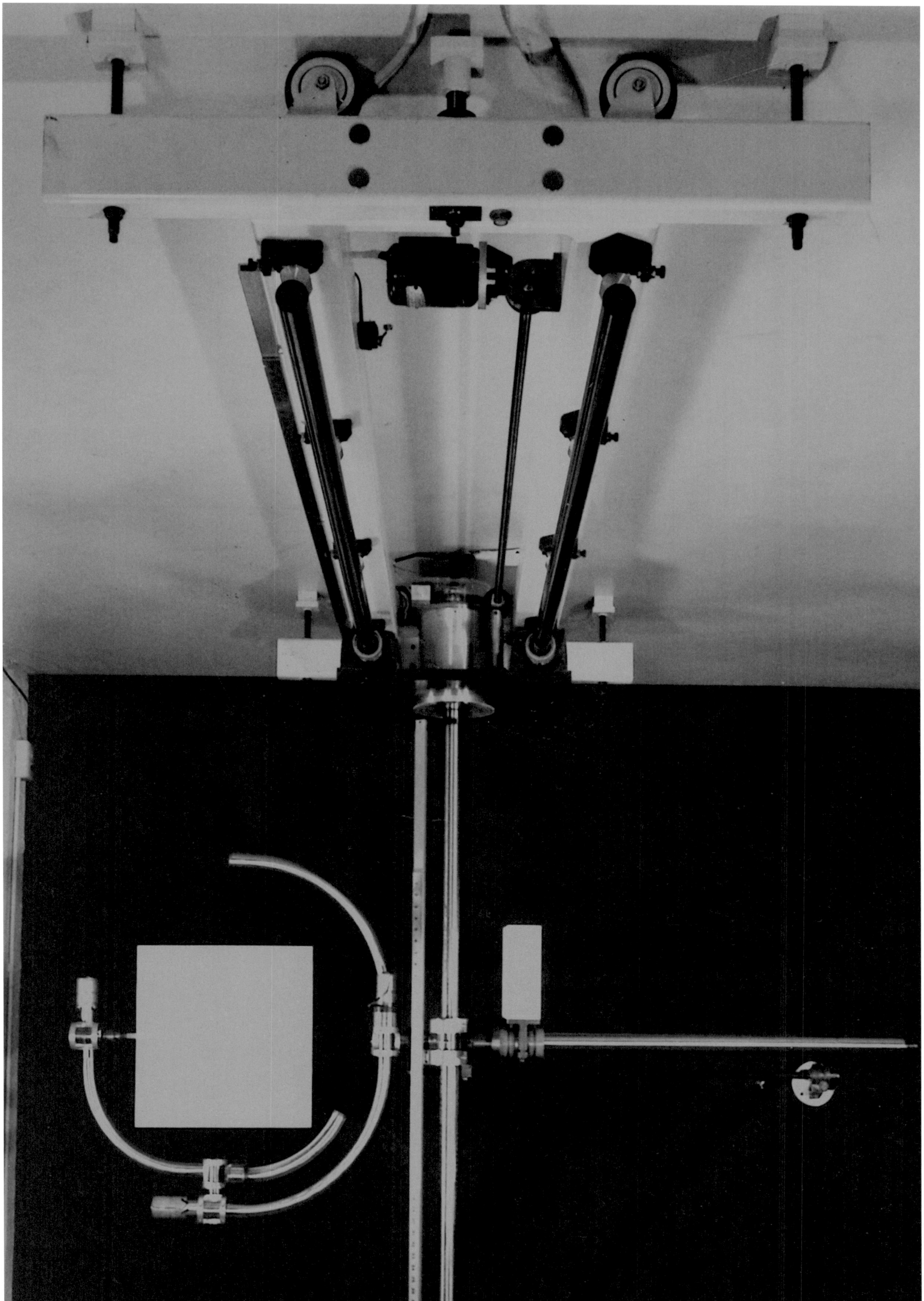

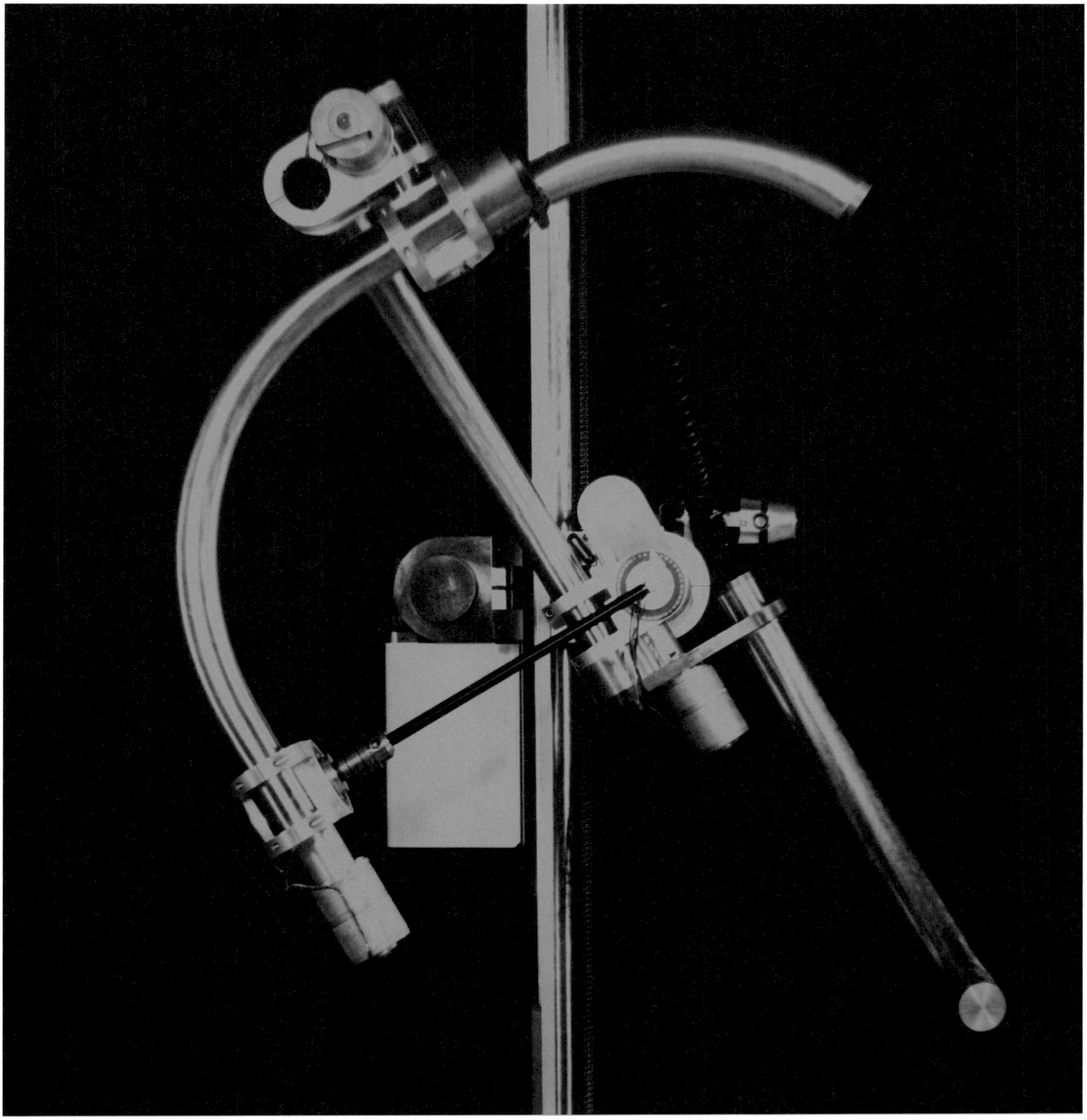

A close up that reveals the long worm screws, one part of the worm gears that are used to transmit movements

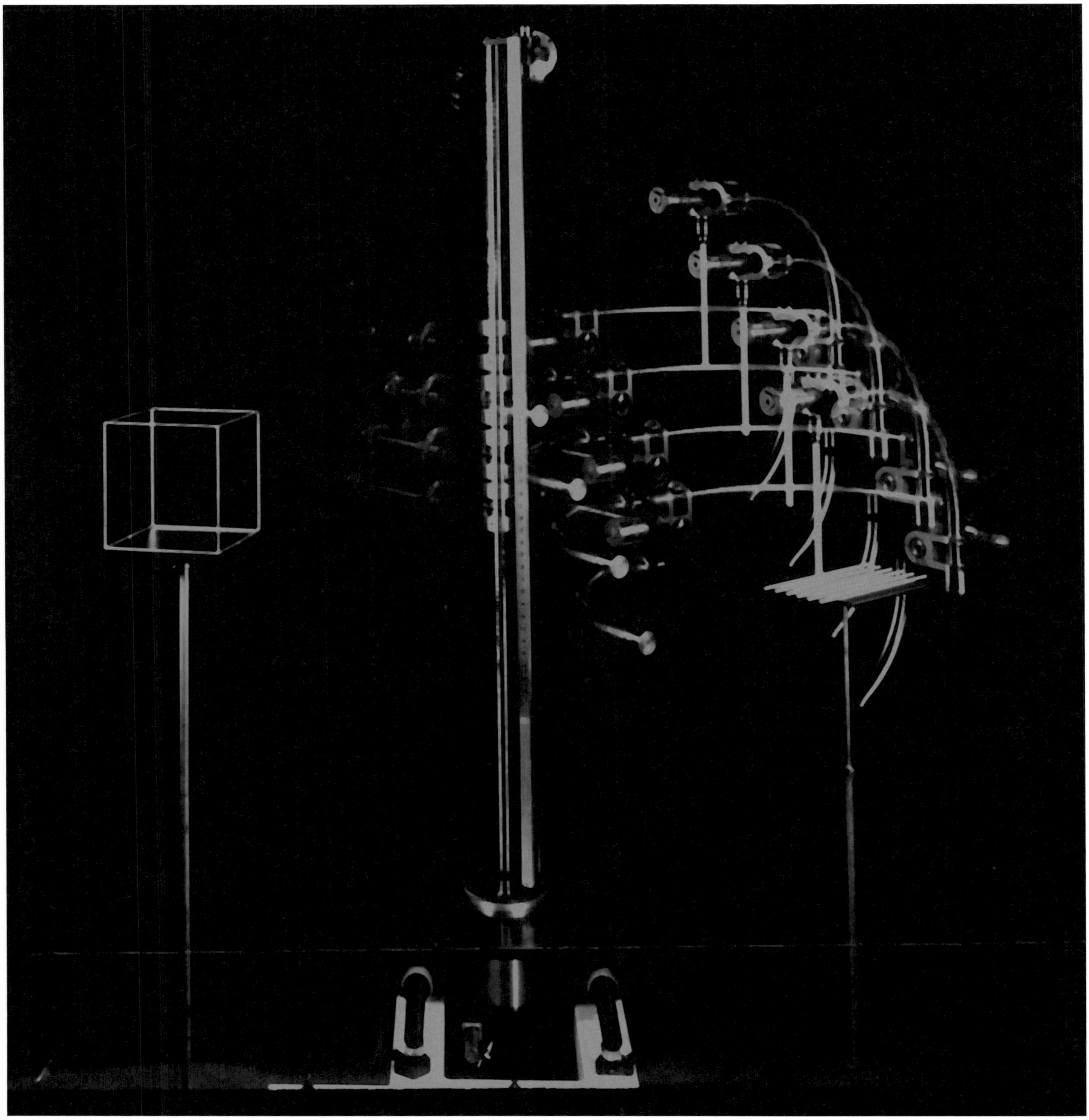

Photographic movement study of LOM's end-effector

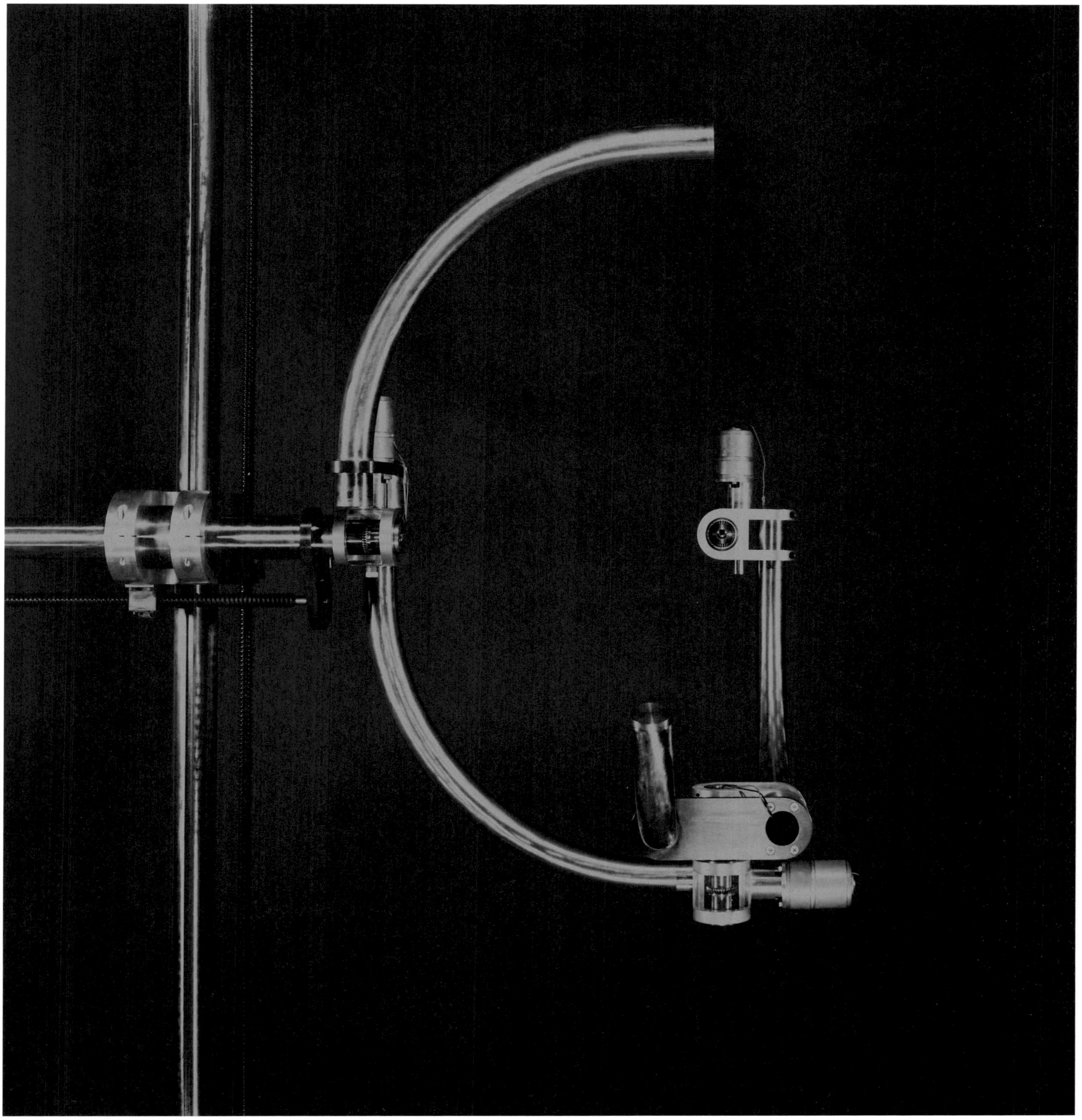

A close up that reveals the long worm screws, one part of the worm gears that are used to transmit movements

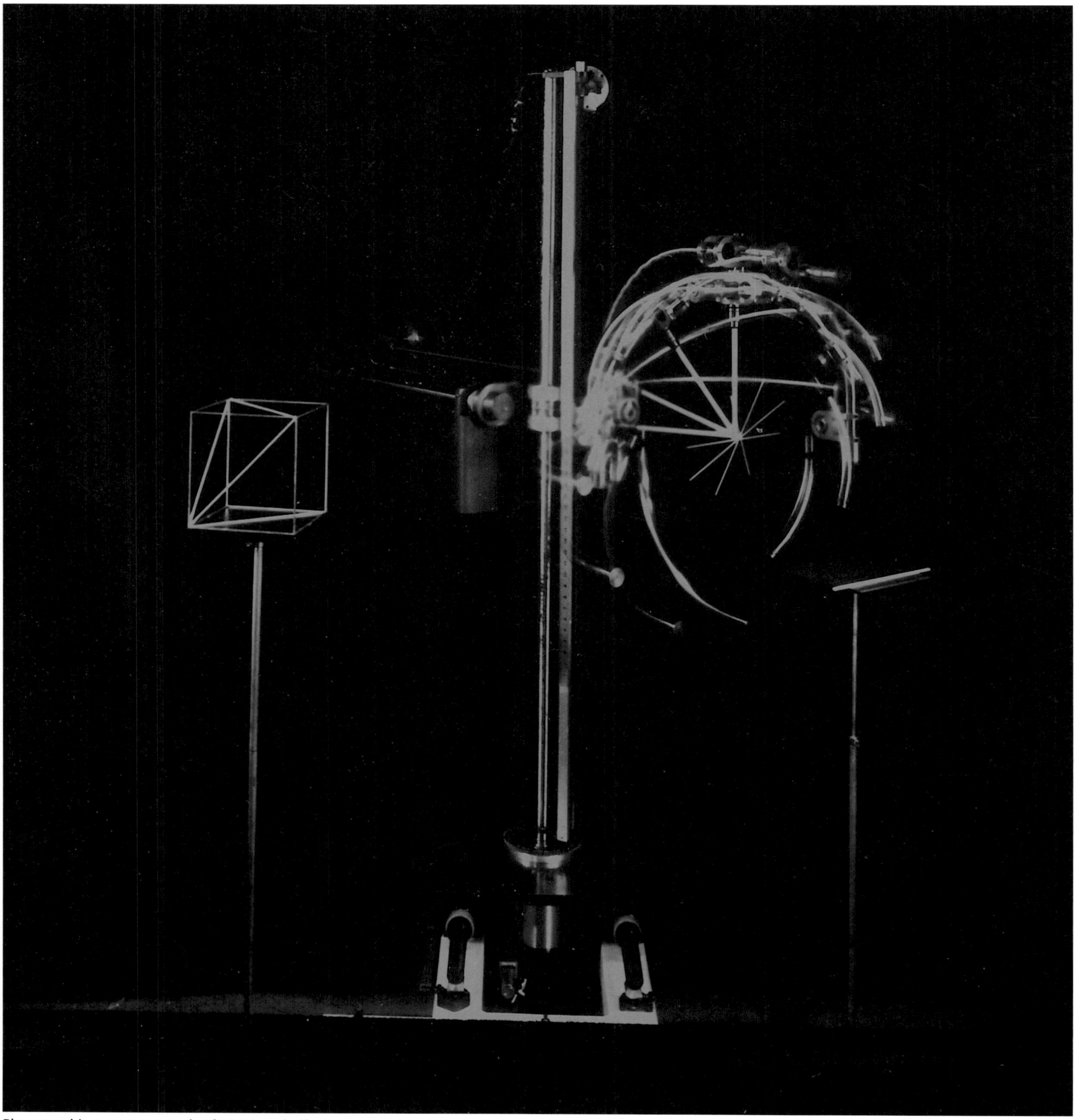

Photographic movement study of LOM's end-effector

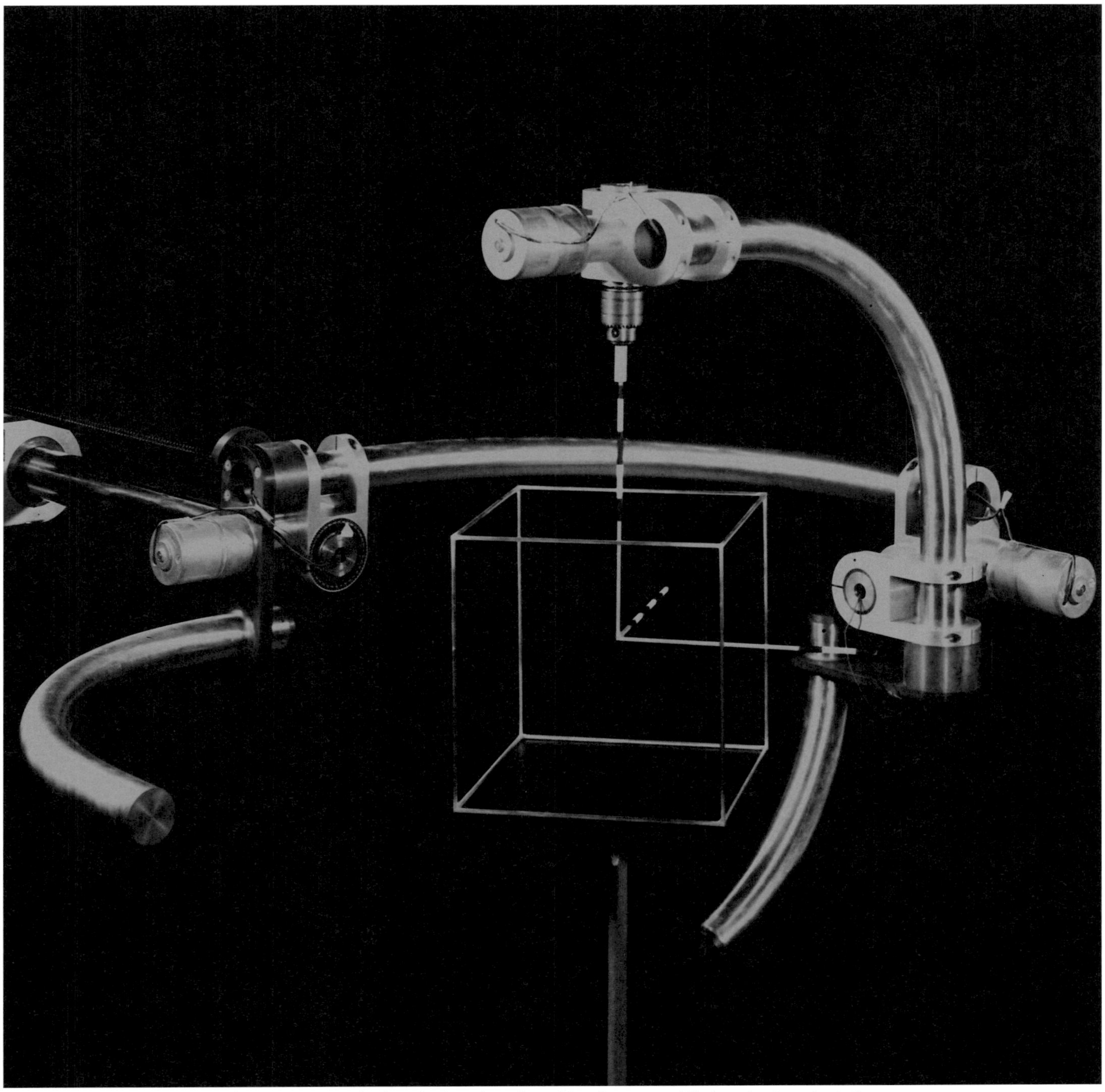

The LOM holding a reference object. It can manipulate the location of an object in space while keeping its orientation

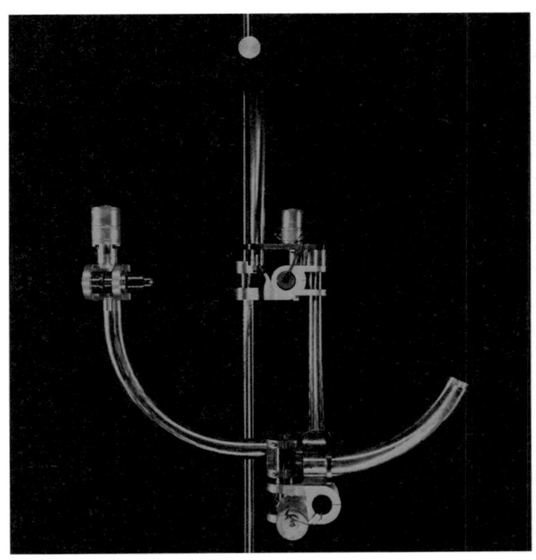

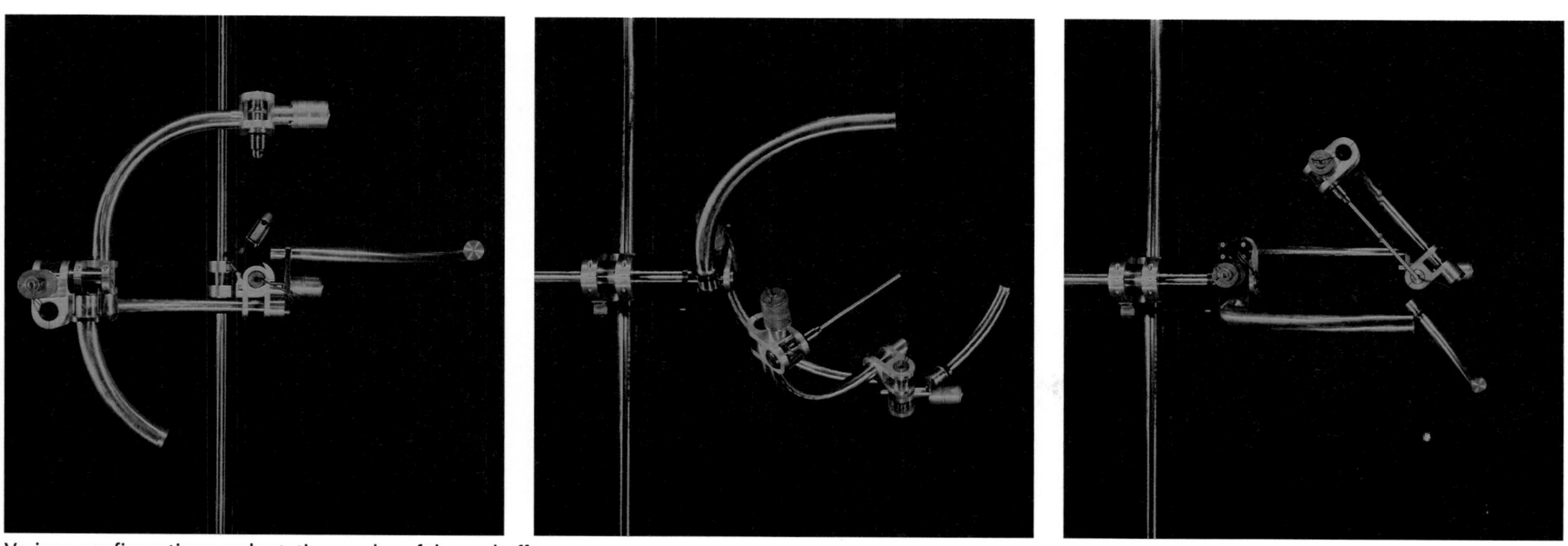

Various configurations and rotation angles of the end-effector

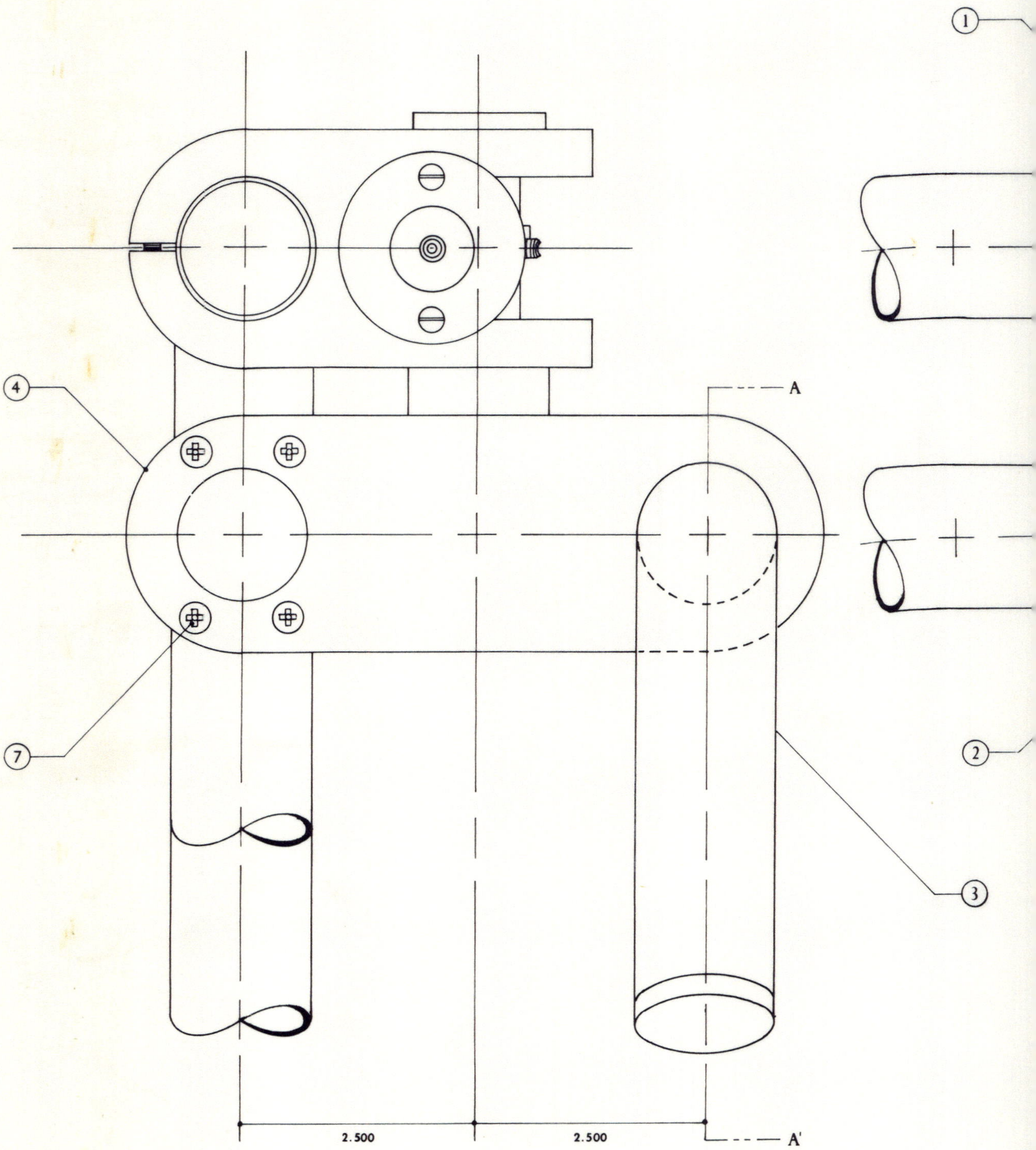

Detail drawing of cross-section and front view of one joint, which is analogue to the other two of the end-effector

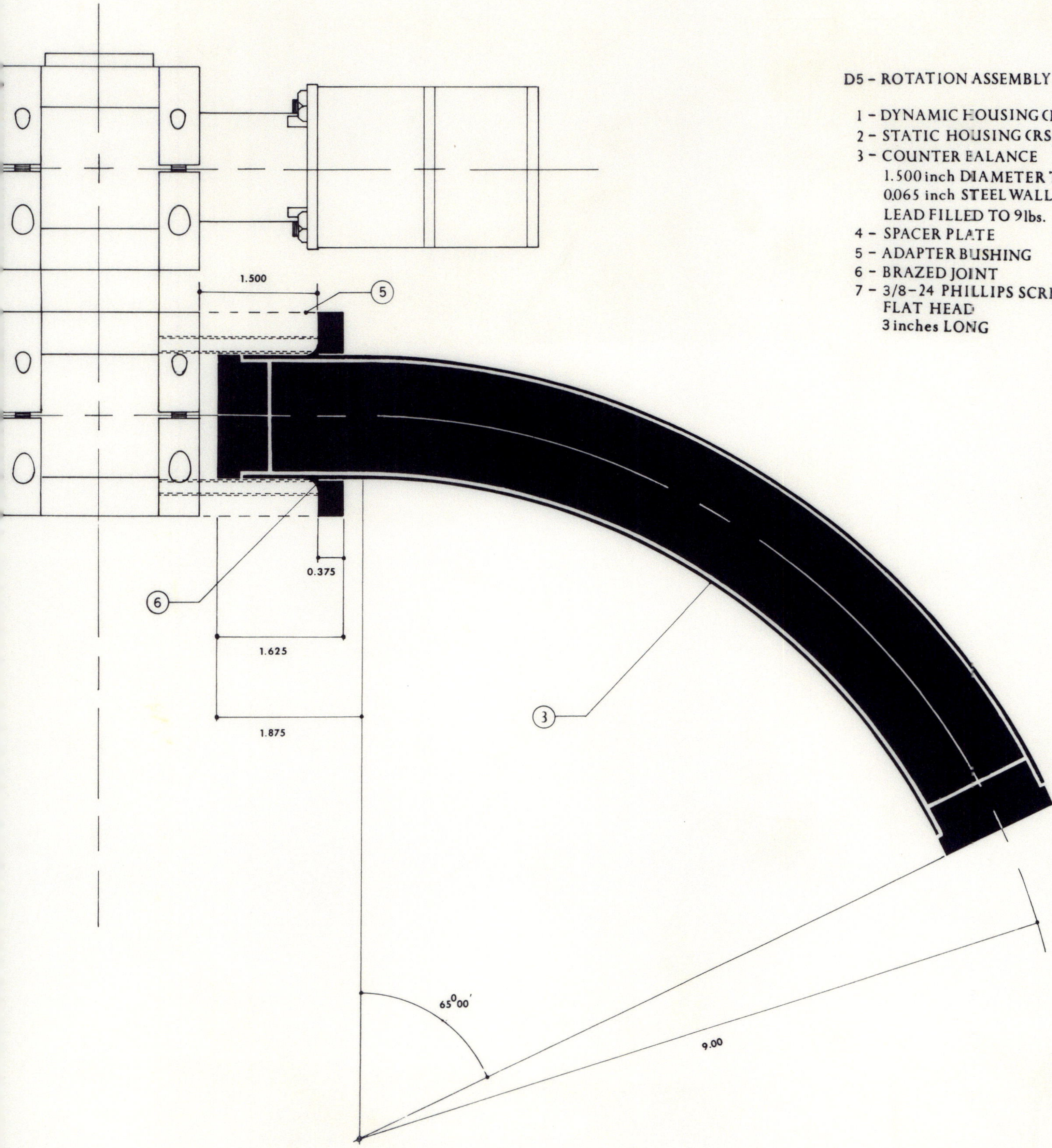

D5 - ROTATION ASSEMBLY

1 - DYNAMIC HOUSING (RD)
2 - STATIC HOUSING (RS)
3 - COUNTER EALANCE
    1.500 inch DIAMETER TUBE
    0.065 inch STEEL WALL
    LEAD FILLED TO 9lbs.
4 - SPACER PLATE
5 - ADAPTER BUSHING
6 - BRAZED JOINT
7 - 3/8-24 PHILLIPS SCREW
    FLAT HEAD
    3 inches LONG

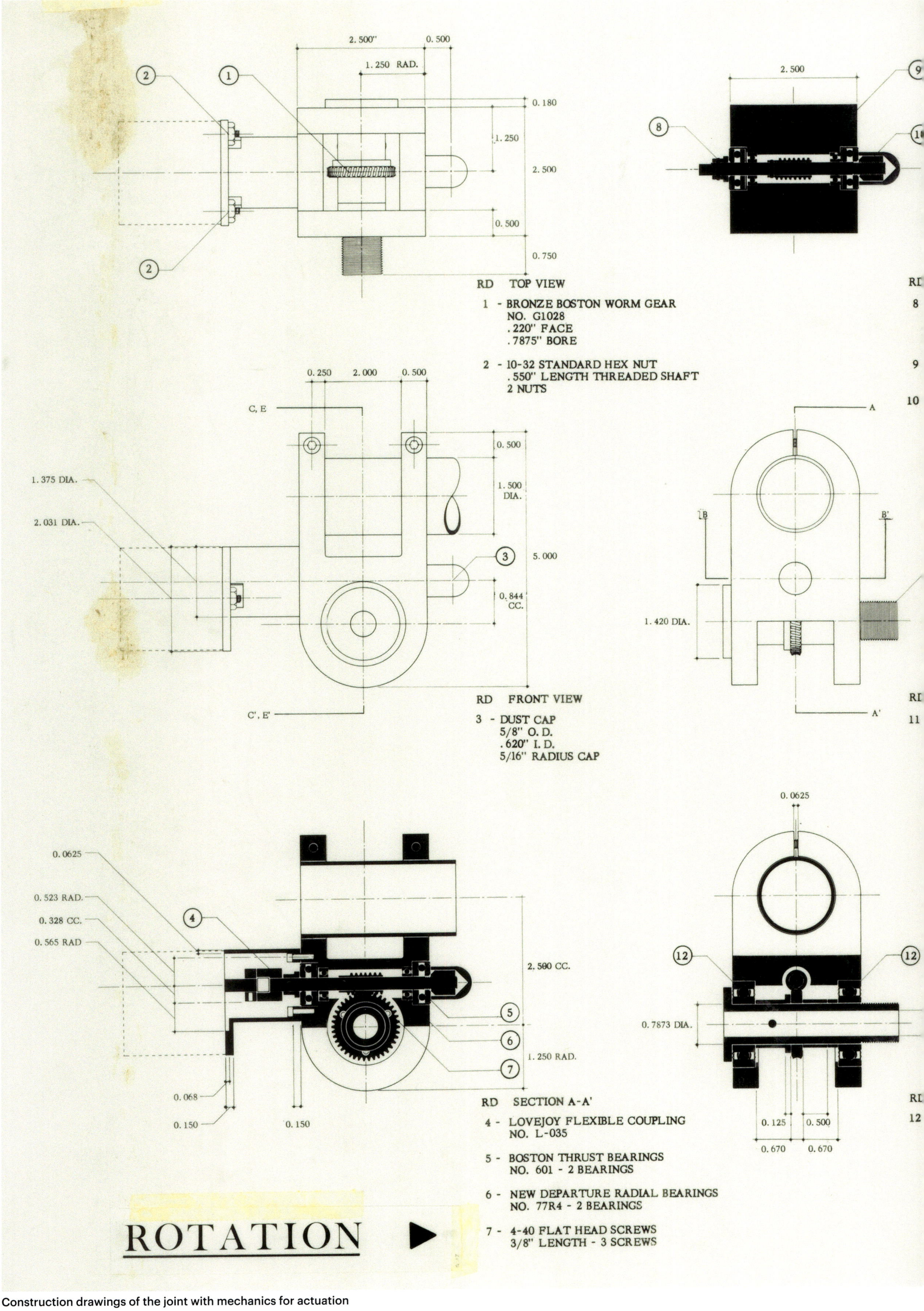

Construction drawings of the joint with mechanics for actuation

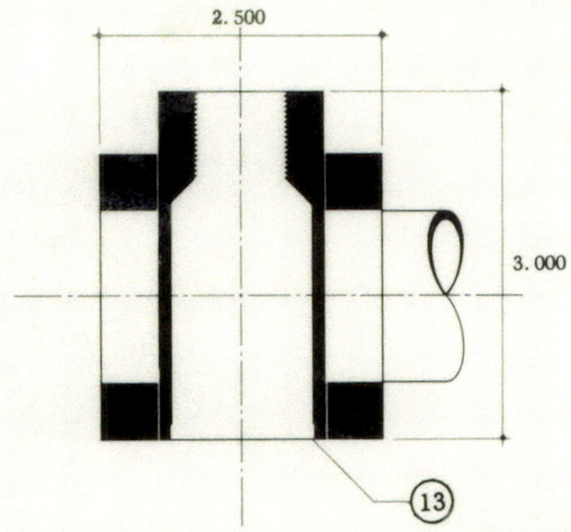

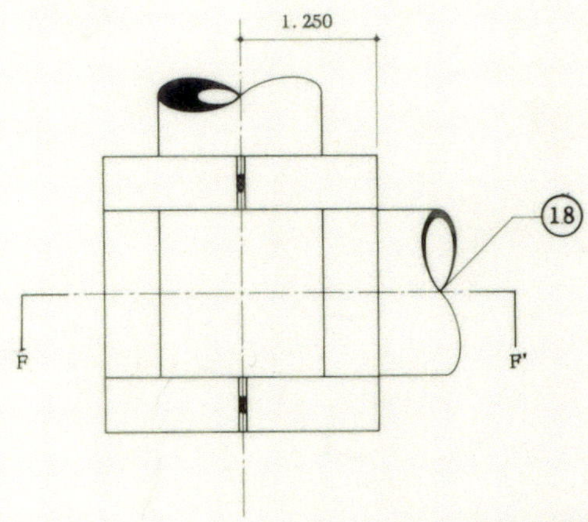

-B'

" LENGTH - .375" O.D.
.00" LENGTH - .500" O.D.
PER PIN

BOSTON WORM
PER PIN

NDARD & SPECIAL
OMBINATION

RS SECTION D-D'

13 - 1/4" RECESS
- RECEIVES 1 1/4" DIA. CAP

RS TOP VIEW

18 - STAINLESS STEEL TUBING
TYPE 304 - 1 1/2" O.D.
.065" WALL

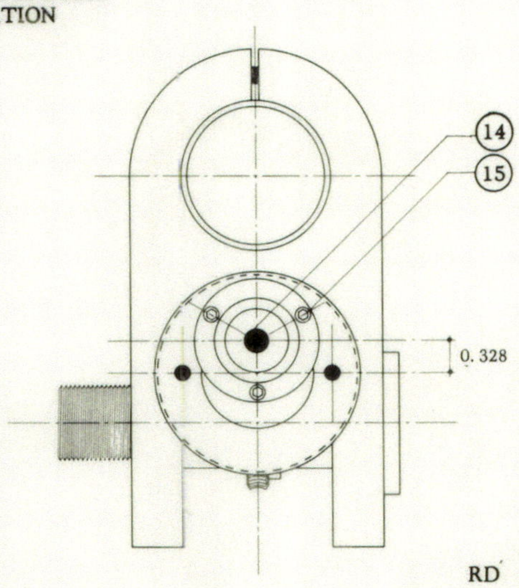

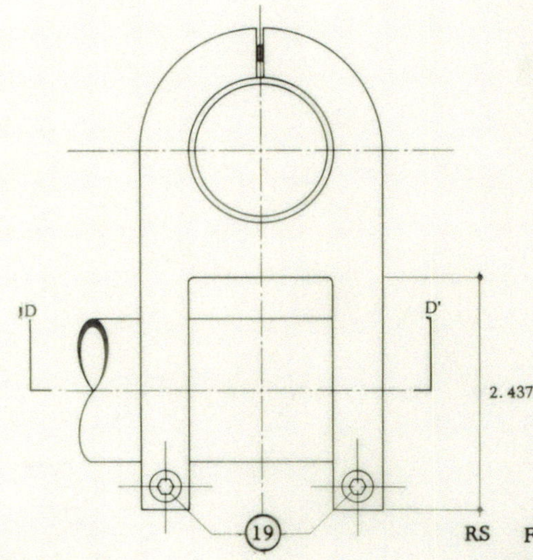

W

READ
TH

RD LEFT VIEW

14 - 1/4" DIA. WORM SHAFT
3 5/8" LENGTH

15 - 4-40 ALLEN CAP SCREWS
1/4" LENGTH
3 SCREWS
0.4725" RAD.

RS FRONT VIEW

19 - 10-32 SOCKET HEAD CAP SCREW
3/4" LENGTH-5/16" DID. HEAD

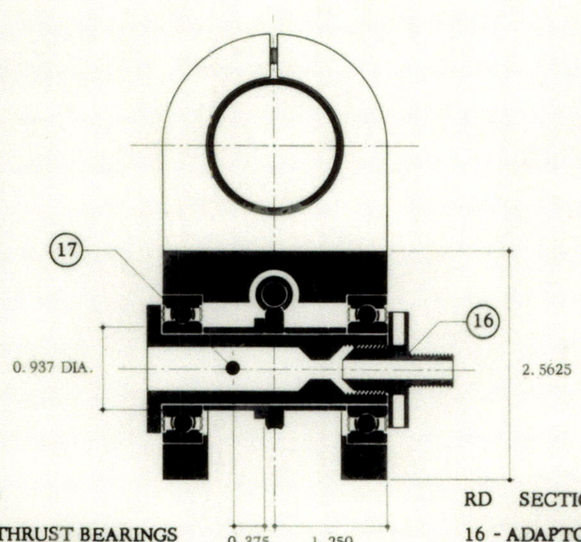

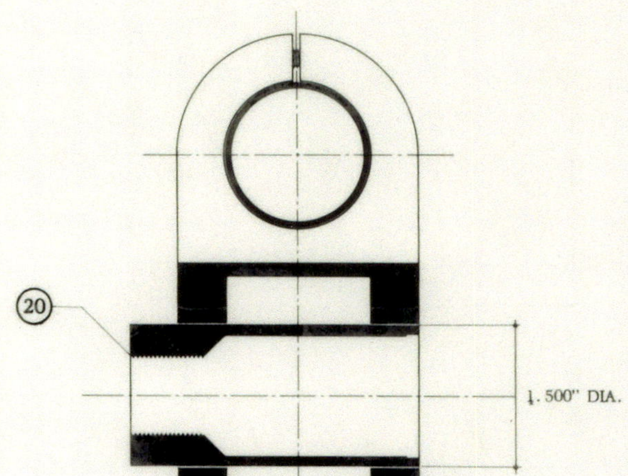

C-C'

L-THRUST BEARINGS
RS-2BEARINGS

RD SECTION E-E'

16 - ADAPTOR
3/8-24 THREAD-1/2" LENGTH
1/2-20 THREAD-3/8" LENGTH
1 5/16" O.D. HUB-3 HOLES
1/8" DIA. 3/8" DEEP
1/8x45° CHAMFER
3/16" BORE

17 - 6/0 TAPER PIN

RS SECTION F-F'

20 - No. 3/4-24 THREAD

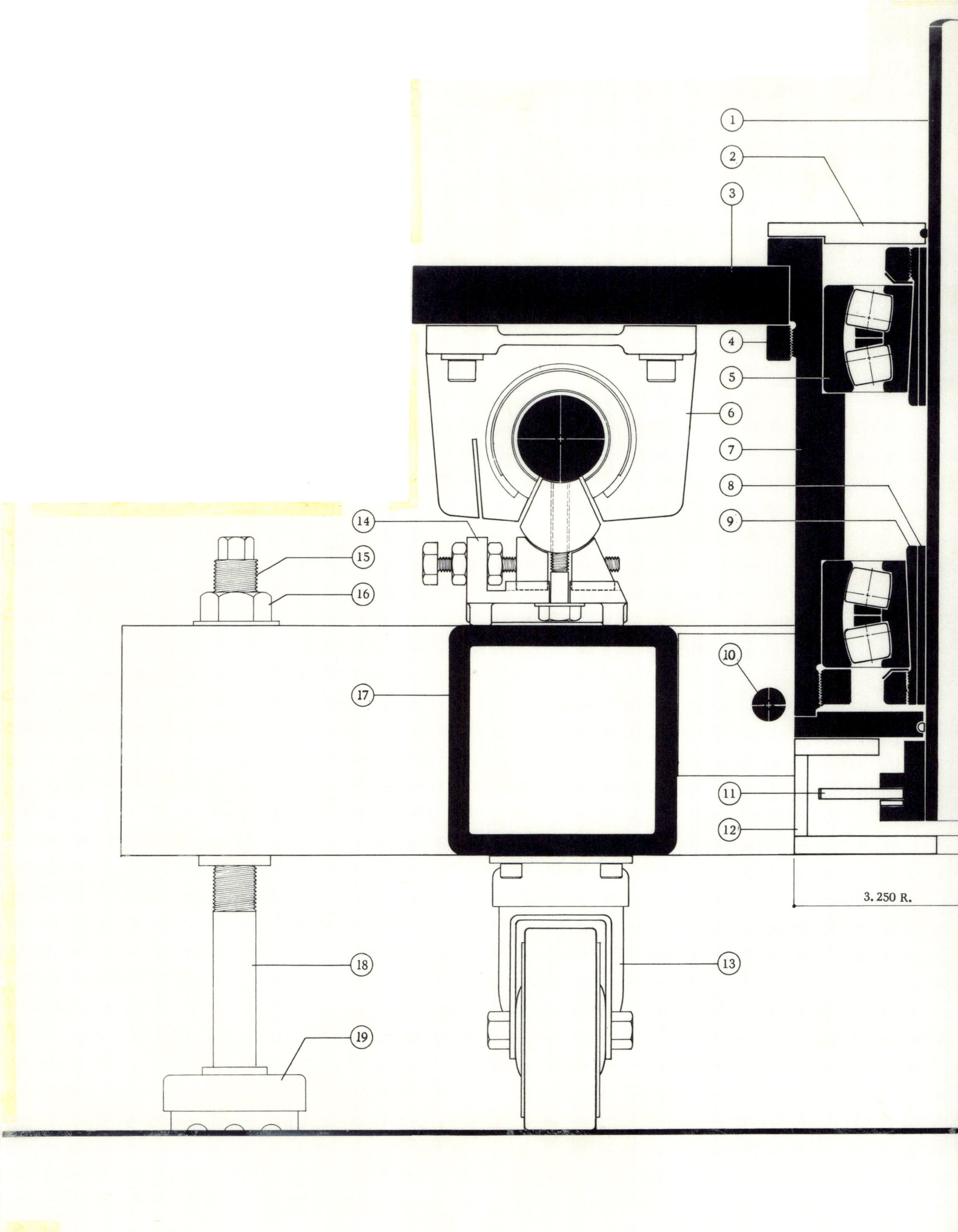

Detail drawing of cross-section of the linear axis on a base with coasters

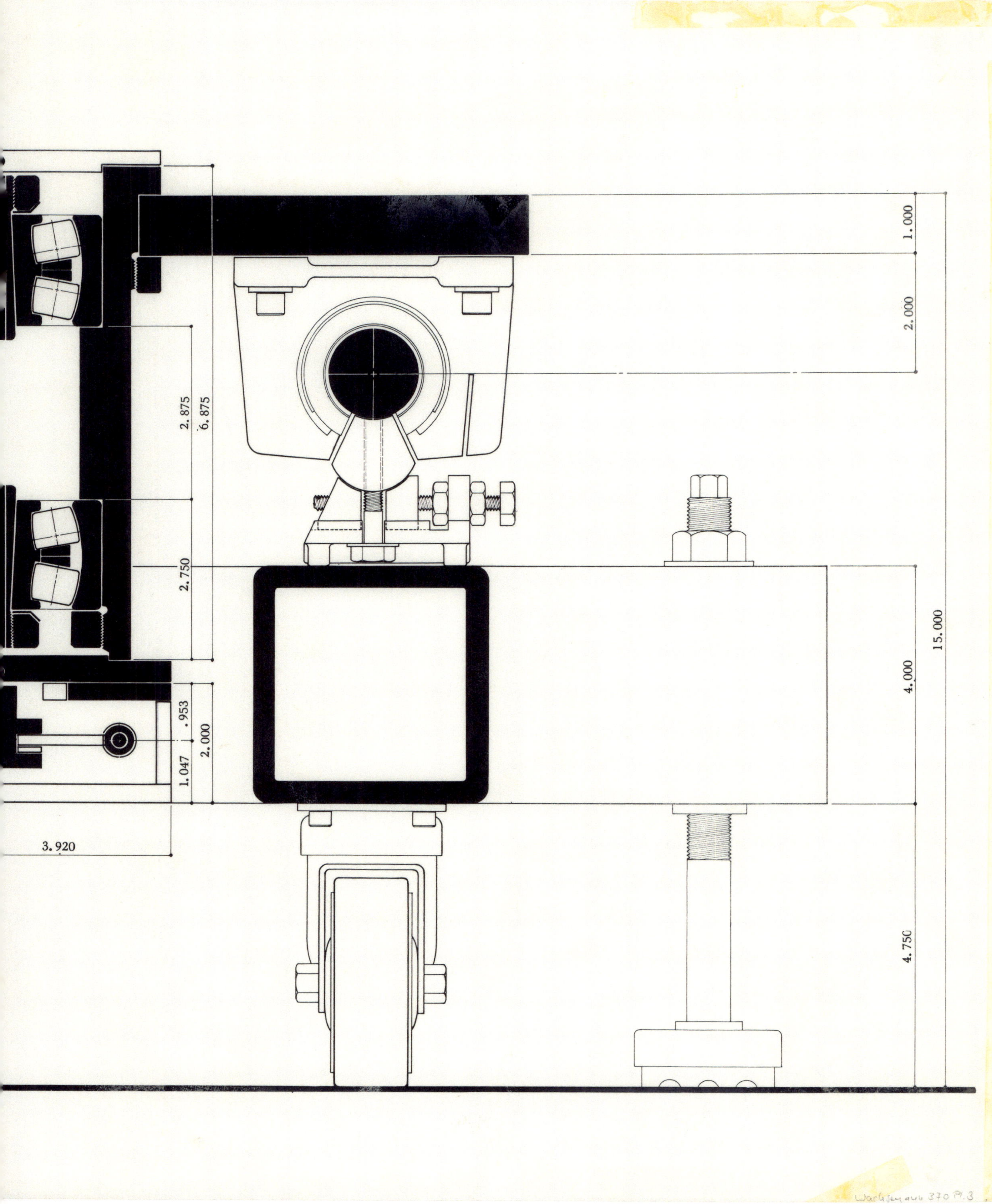
1.000
2.000
2.875
6.875
2.750
15.000
4.000
.953
2.000
1.047
3.920
4.750

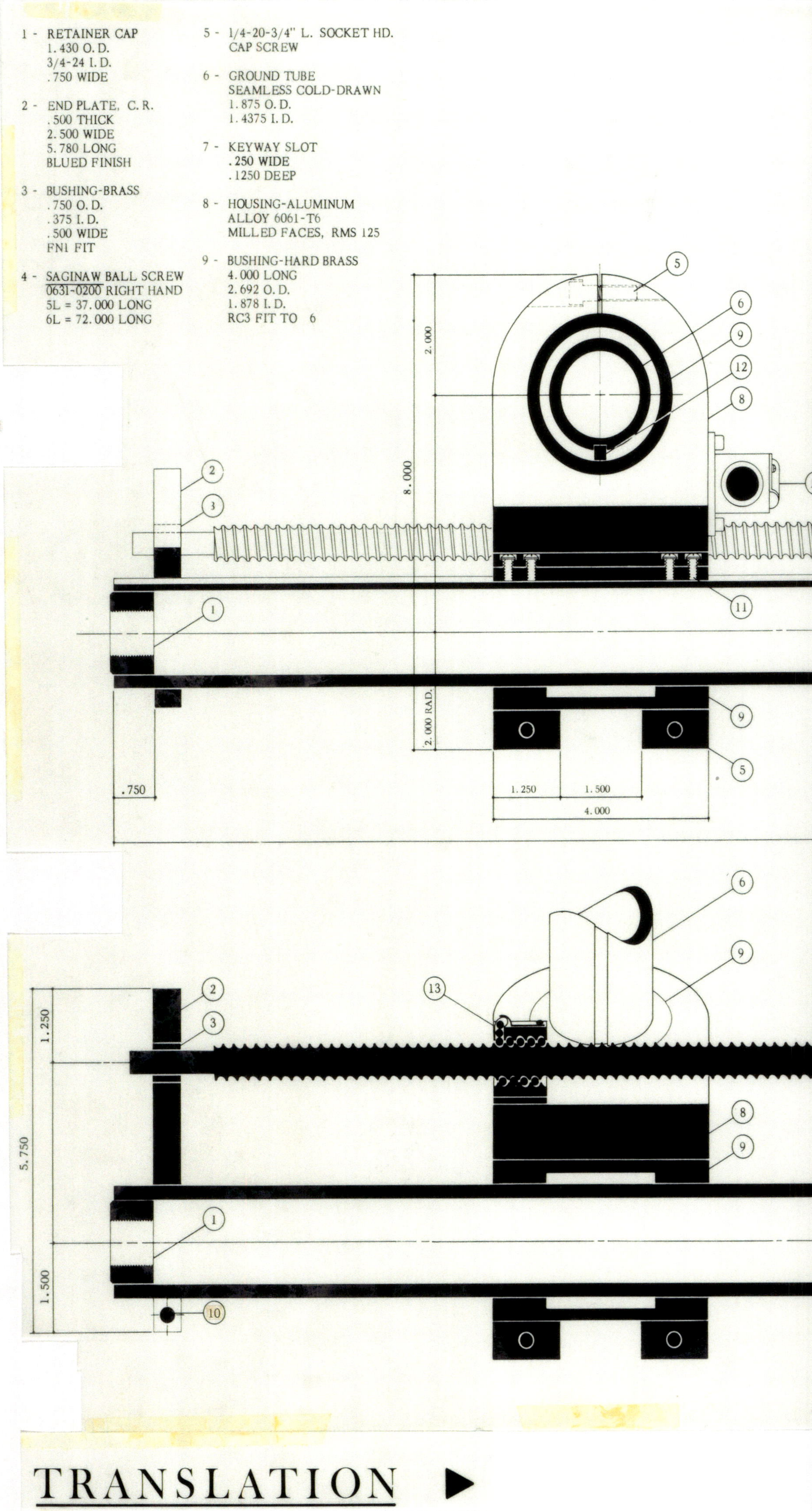

Detail drawing for the actuation of translation

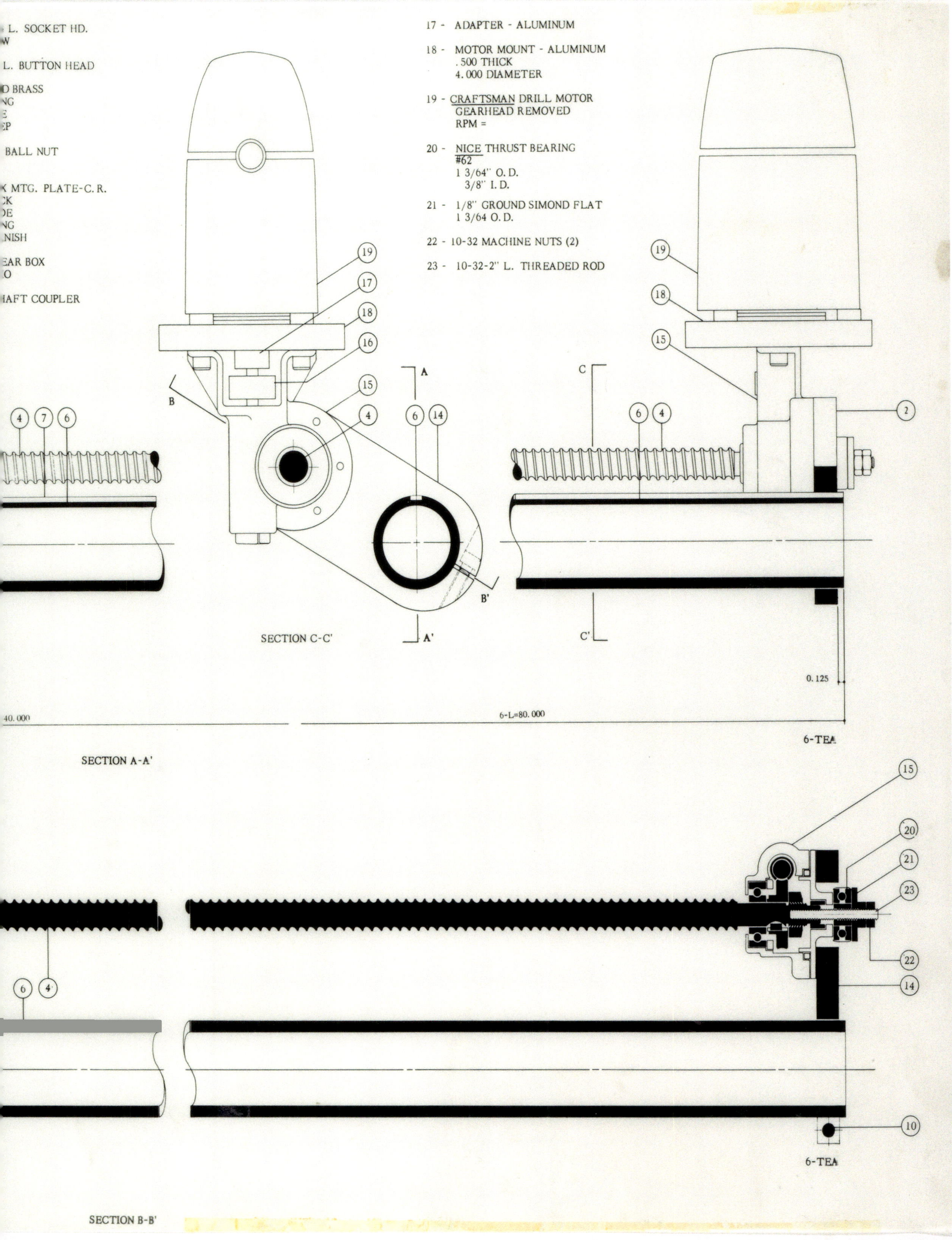
L. SOCKET HD.
W
L. BUTTON HEAD
D BRASS
NG
E
EP
BALL NUT
K MTG. PLATE-C.R.
CK
DE
NG
NISH
EAR BOX
O
HAFT COUPLER
17 - ADAPTER - ALUMINUM
18 - MOTOR MOUNT - ALUMINUM
.500 THICK
4.000 DIAMETER
19 - CRAFTSMAN DRILL MOTOR
GEARHEAD REMOVED
RPM =
20 - NICE THRUST BEARING
#62
1 3/64" O.D.
3/8" I.D.
21 - 1/8" GROUND SIMOND FLAT
1 3/64 O.D.
22 - 10-32 MACHINE NUTS (2)
23 - 10-32-2" L. THREADED ROD
SECTION C-C'
0.125
40.000
6-L=80.000
6-TEA
SECTION A-A'
6-TEA
SECTION B-B'

Salzburg Summer Academy 1959: Hermann Czech in front of the blackboard and Konrad Wachsmann on the left. Photography by Wolfgang Mistelbauer, courtesy Hermann Czech

Konrad Wachsmann
Salzburg 1956 – 1960

Friedrich Kurrent: In the spring of 1956, Konrad Wachsmann (KW) was invited to give a lecture in Vienna that took place in an auditorium on Stubenring. The lecture impressed me deeply. In the same year, the Salzburg Summer Academy was searching for a teacher for the architecture class. The gallery owner Friedrich Welz was organizing the Summer Academy, which had been in existence since 1953. In addition to the famous "School of Seeing" (Schule des Sehens) known for and taught by Kokoschka, from the beginning there had also been an architecture class directed by the Swiss architect Hans Hofmann in 1953 and by Clemens Holzmeister in 1954. After we (*Arbeitsgruppe 4*: Johannes Spalt, Wilhelm Holzbauer and Friedrich Kurrent) had participated in the Summer Academy in 1953 and come into contact with Friedrich Welz, he charged us (Spalt and me) with the renovation of his bookstore. On that occasion, he asked us for the name of an architect for the Summer Academy. We named KW because we had just heard his wonderful lecture, but Egon Eiermann also mentioned his name when declining Welz's invitation to run a master class in Salzburg because of another commitment. This all led to KW's invitation to Salzburg; admittedly, the Summer Academy of 1956 was improvised because of short lead-time. The following year, Welz appointed us KW's assistants and we were able to prepare well for the course by visiting him at the *Hochschule für Gestaltung* in Ulm, where he was a guest professor. He gave us precise instructions for the preparations we had to complete. Our Summer Academy took place in the *Dombögen* in the lower city, not up on the fortifications, with a view towards the cathedral square where Hofmannsthal's *Everyman* is staged. In the very first seminar, he pulled a punch card out of his pocket, waved it around and said: "This is the future of architecture." The word architecture is one he most often avoided. He always spoke about building and about the industrial age. He always showed us his hangar in America with its struts and nodes, which also played a significant role visually. His pedagogic concept emerged from research, and he emphasized teamwork in particular. He directed the seminar from 1956–60 and most of the young Austrian architects came to him (*Arbeitsgruppe 4*: Gsteu, Hollein, Wawrik, Boltenstern, Mistelbauer, Czech, ...). In 1970, KW held a large lecture in Vienna with three projectors and showed a film whose topic was the point in space.

Hermann Czech: The first time I experienced KW was probably through Kurrent and Spalt, in connection with the Summer Academy in 1957. I participated myself in the Summer Academy in 1958 and 1959.
When I participated in my first Summer Academy, the architecture class had already moved into the *Dombögen* and we had no contact with other workshops. KW invited many guests to our class. Among the ones I recall were Frei Otto and the engineer Friedrich Baravalle,[1] but we also heard a lecture by the painters Friedrich Vordemberge-Gildewart,[2] Johannes Itten and Eugenio Carmi.[3]
In general, the guests gave lectures that had no direct connection to the project. Even Frei Otto spoke about his tensile structures although this topic had nothing to do with our assignments. Between Kokoscha's "School of Seeing" and KW's architecture class, there was no exchange or relationship.

Marco Pogacnik: The 50s began with the publication of Sedlmayr's *Loss of the Middle* (Verlust der Mitte) in 1948. It played an important role in Salzburg and for the *Darmstädter Gespräche*,[4] which addressed the question of whether technology and mankind could be reconciled. Kokoschka also had doubts about Modernism and in a text written in 1950, he asserted that we found ourselves "in an era of machine men and de-humanized modern science, which threatens to make the individual, if not the human itself, into an abstraction." The cultural framework within which KW conducted his seminar was in fact not so amenable to his topics.

HC: KW was, in contrast to Kokoschka, very optimistic in his stance towards

Salzburg Summer Academy 1958: Konrad Wachsmann (fourth from the left), Johannes Spalt (fifth from the left) and Friedrich Kurrent (seventh from the left). Taken from: Barbara Wally and Jana Marko (eds), *Die Ära Kokoschka*, Salzburg 1993

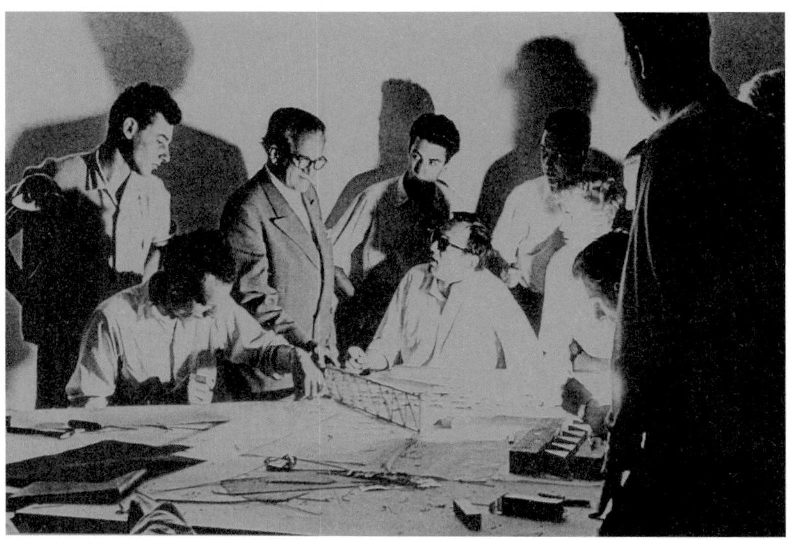

Salzburg Summer Academy 1957: Konrad Wachsmann in the middle. Taken from: Barbara Wally and Jana Marko (eds), *Die Ära Kokoschka*, Salzburg 1993

Modernism. We participants had no opportunity to speak with Kokoschka back then.[5] Kurrent and Spalt certainly had a close relationship[6] to Kokoschka on account of the church project in Parsch. In Sedlmayr's book, it was the images that were more important because they offered representative information about Modern Art. In Austria, Sedlmayr's book was the first information on Modern Art at all back then.

FK: In late 1957 there was an exhibition about KW in Gallery Würthle, which was directed by the sculptor Fritz Wotruba. It included models of designs completed during the Salzburg Summer Academy.[7] The impetus to the exhibition was to make KW's work better known because Welz wanted to found a research institute in Salzburg and make him the director. Many established architects were asked to voice their opinion on it (Roland Rainer, Karl Schwanzer, Eric Boltenstern) but the results were negative. The cultural political climate was disadvantageous. It would have been vital to bring people such as Kokoschka, Josef Frank and Arnold Schönberg back to Austria immediately after the war. But that was obstructed.[8]

MP: How was the Summer Academy organized? It's important to note that all applicants were trained architects.

HC: KW accepted the first twenty-one who registered and there was no application review process or choice. The twenty-one participants were then subdivided into groups with three members. There were always two days on which the groups worked together as a trio and then came a reporting day, on which everyone sat down together and reported on the work completed. Thereafter, the topics given by KW were rotated to other groups so that all groups had to work on all the topics. There was no hierarchy among the groups.

MP: In the publications about the Summer Academy, it says that the 1958 topic was "a study on the development of a building system that uses an industrially produced, standardized panel; is based on tension cables and pre-tensioned locks; and does not use columns, beams, horizontal supports and their like." How did KW present this topic to the participants?

HC: At the beginning of the seminar, there was no program or assignment. KW introduced the seminar using general lectures on the topic of construction as well as topics such as those in the book *The Turning Point of Building*. The groups of three were then given very general topics: connection, materials and methods, construction, modules, elements, installation, definitions. In 1958, my group included Peter Schmid and Rainer Reinisch. I recall one discussion with Peter Schmid about the required number of columns in a building; we first asserted that four columns were required, then came the insight that three were necessary. Later we made do with two until Peter Schmid decided that one column was enough. All ideas were laid out on *Aquafix* sketch paper. The paper came in a 60 cm long roll and was cut down into A2 format. Drawings were only made on these sheets of paper, as were all notes. All these sheets were then preserved and not thrown away so that the working process could always be reconstructed. Every third day, following general discussion, the topic was rotated and the design process increasingly enriched step by step. At the end, as if miraculously, an object was generated, a hall or something similar. In a photo that Mistelbauer took (Fig. p. 133) I'm standing in front of a board and describing the roles assumed by elements and connection. The consideration I described is that even the connections have to be considered as an element and thus can leave behind an orthogonal grid. That's the kind of discussions we had.

MP: KW wrote that "no attempt, no sketch, no drawing, no model, no text that was generated during work [may] be destroyed ... For that reason, trash cans are not permitted in the work spaces just as in this work process, the concept 'trash' no longer exists." How should we imagine a working process without decisions?

FK: Even the eraser was forbidden! No one decided or determined anything. The constellation of three is always the best. In a group of two it is much more difficult, since it often occurs that the two don't speak to each other for quite some time. The other thing that characterized the "teamwork" is that there were no leaders. "Teamwork" seemed self-explanatory to all of us.

HC: Deciding doesn't mean that you have to throw something away. More often in a working process, you have to return to a point in the past, which can be recalled by means of documentation.

MP: How did you arrive at a result? The work that is published includes gorgeous drawings, imposing models, even cast metal prototypes of the connections. How were these results achieved in only 21 days?

HC: The work took weeks after the first three weeks, at least as long again. The work developed slowly, collaboratively, almost inevitably, and the results were experienced as something that could not have been any different. That can be seen in the results from the first Salzburg Seminar in 1956 (in which I did not participate): apparently someone suggested the topic of the cantilever, and it was developed further. A square roof would cantilever off two columns, assuming that these columns were anchored to the ground solidly. In developing this cantilever, it became clear that the forces decrease progressively towards the outer edge, and for that reason, the number of beam elements becomes smaller. The transverse beams in the other direction respond respectively to their distribution of loads (Fig. p. 147).

MP: In 1958, the result was "develop a building system that uses an industrially produced, standardized panel; is based on tension cables and pre-tensioned locks; and does not use columns, beams, horizontal supports and their like."

HC: In 1959, on the other hand, the idea to make something out of concrete emerged. We studied a concrete press that actually existed. The fluid concrete was pressed into a shape and at the same time, the steel reinforcing was threaded through. Two profiles were developed: one for an additive wall panel and the other that could be used for a floor slab as well as for a column also conceived as additive.

MP: With regard to his hangar, KW wrote about the working process that "statics experiments were conducted independent of the actual development work and accordingly had almost no influence on the project's direction. Instead, these were strongly inspired by the laboratory experiments on models." In this sense, statics never decided the direction for him.

HC: Yes, in his case, construction-based thinking was determinative. KW explained this to us in one particularly elegant sentence: "If the model holds, that is not proof that the structure will hold in reality. But if the model doesn't hold, then it will definitely not hold in reality."

MP: That seems to lead to a different kind of design concept. It assumes an anonymous working process, not the genius creative force of an individual. The design product is almost a byproduct. During the working process, KW never described a solution as good or bad; he spoke instead of advantages and disadvantages.

HC: The intensive "teamwork" meant that everyone identifies with everything. In other words, everyone thinks everything is his brainchild. No one can say definitely which contribution is whose. That demanded a certain discipline around authorship. All in all – I grew up with the conviction that design is a series of decisions in which every thinking person has to come to the same conclusion. It is, by contrast, an interesting experience that this is not the case, that other people proceed in entirely different ways, but that doesn't mean it is arbitrary.

MP: KW developed his team concept within the framework of a didactic experience. Did you ever consider applying this kind of work system in the normal professional conditions of an architecture office?

HC: That could only work if the design team has worked together for years. The design process with temporary associates is not democratic, even if those associates are always able to introduce their own thoughts. In the end, however, someone has to decide. KW decided in the end, but he did that imperceptibly by giving reasons for everything in a way that was logical for everyone and could not be doubted.

MP: For almost a decade, over the course of the entire 1950s, KW dedicated himself to the experience of "teamwork." He began in Chicago at the Institute of Design (1952–55) then came Karlsruhe (1954, at the invitation of Egon Eiermann), Tokyo (1955, invited by Kenzo Tange) and finally from 1956–60 Salzburg (in 1959 he was also in Lausanne). The Salzburg experience seems to have had special meaning. That is also the period in which he was working on his book *The Turning Point of Building*, which was published in 1959. What aspects of his theoretically demanding book came through in the Salzburg seminar? Did he point to historic precedents during discussions?

HC: I don't recall that he showed photographs. He often mentioned Joseph Paxton. He didn't rely heavily upon historic precedent. If he was speaking about modularity, he made a comparison to the Gothic cathedral or referred to a Renaissance palace in order to clarify the problem of the corner. But nothing more.

MP: The visual played an important role for KW. Consider his juxtaposition of the Graz circular stair with the project for the Grapevine; the two have not even the slightest to do with each other in structural terms. The foundation for this way of thinking is geometry. Material and statics did not influence the project, even if that seems strange. Geometry seems, in the case of Le Corbusier, to have been imposed on the architecture after the fact, in contrast to KW, for whom geometry exercised a generative force.

HC: That might perhaps have first been totally clear in his book. Back then, we did not separate at all between geometry and static loads. His methodology was a rational, systematic and conscious way of looking at construction. There was never a one-sided approach to building but rather an entire world reflected in it.[9] In the book *Aspekte*, he tested his wealth of visual associations many times over. For example, the cover image in which he notices that "water forms itself in honeycomb-like waves for the sake of the bees, the heraldic animal of the Barberinis," an effect that is caused by the concave niche along the fountain's edge.

FK: KW was completely fascinated by the double helix spiral stair in Graz and he often spoke about it. This kind of analogy was, however, never discussed at the Summer Academy.

MP: How should one position KW within the panorama of that era? Prouvé was a constructeur, Fuller was a visionary, how should KW be characterized? He came from practice and knew the construction market, construction site and work processes well. He was not an impractical dreamer; nonetheless it is hard to imagine two architects as radically different as KW and Prouvé. KW argued for industry, Prouvé for crafts-based production; KW worked towards the unification of all construction elements, Prouvé worked with heterogeneous bearing elements in which each element maintained its own physiognomy. One difference is that KW's thinking began to develop so radically at a certain point that it prevented him from building. That was also the period in which he developed his theoretical efforts around "teamwork."

HC: That which KW produced at all times was basic research, which is also important for a practice-oriented career. If we take the example of his design for a city hall in California (1966): he designed a hall whose roof used only tension members but he nonetheless assumed that it would be horizontal, a quality that is only possible under infinite tensile force. That might already be considered a trajectory that tends towards un-buildability.

FK: The last craftsman is the toolmaker, an idea that KW repeated. Within that family of architects, there was also Egon Eiermann, although when he recommended KW for the Summer Academy, he noted, "Ask KW. He's ruining my students for me anyway." In the 1970s, I was at a public discussion with Ottokar Uhl in Karlsruhe, where Uhl was professor. The discussion was between Prouvé and KW. At that time, I had the impression that Prouvé had bested him because he could show his buildings with their steel components, whereas KW remained on a theoretical level because he hadn't built anything more. That might also have bothered Friedrich Welz and hemmed in his plans for an architectural institute in Salzburg, for which KW would have been director. KW was removed from designs with a capacity for realization. His vision was separated from realization by a chasm.

MP: The fact is that KW enriched our tectonic perception of building. Writing about his design for the Grapevine, he claimed that the project's intention was "to dissolve the column as a concept."[10] In this design, we can thus consider the column as a node, as a connective element, which binds together ceiling and floor. That reminds me of an equivalency that HC made earlier between element and connection while discussing the topic of the grid. The same could be expanded to the treatment of wall, ceiling and floor as interchangeable elements.

HC: Yes, that derives from the ambivalence of elements. It is actually correct to assert that KW deeply enriched our perception of architecture in this way.

MP: KW conducted anonymous "teamwork" in Chicago, Lausanne and Tokyo but Salzburg represented a special case in his scientific biography. One might even say that KW has as much a right to belong to Austrian architectural history as does Loos, Wagner or Josef Frank.

HC: In Austria, his teaching around teamwork had a sustained effect. Every well-known architect participated in his seminars. KW generated an impulse towards rationality and truth. His architecture and his enthusiasm for technology cannot be compared with other contemporary architects such as, for example, Archigram. Wachsmann wrote, that it "will likely be less visible, but the little will therefore be more meaningful." That is exactly the opposite of the qualities for which Banham praised Archigram. In that case, there was plenty to see but the more there is to see, the less meaningful it is.[11]

MP: If we think about KW's final designs, he tried to achieve a certain monumentality. Although he worked quite a bit on the topic of housing early in his career, it played no role at all in his later designs.

HC: He did not think in functional terms.

MP: KW spoke about the design process in the following way: "[one can] change nothing fundamentally if one makes good architecture instead of bad. Because it is actually the productive work process that decides everything, that preempts it." Is it not fair to say that this premise questions our concept of architecture? That also has something to do with the concept of an anonymous design process, which presumes "teamwork." A final comment on KW's design process. He spoke quite a lot about industrialization and the unification of building elements, but his working method always took him towards individual solutions, which were questioned anew time and again. It was enough to introduce a barely noticeable change in order to lead the entire design process into a fundamentally new trajectory.

1
Professor at the Academy of Fine Arts (*Akademie der bildenden Künste*) he contributed as engineer to many projects of Arbeitsgruppe 4. He was famous for his designs and urban planning for the Vienna municipal hall (Wiener Stadthalle).

2
Friedrich Vordemberge-Gildewart began his career with a cabinetry apprenticeship in Osnabrück; studied architecture, sculpture and painting at the TU Hanover; was employed by the journal *Der Sturm*; a member of the *De Stijl* group; co-founder of the group "abstracts hanover" with Kurt Schwitters; a member of the group "Abstraction-Creation" with Naum Gabo, A. Pevsner, G. Vantongerlo; and a participant in the first *documenta* art exposition in Kassel (1. 1951, 2. 1959).

3
The following lectures are noted in HC's calendar: Friedrich Baravalle 28. 7. 1958; Johannes Itten 2. 8. 1958; Victor Gruen 7. 8. 1959; Eugenio Carmi 11. 8. 1959. KW had met the painter and graphic designer Carmi in Genoa where he was working later on a large project for the company Finsider in 1961–63.

4
Darmstädter Gespräche: 1.1950, "The Image of Man in our Time" (Adorno, Sedlmyer, W. Baumeister); 2.1951 "The Human Being and Space" (Otto Bartning, E. Neufert, Ortega y Gasset, R. Schwarz, Heidegger, Scharoun); 3.1952 "The Human Being and Technology" (Otto Bartning, E. Eiermann).

5
KW and Kokoschka had met in Dresden in 1923, while KW was studying with Tessenow. KW spoke about Kokoschka in critical terms. Grüning (1986), p. 383–390. On Salzburg, Grüning p. 549.

6
Kokoschka had submitted the drawing for a relief in the church's concrete door, and at Kokoschka and Welz's request, *Arbeitsgruppe* 4 had prepared a project in 1953 for the workshop buildings for a summer academy at the fortifications.

7
The exhibition catalogue is entitled *Building in our Time* (*Bauen in unserer Zeit*), Salzburg, Galerie Welz, 1957.

8
The events around the portrait Kokoschka painted of Mayor Körner – which was left to the city of Linz – were quite representative.

9
The reflection on geometry, construction and modularity expressed as a moebius strip or tessellation was later developed by Gsteu based upon his experience in KW's seminar.

10
KW, *Wendepunkt im Bauen*, Krausskopf-Verlag, Wiesbaden 1959, p. 194.

11
HC, *Future and Architecture*, in "Die Furche," 9/1967.

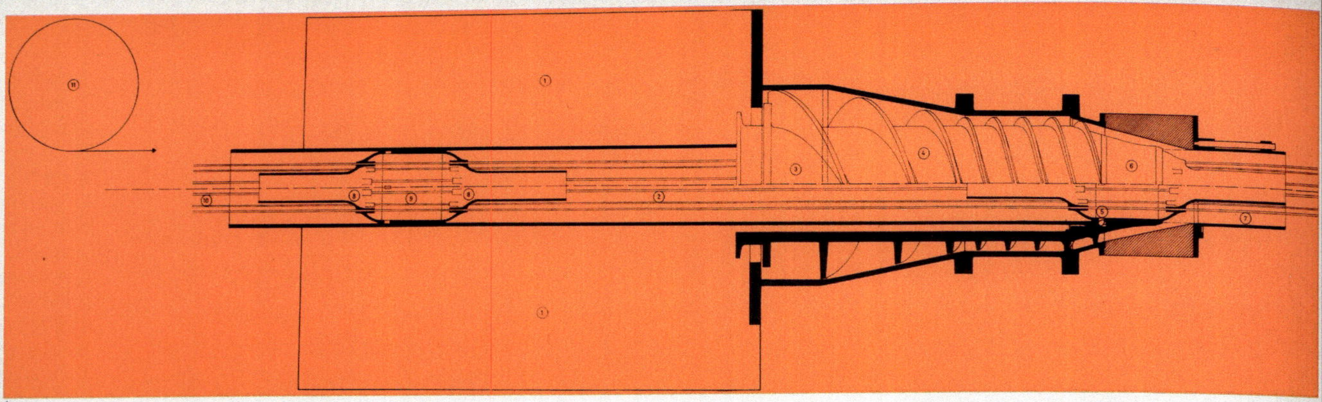

1

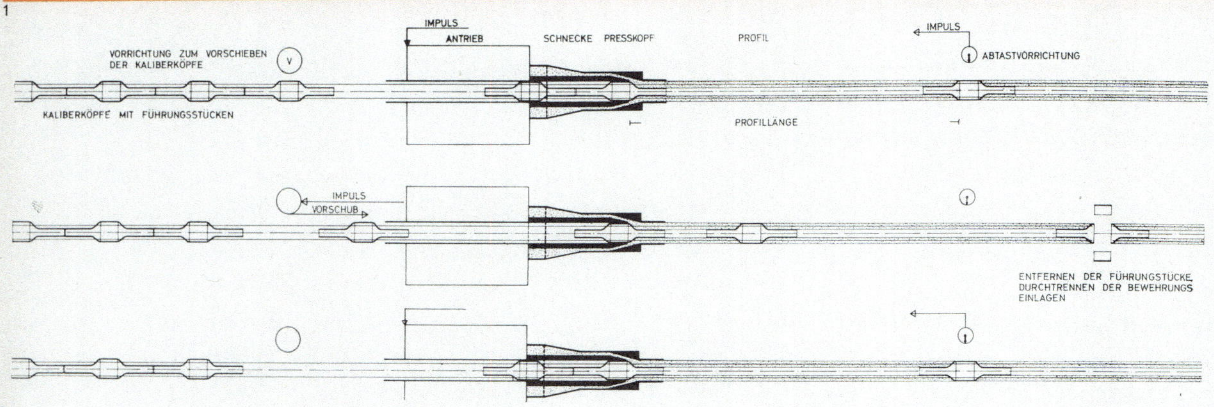

2

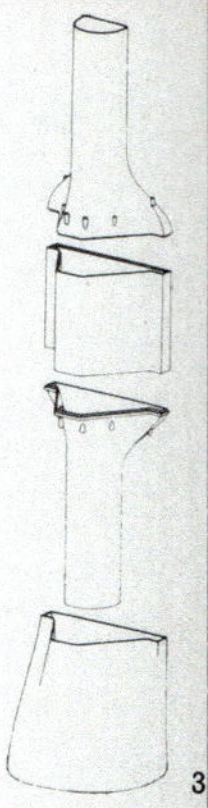

3

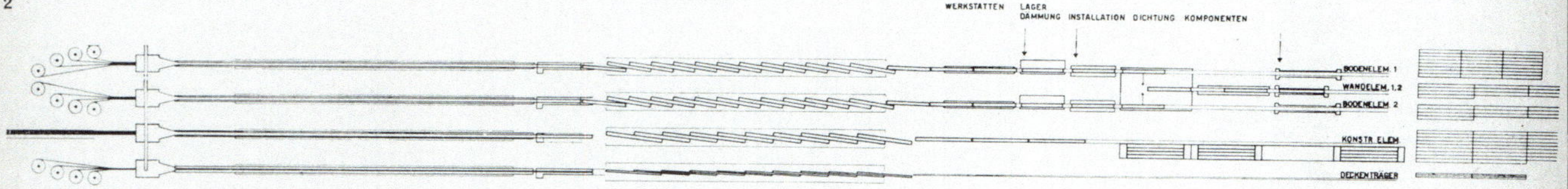

4

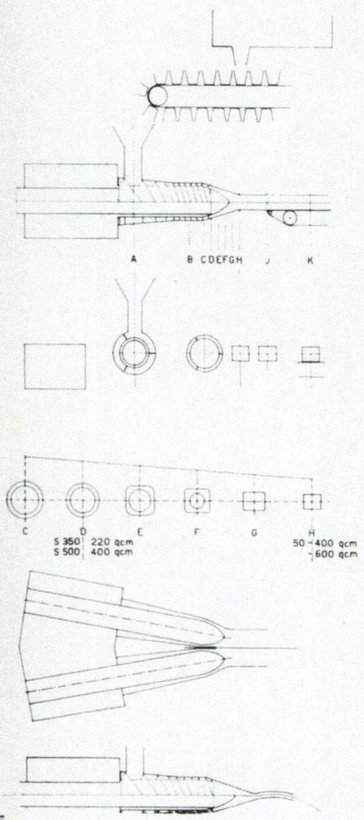

5

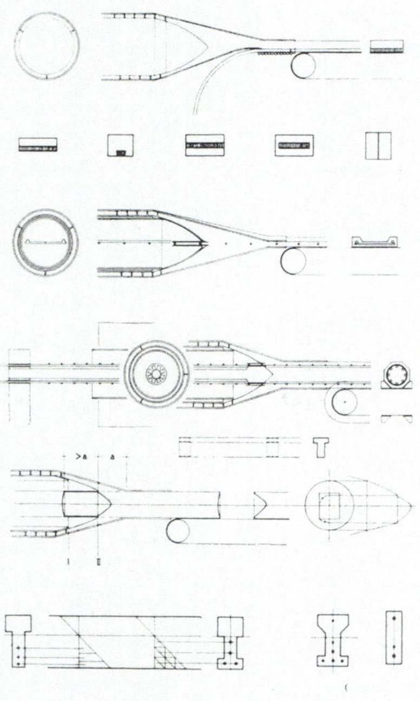

6

Teamarbeit an der Internationalen Sommerakademie in Salzburg

15. Juli bis 15. August 1959

Die Studien dieses Teams, das sich aus Teilnehmern vieler europäischer Länder zusammensetzte, befaßten sich mit der spezifischen Untersuchung einer Betonstrangpreßmaschine, deren Produkt unter dem Namen Pressolit bekannt ist.

Das Hauptproblem bildete die Frage, ob es möglich ist, Betonkonstruktionen ohne irgendwelche Schalungen herzustellen. Zuerst wurde die Maschine vom Team weiterentwickelt; es ergaben sich neue Vorschläge der Produktionstechnik; ein spezielles Profil für die Konstruktionsstäbe und ein Profil für die vertikalen und horizontalen Flächenelemente wurden entwickelt. Das Arbeitsergebnis bestand darin, daß spezielle Kaliberköpfe, das heißt vorgeformte Kunststoff-Endungen der Profilstäbe entwickelt wurden. Es entstand ein universelles Bausystem, das sowohl bei eingeschossiger Bauweise als auch bei Hochbauten verwendet werden kann.

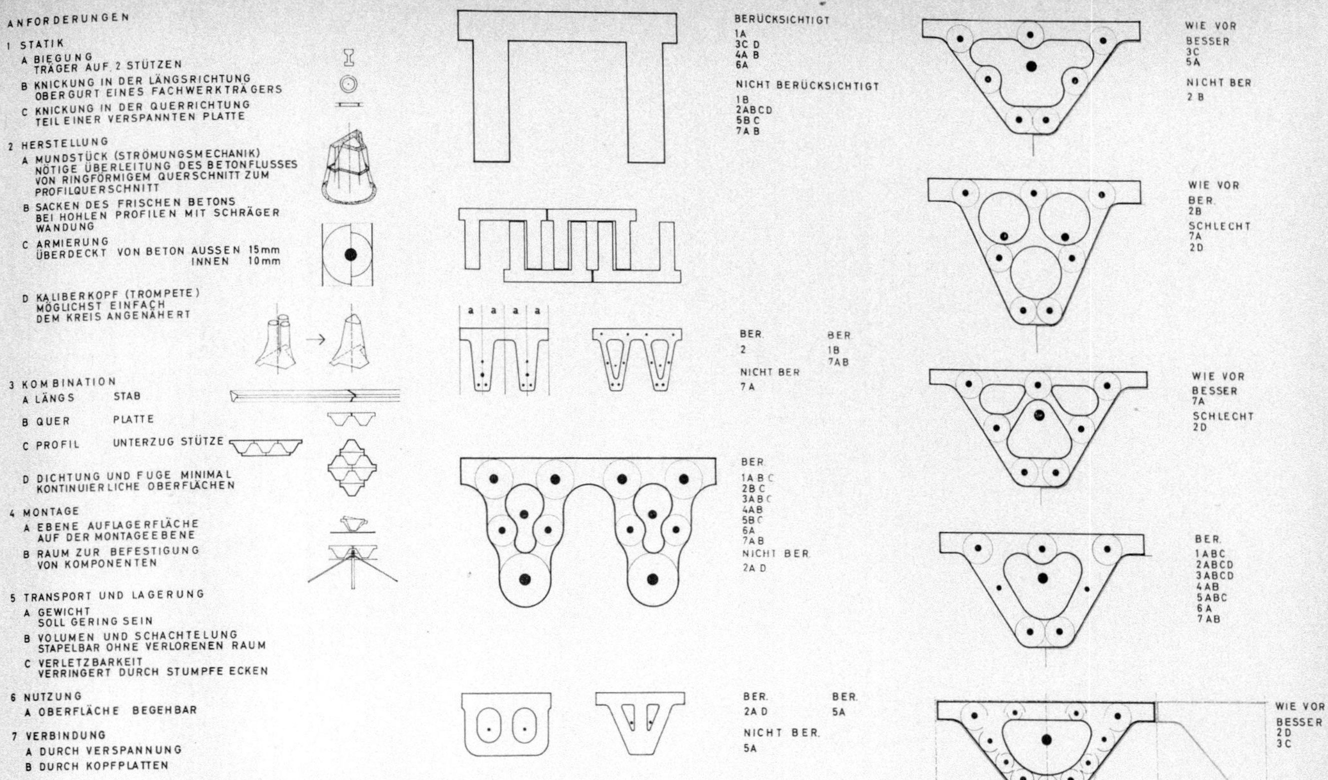

7

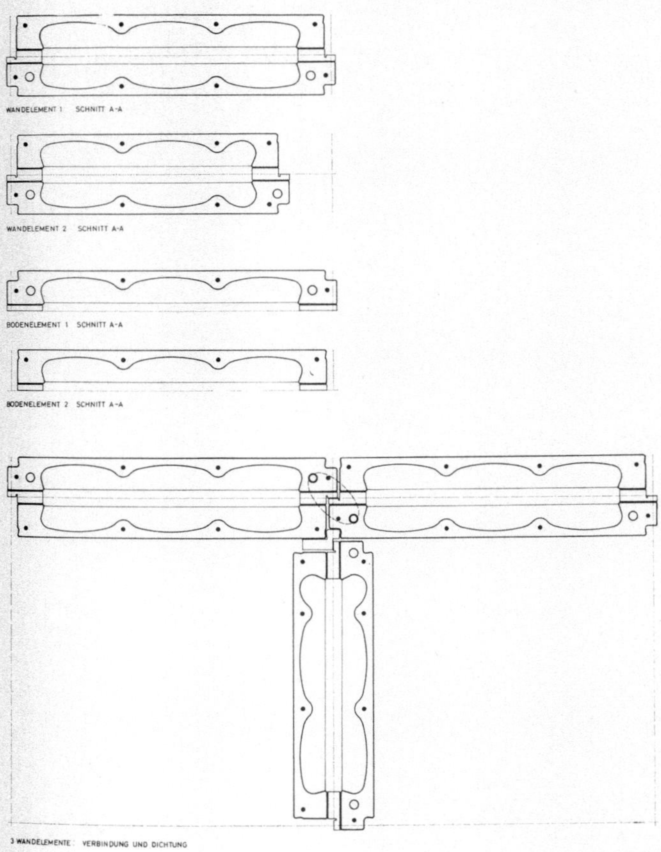

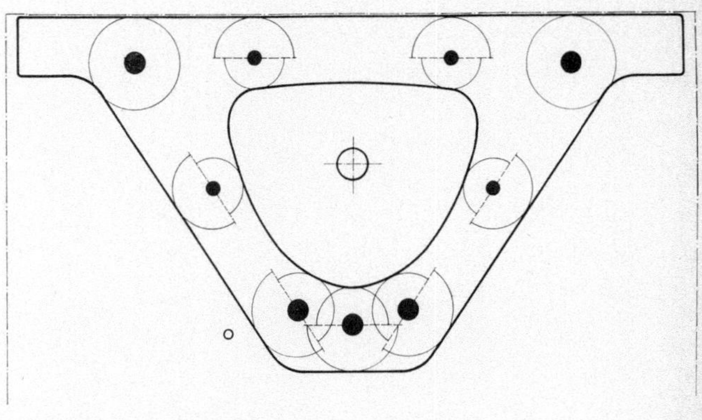

GEWÄHLTES PROFIL
FLÄCHE 183.5 cm^2
GEWICHT 45.8 kg/lm
220.0 kg/ELEMENT
STAHL 5/10 mm Ø
4/ 6 mm Ø

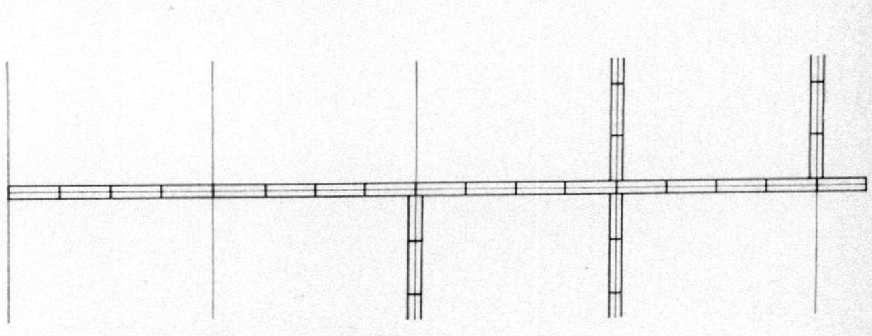

KOMBINATIONSSCHEMA WANDELEMENTE

8

1
Der Schnitt durch die Maschine zeigt, wie durch einen Schneckengang der Beton verdichtet und zur Öffnung gepreßt wird und wie sich zugleich von hinten die Armierungsstäbe und Kaliberköpfe durch die Maschine bewegen.

Section d'une machine montrant le fonctionnement de la spirale pressant le béton vers l'ouverture de sortie tout en laissant passer les fers d'armature.

Section through the machine showing how the cement is solidified through a spiral and pushed towards the aperture at the same time as reinforcing rods and ring heads move through the machine from behind.

2 und 3
Die Position der Stab-Endungen im Produktionsprozeß und die Kunststoff-Endung selbst mit den Durchlässen für die Metallbewehrungen.

Position des têtes de tringle dans le processus de production et terminaisons en matière plastique.

The position of the rod ends in the production process and the end of the synthetic material itself with the space for the metal reinforcements.

4
Eine Fabrikationsanlage auf der Basis eines kontinuierlichen Arbeitsprozesses mit Dampfhochdruck-Trockentunnel und Nachbearbeitungsaggregaten.

Usine sur la base d'un processus de travail continu avec tunnel d'asséchage de vapeur à haute pression.

A production plant on the basis of continuous work with high-pressure steam tunnel drier and subsequent processing units.

5 und 6
Analyse der Maschine und der Stab-Endungen.

Analyse de la machine et des têtes de tringle.

Analysis of machine and rod ends.

7
Analysen und Entwicklungsstadien eines Konstruktionsprofils, das sowohl als Balken oder Stütze als auch einzeln und in Kombination verwendet werden soll.

Analyses et étappes d'évolution d'une construction profilées pouvant servir de sommier et pilier.

Analyses and development stages of a construction profile to be used either as girder or support both singly and and combined.

8
Die aus Halbschalen zusammengesetzten vertikalen Elemente.

Eléments verticaux formés de demi-sphères.

The vertical elements composed of semi-circular shells.

Teamarbeit an der Internationalen Sommerakademie in Salzburg

15. Juli bis 20. August 1958

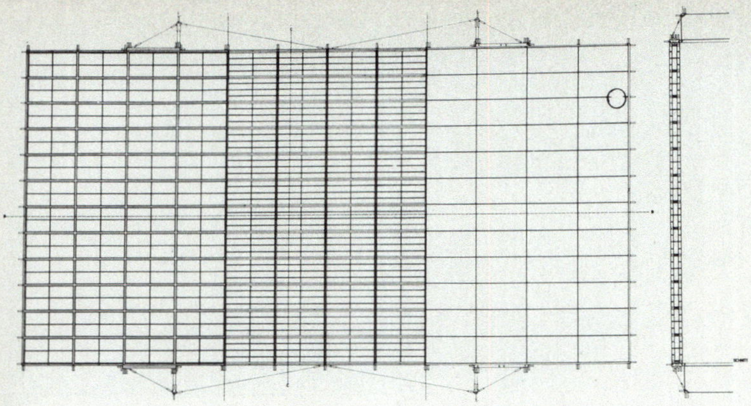

1

Studie über die Entwicklung eines Bausystems, das auf der Verwendung einer industriell hergestellten, standardisierten Bauplatte, von Spannkabeln und Vorspannschlössern beruht, ohne Benützung von Stützen, Balken, Unterzügen oder dergleichen.

Die dominierenden Spannschlösser und Kabel werden einleuchtend im Projekt für ein als Kulturzentrum gedachtes Gebäude, in dem durch simultane Projektionen Bilder oder Filme, Band- oder Plattenübertragung von Sprache und Musik eine Art mechanisches Museum entsteht, das kulturelle Informationen bis in den hintersten Winkel tragen kann.

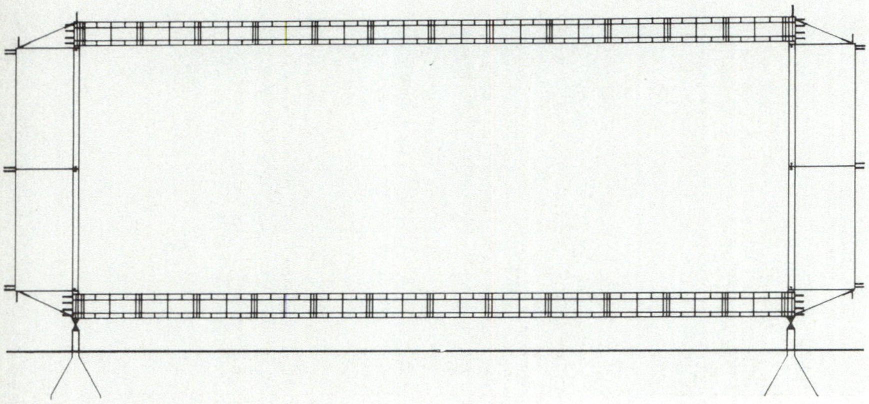

2

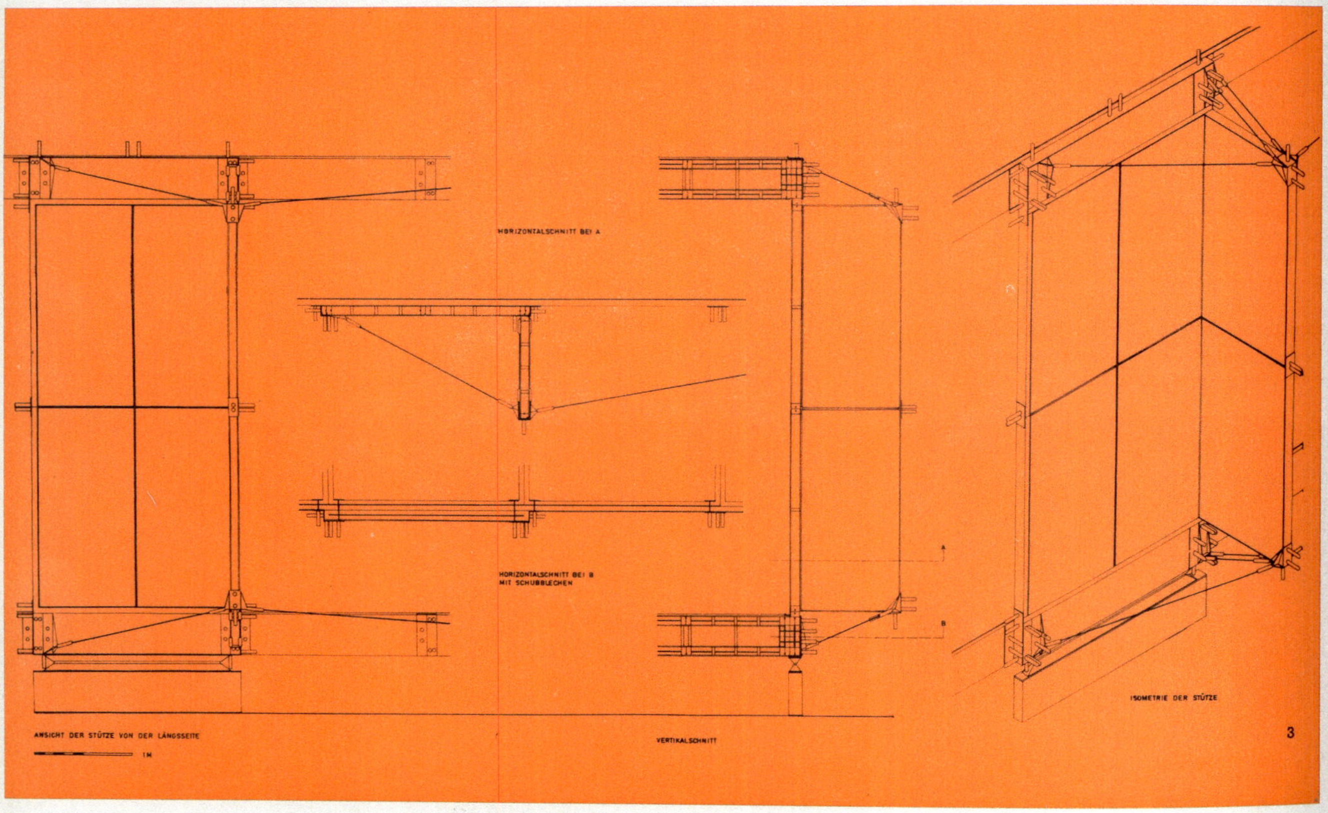

3

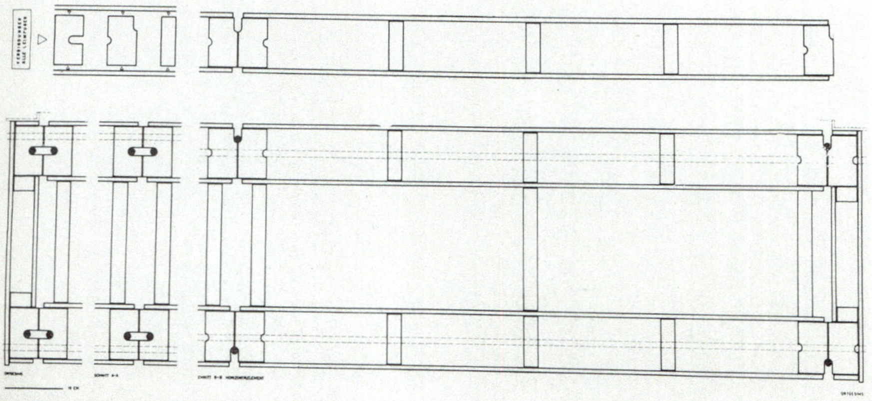

4

5

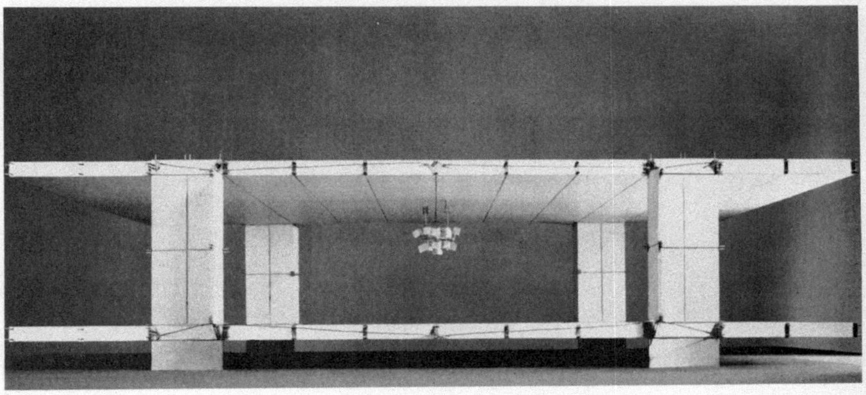
6

7

Seite 376/page 376

1
Aufsicht auf die horizontale Fläche und Einblick in ihre Konstruktion, in zwei verschiedenen Ebenen geschnitten.

Vue sur la surface horizontale avec deux sections détaillées sur plans différents.

View on to the horizontal surface alongside two views of the construction cut along two different planes.

2
Querschnitt der Halle.

Section de la halle.

Cross section of shed.

3
Details der Spannschloßverteilung und der Verspannung der als Windverstrebung dienenden vertikalen Elemente.

Raidissement des éléments verticaux et répartition des raidisseurs.

Details of the distribution of coupling nuts and the bracing of the vertical elements acting as wind brace.

4
Die aus Sperrholz und Balken aufgebaute Standard-Sandwichplatte mit den Anschlüssen der Verspannungsdrähte und der Kombination von zwei solchen Platten für Fußboden und Dachkonstruktion.

Plaque-sandwich en contre-plaqué et bois avec câbles de précontrainte; combinaisons sol et plafond.

The sandwich panels constructed of plywood and beams with the attachments for bracing wires and the combination of two of these panels for the construction of floors and roofs.

Seite 377/page 377

5
Aufsicht auf einen Teil des Daches.

Vue sur une partie du toit.

View on to part of the roof.

6
Der eigentliche Baukörper ohne die beweglichen vertikalen Flächen.

Le bâtiment sans éléments mobiles verticaux.

The actual body of the building without the movable vertical surfaces.

7
Einige Variationen von Kombinationsmöglichkeiten der beweglichen Elemente und der zentrale Projektionsapparat.

Quelques variations et combinaisons possibles des éléments mobiles et appareil de projection central.

Some variations in combination possibilities of the movable elements and the central projection apparatus.

1

1 und 2
Die Entfernung vertikaler Elemente ermöglicht die Verwendung des Gebäudes als Podium oder Freilichtbühne.
Der geschlossene Raum, dessen vertikale Elemente jeder gewünschten Position angepaßt werden können.

La distance des éléments verticaux permet également l'emploi du bâtiment comme podium ou scène à ciel ouvert. L'espace fermé, dont les éléments verticaux peuvent être réglés.

The removal of the vertical elements also allows the building to be used as a podium or open-air stage.
The enclosed space, the vertical elements of which can be adjusted to any desired position.

2

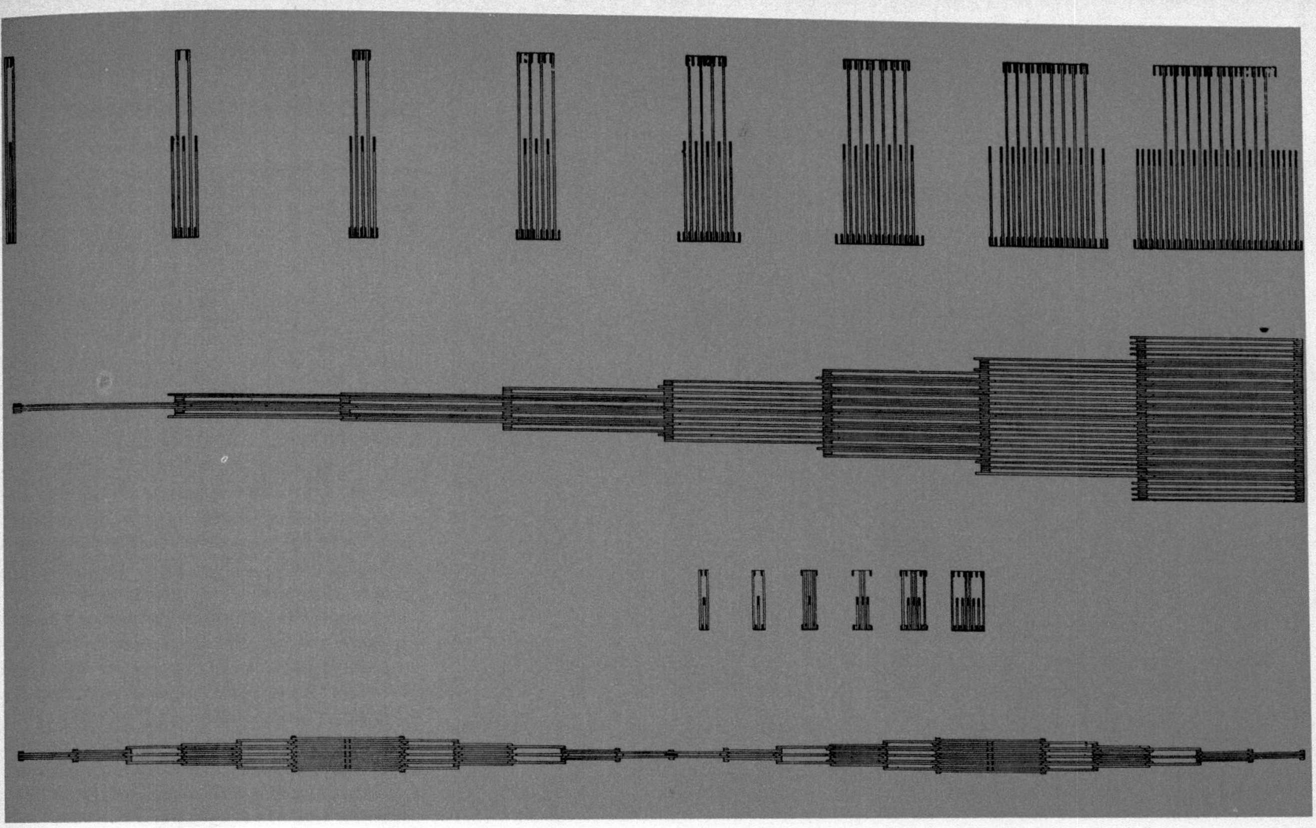

1

1
Der große Hauptträger, von oben gesehen, mit allen vertikalen Schnitten. Die Nebenträger, von oben gesehen, mit den vertikalen Schnitten.

Le grand sommier principal vu du haut avec toutes les sections verticales. Les sommiers secondaires et sections verticales.

The large main girder seen from above with all the vertical sections. The auxiliary girder seen from above with the vertical sections.

2
Die an zwei Stützen befestigte Dachkonstruktion mit einer freitragenden Spannweite von 32 m.

Construction de toit d'une portée de 32 mètres.

The roof construction is secured to two supports and has a self-contained span of 32 m.

3 und 4
Ansichten von oben zeigen die Beziehungen der Holzkonstruktion zum Betonkern.

Vues du haut montrant les rapports entre construction de bois et noyau de béton.

Views from above show the relations of the wood construction to the concrete core.

Teamarbeit an der Internationalen Sommerakademie in Salzburg

13. Juli bis 28. Juli 1956

2

Die Hauptaufgabe dieser Studie bestand darin, die Veränderung der statischen Charakteristiken eines einfachen Holzprofils zu untersuchen, wenn dieses, mit anderen zu großen Konstruktionen verbunden, statisch verschiedenartig beansprucht wird.

Die Entwicklung des Profils, die Bestimmung der Stablängen und eine spezielle Tellerdübelverbindung führte zur Projektierung einer offenen Konzerthallenüberdachung, die nur an zwei Betonstützen befestigt ist.

3

4

Teamarbeit an der Internationalen Sommerakademie in Salzburg

15. Juli bis 20. August 1957

Das Projekt dieses Teams bezog sich auf die Entwicklung einer Aluminiumröhrenkonstruktion mit identischen Knotenpunkten und immer gleichen Stablängen, auf die Verwendung räumlich angeordneter Verspannungskabel und auf die Entwicklung vertikaler und horizontaler beweglicher, raumbildender Flächen. Das Resultat der Untersuchungen des Teams war dann ein Projekt, das in seinem dynamischen Charakter kaum mit dem vom Team gewählten Wort »Salzburg-Halle« richtig bezeichnet ist. Denn die hier entwickelten Prinzipien würden eine solche Fülle von Anwendungen und Anpassungen ermöglichen, daß die Salzburg-Halle nur eine von vielen Kombinationsmöglichkeiten darstellt.

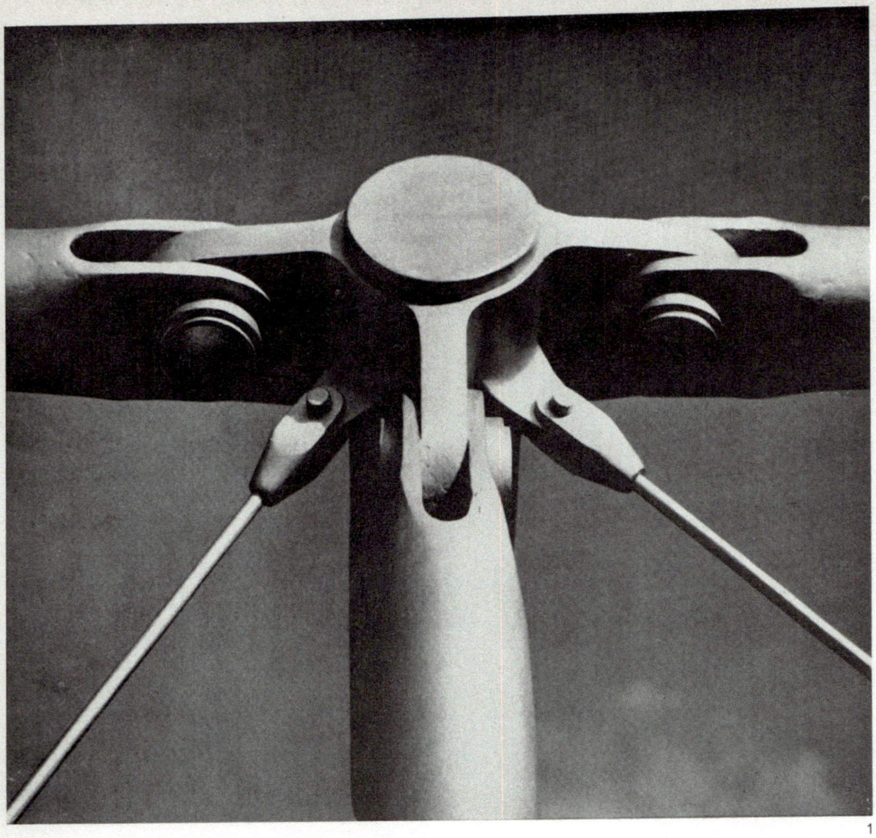

1

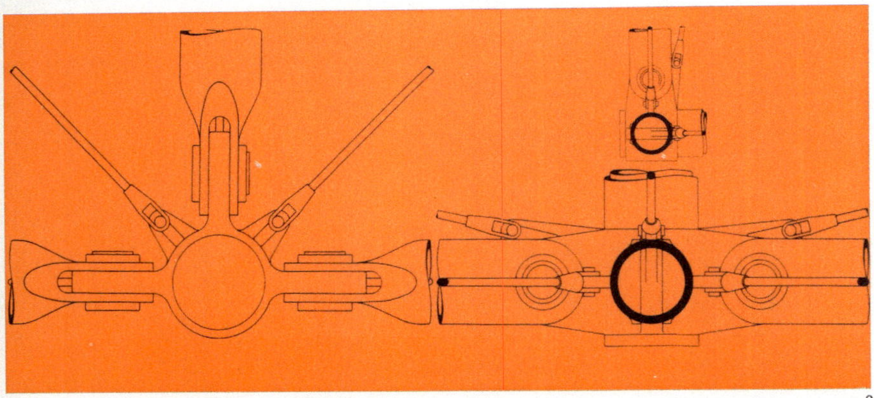

2

3

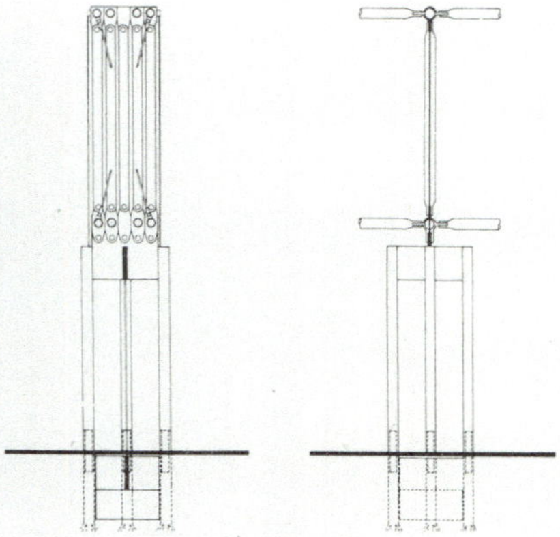

4

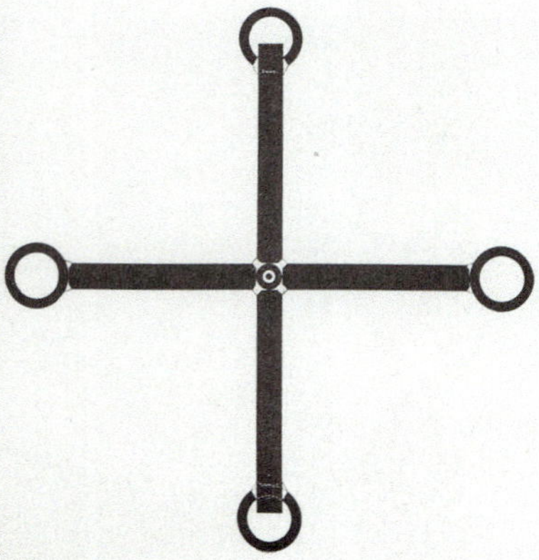

5

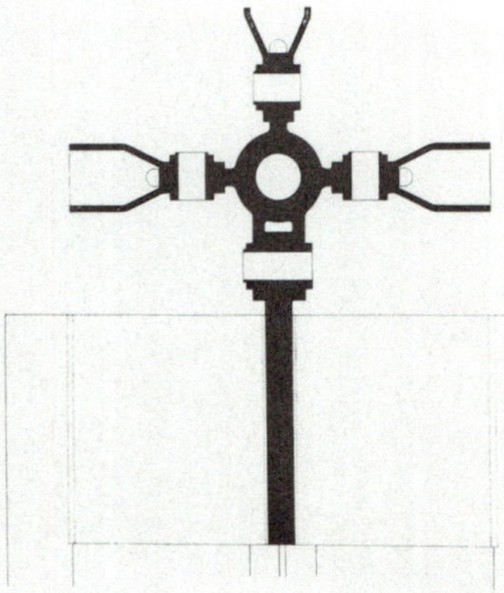

6

1 und 2
Der Standardknotenpunkt, geformt aus den flachgedrückten, geschlitzten und gestanzten Rohr-Enden und einem Aluminiumgußkern, an dem die räumlichen Verspannungskabel angebracht werden.

Point de croisement standard. Construction et câbles de précontrainte.

The standard knot shaped from flattened, slotted and punched tube ends and a moulded aluminium core to which the bracing cable is fixed.

3–6
Das aus vier Rohren bestehende, mit einer Kreuzplatte verbundene Stützenaggregat in seiner Beziehung zum Hauptbinder.

Plaque de croisement des 4 tubes du pilier et raccord au sommier principal.

The support unit of four tubes and cross plate in its relation to the main header.

1
Die quadratischen Felder des 3 m hohen Binders, die durch sich überkreuzende räumlich angeordnete Verspannungskabel verstrebt sind, und seine Auflage auf dem Stützenaggregat, durch dessen Mitte ein Vorspannseil die ganze Konstruktion an das Fundament zieht.

Construction du sommier, câbles de précontrainte croisés, piliers et fondation.

The square fields of the 3 m. high header, which are braced by spatially ordered bracing cables crossing them and the position of the header on the support unit, through the middle of which a cable holds the whole construction to the foundation.

2
Seiten- und Frontansicht des Binders mit Aufsicht auf Ober- und Untergurt und den Variationen der Querschnitte, welche die Anordnung der Konstruktionsstäbe in den verschiedenen Feldern in bezug auf ihre statische Beanspruchung deutlich zeigt.

Vue frontale et latérale du sommier et variations des sections transversales montrant la répartition des profils suivant les charges statiques.

Side and front view of the header with view on to the upper and lower flanges and the variations in the cross sections, which clearly shows the arrangement of the construction rods in the various fields in relation to their static requirements.

3
4 Stützen und 2 Binder: die einzigen feststehenden Elemente des Bauwerks.

4 piliers et deux sommiers, les seuls éléments fixes du bâtiment.

4 supports and 2 headers, the sole stationary elements of the structure.

1

2

3

Biographies

Andreas Burkhalter

Andreas Burkhalter was born in Thalwil/Switzerland. He studied Zoology at the University of Zurich and received a BS for work with Rüdiger Wehner on the navigation of desert ants in Tunesia. Burkhalter received a Ph.D. in Neuroscience based on work performed on the bird visual system at the Brain Research Institute of the University of Zurich. In 1980, Burkhalter joined the laboratory of David Van Essen at the California Institute of Technology in Pasadena CA/USA as Postdoctoral Fellow. In 1983, he moved to the Department of Neurobiology at Harvard Medical School in Boston, MA/USA for further postdoctoral training. In 1985, Burkhalter joined the faculty at Washington University School of Medicine in St. Louis, MO/USA where he is Professor of Neuroscience. Burkhalter is an international leader in the field of neuroscience research. He is known for his fundamental discoveries to advance our understanding of the organization and function of the mammalian visual cortex. In 2013 Burkhalter served as Wiersma Visiting Professor at the California Institute of Technology and in 2018 has received the Distinguished Investigator Award from Washington University.

Marianne Burkhalter

Since 1984, Marianne Burkhalter has run an architectural practice in Zurich with Christian Sumi, and in partnership with Yves Schihin (since 2009) and Urs Rinklef (since 2012). The most recent publication of work is burkhalter sumi architekten (Electa documenti di architettura 198, Milano 2016). She practiced as an architect in Florence (Super-studio), New York and Los Angeles (Studio Works), and was an auditor at Princeton University. She has taught at SCI-ARC in Los Angeles and the Lausanne Polytechnic EPFL. From 2008–2016, she maintained a full professorship at the Accademia di Architettura Mendrisio AAM. Between 2009 and 2014, she completed a research project together with Christian Sumi (Swiss cooperation program in architecture) entitled "Der Gotthard. Il Gottardo, – landscape myths technology," published in 2016 by Scheidegger und Spiess. She serves as a member of various committees (Baukollegium der Stadt Zürich, Gestaltungsbeirat Salzburg) and juries.

Fabio Gramazio, Matthias Kohler

Fabio Gramazio and Matthias Kohler are architects with multi-disciplinary interests ranging from computational design and robotic fabrication to material innovation. In 2000, they founded the award-winning architecture practice Gramazio & Kohler. Current projects include the design of the Empa NEST research platform, a future living and working laboratory for sustainable building construction. They are both full professors at ETH Zurich leading Gramazio Kohler Research, a pioneering group of researchers at the forefront of digital fabrication. They initiated the world's first architectural robotic laboratory at ETH Zurich, creating a new research field merging advanced architectural design and additive fabrication processes through the customized use of industrial robots. This ranges from installations such as Remote Material Deposition, Rock Print or Flight Assembled Architecture to the computational design and robotic fabrication of full-scale building elements such as the Sequential Roof for the Arch_Tec_Lab at ETH Zurich and the three storey DFAB HOUSE for the NEST building. The work of Gramazio Kohler Research is presented and theoretically framed in the book The Robotic Touch: How Robots Change Architecture. From 2014 to 2017 Matthias Kohler was the founding director of the National Centre of Competence in Research (NCCR) in Digital Fabrication.

Hannes Mayer

Hannes Mayer is co-publisher of the architecture magazine manege für architektur and a Senior Researcher of Gramazio Kohler Research at ETH Zurich, where he also directs the Master of Advanced Studies in Architecture and Digital Fabrication. Prior to joining Gramazio Kohler Research, Hannes Mayer was the Roland Rainer Chair 2014/15 – Professor for Architectural Design and Research at the Academy of Fine Arts in Vienna and taught design studios and postgraduate design research at the Bartlett School of Architecture, University College London as well as University of Westminster, London. At the same time, he was the director and editor-in-chief of the thematic review for architecture archithese until 2014. In 2016, he was artist in residence at Villa Kamogawa, Goethe Institut Kyoto.

Marko Pogacnik

Marko Pogacnik is currently professore associato for history of architecture at the University IUAV in Venice. He was DAAD Gastprofessor at the Faculty of Architecture of the Fachhochschule of Potsdam, visiting professor in Dortmund, Innsbruck and at the University in Kaiserslautern. He has held lectures and seminaries in many European universities including TU-Graz, RWTU Aachen, Academy of Architecture, Mendrisio, University of Geneva, ETH Zürich, University of applied arts in Vienna, Faculty of Architecture of Cottbus, ILEK in Stuttgart, TU Munich, TU Berlin, and TU Delft. In September 2007, he served as chairman of the commission for the Jurkovic Prize, Bratislava. In March 2008, he held the Schinkel lecture, Potsdam. Invited by the National Museum of Contemporary Art of Seoul, he participated in the competition jury for the new MoCA Seoul, january 2010.

Christian Sumi

Since 1984, Christian Sumi has run an architectural practice in Zurich with Marianne Burkhalter, and in partnership with Yves Schihin (since 2009) and Urs Rinklef (since 2012). The most recent publication of work is burkhalter sumi architekten (Electa documenti di architettura 198, Milano 2016). He graduated from the Zurich Polytechnic, where he worked for the Institute of History and Theory of Architecture gta. He has taught at Harvard University GSD, the Lausanne Polytechnic EPFL and the University of Strathclyde in Glasgow. From 2008–2016, he maintained a full professorship at the Accademia di Architettura Mendrisio AAM. He is the author of studies on, among others, Giulio Minoletti and Marco Zanuso, both in collaboration with the Archivio del Moderno AdM at AAM, and on Konrad Wachsmann, Jean Prouve, Le Corbusier, Otto Rudolf Salvisberg, Flora Crawford and Rudolf Steiger.

Bibliography

Selected Publications by Konrad Wachsmann

Konrad Wachsmann, *Holzhausbau. Technik und Gestaltung* [1930], new edition, Birkhäuser Verlag, Basel 1995 [English edition: *Building the Wooden House. Technique and Design*].

Konrad Wachsmann, *Bauen in unserer Zeit*, Kunstgewerbemuseum Zürich/Galerie Welz, Salzburg 1958.

Konrad Wachsmann, *Wendepunkt im Bauen*, Krausskopf-Verlag, Wiesbaden 1959.

Konrad Wachsmann, *The Turning Point of Building*: Structure and Design, Reinhold, New York 1961.

Konrad Wachsmann, *Aspekte*, Krausskopf-Verlag, Wiesbaden 1961.

Publications by Christian Sumi about Konrad Wachsmann

Christian Sumi, "Holzhausbau heute," in: *Holzhausbau. Technik und Gestaltung*, 1995, pp. 19–27; "Building the Wooden House Today," pp. 19–27 in the English edition.

"Konrad Wachsmann," in: *Marianne Burkhalter & Christian Sumi – Die Holzbauten*, gta Verlag, Zurich 1995, pp. 31–33 [English edition: *Marianne Burkhalter & Christian Sumi – The Timber Buildings*; Dutch edition: *Marianne Burkhalter & Christian Sumi – De Houtbouw*].

Christian Sumi with Regina Böhm, Daniela Däumler, and Tobias Haag, "Konrad Wachsmann: Architekt und Pionier des industriellen Bauens," in: "Konservierung der Moderne?," *Icomos Hefte des Deutschen Nationalkomitees*, no. 24, Munich 1998, pp. 56–62.

Christian Sumi, "Holzhausbau heute," in: *Der Architekt* 11/1999, pp. 26–29; abridged text from *Holzhausbau* 1995.

Christian Sumi, "Direktorenhaus in Niesky," in: *Die unbekannte Moderne*, Philo&Philo Fine Arts, Berlin 2004, pp. 84–91.

Christian Sumi, "Building the Wooden House Today," in "Details/Detaljer," *B—Arkitekturtidsskrift/B Architectural Magazine*, no. 54, 2005, pp. 36–47 [English and Danish version of *Holzhausbau* 1995].

General Publications

Gilbert Herbert, *The Dream of the Factory-Made House, Walter Gropius and Konrad Wachsmann*, MIT Press, Cambridge MA 1984.

Barry Bergdoll, Peter Christensen (eds), *Home Delivery: Fabricating the Modern Dwelling*, The Museum of Modern Art, New York 2008.

Wendepunkt(e) im Bauen – von der seriellen zur digitalen Architektur, Edition Detail, Munich 2010.

Franz Graf, Yvan Delemontey (eds), *Architecture industrialisée et préfabriquée*: connaissance et sauvegarde, Presses polytechniques et universitaires romandes, Lausanne 2012.

Akos Moravanszky, *Stoffwechsel. Materialverwandlung in der Architektur*, Birkhäuser, Basel 2018.

Publications about Konrad Wachsmann / Fritz Haller

Michael Grüning, *Der Architekt Konrad Wachsmann. Erinnerungen und Selbstauskünfte*, Löcker Verlag, Vienna 1986.

Otto Maier, *Die räumliche Syntax. Konrad Wachsmanns Beitrag zum Bauen in unserer Zeit*, Dissertationsschrift, Universität Karlsruhe 1989, Referent Prof. Fritz Haller, Koreferent Prof. Ottokar Uhl.

Barbara Dafft, *Autopoisesis, Die Genese des "Grape Vine Project" (1953) von Konrad Wachsmann*, Masterarbeit / MAS ETH Geschichte und Theorie der Architektur Silvia Claus/Kathrin Siebert, 2009.

Georg Vrachliotis, Laurent Stalder (eds), *Fritz Haller Architekt und Forscher*, gta Verlag, Zurich 2015.

Image Credits

Cover: Akademie der Künste, Berlin, Konrad-Wachsmann-Archiv (KW 126/16)

Akademie der Künste, Berlin, Konrad-Wachsmann-Archiv: pp. 2, 3 (KW 126/16), 4, 5 (KW 125/5a, KW 125/4a) , 6, 7 (KW 127/24, KW 127/40a, KW0127/3a), 8, 9 (KW 127/42), 10 (KW 205/121), 14, 15 (KW 87 F.1 -15, F.20), 34 (KW 118/23), 37 (KW 118/1-8, KW 118/9a–12a), 42 (KW 125/4a), 47 (KW 130/11, /8, /12), 49 (KW 122/5a), 51 (KW 121/29a, KW 122/7, KW 121/30a, KW 121/10a), 53 (KW 122/15, KW 121/7, KW 122/16), 81 (KW 164/26), 82, 83 (KW 318 Pl.8), 87 (KW 0164/13), 89 (KW 318/4), 91 (KW 318/6), 116 (KW 169/80), 117 (KW 169/79), (KW 205/207), 118 (KW 169/05), 119 (KW 169/70), 120 (KW 169/17), 121 (KW 169/75), 122 (KW 169/25, 169/12), 123 (KW 169/11, /10, /15), 124, 125 (KW 370/2) 126, 127 (KW 370/1), 128, 129 (KW 370/3), 130, 131 (KW 370/4), 152

For all works by Richard Paul Lohse: © 2018, ProLitteris, Zurich

Harry Callahan, © The Estate of Harry Callahan; courtesy Pace/MacGill Gallery, New York: pp. 2,3 (KW 126/14a)

Konrad Wachsmann, *Una svolta nelle costruzione*, Il Saggiatore, Milan 1960: p. 12

Konrad Wachsmann, *The Turning Point of Building*, Reinhold, New York 1961: p. 12

Konrad Wachsmann, *Wendepunkt im Bauen*, Krausskopf-Verlag, Wiesbaden 1959: pp. 12, 28, 30, 31, 35, 40–43, 84, 85, 86, 87, 89

Burkhalter Sumi Architekten, Zurich: pp. 14, 32, 33, 38, 46, 48, 50, 52, 60, 66–68, 88

Courtesy of the Aaron Siskind Foundation: pp. 17 (KW 123/1), 45 (KW 123/4a)

Werk, 3/1974, pp. 350–354: pp. 18–22

Gottfried Semper, *Der Stil in den technischen und tektonischen Künsten oder Praktische Ästhetik*, Frankfurt a. M./Munich 1860–63: pp. 25–27

USM U. Schärer Söhne AG: pp. 25, 29

Lorenzo Fassi, Niccolo Bononi Baraldi aam: pp. 25, 44, 55, 56, 60

Heinrich Helfenstein; gta Archiv / ETH Zurich (Archiv Heinrich Helfenstein): pp. 38, 39

Heinz Unger, Zurich: pp. 54–79

Gramazio Kohler Research, ETH Zürich: pp. 92–97

Erne Holzbau, Laufenburg: pp. 98–101

Pietro Maria Romagnoli: pp. 99–101

Video *Bosque Neuronal* (Cajal Blue Brain Project): pp. 103, 107

Cajal Institute-CSIC, Madrid, Spain: pp. 105, 109.

Laurent Stalder, Georg Vrachliotis (eds), *Fritz Haller Architekt und Forscher*, gta Verlag, Zürich 2015: p. 113

Hermann Czech, Vienna: p. 133

Barbara Wally and Jana Marko (eds), *Die Ära Kokoschka*, Salzburg 1993: p. 135

Bauen und Wohnen, 10/1960, pp. 363–384: pp. 140–147

Imprint

Acknowledgments

Our main partners and sponsors have been instrumental in making this project a reality, and we express our gratitude to the USM Foundation for their generous support of the catalog, Erne Holzbau and KT Color for the realization of the Grapevine Structure in Venice, together with Sherpa Connector, Schilliger Holz, Krinner Das Schraubenfundament, and Planzer Transport AG.

A special thanks goes to the Akademie der Künste Berlin, Mrs. Dr. Barkhofen and Mrs. Morgenstern for the fruitful cooperation and their support, as well as to Fabio Gramazio, Matthias Kohler, Hannes Mayer, Sarah Schneider, Matthias Helmreich (Gramazio Kohler Research, ETH Zürich) for their invaluable help in the development of the Grapevine Structure.

We would also like to thank the authors Andreas Burkhalter, Fabio Gramazio, Matthias Kohler, Hannes Mayer, and Marko Pogacnik for their contributions, photographer Heinz Unger for his striking images of the mock-ups, as well as the staff and interns of our studio, in particular Pietro Maria Romagnoli for being at the helm of this project.

We are grateful to Park Books, Thomas Kramer in particular, for realizing the book in the very short time we had, to Lynnette Widder for her precise translations, and to graphic designer Viola Zimmermann for her patience and careful work on the layout.

Last but not least, we would like to thank the two curators, Yvonne Farell and Shelley McNamara, for their invitation to participate in the Venice Biennale 2018, which is what brought forth this publication in the first place.

Concept:
Marianne Burkhalter,
Christian Sumi

Translations and copy editing:
Lynnette Widder

Proofreading:
Louise Stein

Design:
Viola Zimmermann, Zurich

Lithography:
Widmer & Fluri GmbH, Zurich

Printing and binding:
DZA Druckerei zu Altenburg GmbH,
Thuringia

Park Books
Niederdorfstrasse 54
8001 Zurich
Switzerland
www.park-books.com

Park Books is being supported by the Federal Office of Culture with a general subsidy for the years 2016–2020.

ISBN 978-3-03860-110-4

June 9, 1980

Creative Resources &

Jackie Dubey

8322 Beverly Boulevard
Los Angeles, California 90048
Telephone: (213) 651-5511

Konrad Wachsman
10347 Calvin Avenue
Los Angeles, California 90025

Dear Konrad,

Thank you for making this a special day, April 8, 1980.
(Left to right): Frank Gehry, Berta Gehry, Doreen Nelson, Bernard Zimmerman, Jackie Dubey, Margie Gordon, Eric Zimmerman, David Cloud, Bucky Fuller, John Cage, Konrad Wachsman, Anne Fuller.

Regards,

Jackie Dubey

Consultant
Bernard Zimmerman, F.A.I.A.